FINANCIAL ACCOUNTING

STUDY GUIDE • STEPHEN C. SCHAEFER

FOURTH EDITION

FINANCIAL ACCOUNTING

Harrison • Horngren

Prentice
Hall

Upper Saddle River, New Jersey 07458

Acquisitions editor: Deborah Hoffman
Associate editor: Kathryn Sheehan
Production editor: Leah Crescenzo
Manufacturer: Victor Graphics, Inc.

ISBN 0-13-018852-2

10 9 8 7 6 5 4 3 2 1

CONTENTS

PREFACE

This Study Guide will assist you in mastering FINANCIAL ACCOUNTING by Walter T. Harrison, Jr., and Charles T. Horngren. The thirteen chapters in this Study Guide correspond to the thirteen chapters in the textbook. Each chapter of this Study Guide contains three sections: Chapter Review, Test Yourself, and Demonstration Problems.

Chapter Review. The Chapter Review parallels the chapter in you textbook. It is organized by learning objective and provides a concise summary of the major elements in each objective. Emphasis is given to new terms and concepts, particularly in the earlier chapters where it is essential for the student to be conversant with accounting terminology. A Chapter Overview links each chapter to previous or subsequent topics.

Test Yourself. The test yourself section is divided into six parts: matching, multiple choice, completion, true/false, exercises, and critical thinking. Answers are provided for each section along with explanations, when appropriate. The six sections provide a comprehensive review of the material in each chapter and should be used after you have read each chapter thoroughly to determine which topics you understand and those requiring further study.

Demonstration Problems. Two demonstrations problems are provided for each chapter. These problems attempt to incorporate as many of the topics in the chapter as possible. For some chapters, the first demonstration problem must be completed before the second one is attempted. For those chapters, complete the first one, check your answers, make any necessary corrections, then go on to the second problem. The solutions to the demonstration problems provide explanations as well.

THIS STUDY GUIDE IS NOT A SUBSTITUTE FOR YOUR TEXTBOOK. It is designed as an additional support tool to assist you in succeeding in your accounting course.

Comments about the Study Guide are encouraged and should be sent to me in care of the publisher.

Stephen C. Schaefer
Contra Costa College

ACKNOWLEDGMENTS

Thanks to Loc Huynh, a former student and graduate of the Walter A. Haas School of Business at the University of California-Berkeley, for his invaluable assistance in the preparation of this Study Guide. Loc did all the word processing and his comments and suggestions were always thought-provoking and worthwhile. Thanks to current and former students who are a constant source of inspiration and challenge. Thanks also to Melanie Yeung, a former student now attending San Francisco State University, for her contribution to the accuracy of the Study Guide.

CHAPTER 1—THE FINANCIAL STATEMENTS

CHAPTER OVERVIEW

Chapter 1 introduces you to accounting and its use in decision making. Some of the topics covered in this chapter are the types of business organization, the basic accounting equation, and financial statements. Like many disciplines, accounting has its own vocabulary. An understanding of accounting terminology and the other topics covered in this chapter will give you a good foundation towards mastering the topics in upcoming chapters. The specific learning objectives for this chapter are to

1. Understand accounting vocabulary and use it in decision making
2. Analyze business activity with accounting concepts and principles
3. Use the accounting equation to describe an organization's financial position
4. Evaluate a company's operating performance, financial position, and cash flows
5. Explain the relationships among financial statements

CHAPTER REVIEW

Objective 1 - Understand accounting vocabulary and use it in decision making.

Accounting is the information system that measures business activities, processes that information into reports, and communicates the results to decision makers.

There are many users of accounting information. Individuals use accounting information to make decisions about purchases and investments and to manage their bank accounts. Businesses use accounting information to set goals for their businesses and to evaluate progress toward achieving those goals. Investors use accounting information to evaluate the prospect of future returns on their investments. Creditors use accounting information to evaluate a borrower's ability to meet scheduled repayments of money loaned. Accounting information is also used by government regulatory agencies, taxing authorities, nonprofit organizations, and others, such as employee and consumer groups.

While there are many users of accounting information, they can be grouped into two broad categories—external users and internal users. **Financial accounting** provides information useful to managers and individuals outside the organization while **management accounting** provides information exclusively to internal decision makers.

The **American Institute of Certified Public Accountants (AICPA)** has adopted a Code of Professional Conduct that serves as a guide to produce accurate information for decision making.

$$\text{Ethical behavior} \Rightarrow \text{reliable information} \Rightarrow \text{decision}$$

The three forms of business organization are:

1. **sole proprietorship** - a business owned by one person.
2. **partnership** - a business owned by two or more individuals.
3. **corporation** - a business owned by shareholders whose liability for business debts is limited to the amount the stockholder invested in the corporation.

In the United States, proprietorships are numerically the largest form of business, whereas corporations are the dominant form in terms of total assets, income, and number of employees. (Helpful hint: review Exhibit 1-2 in the textbook.)

A corporation is formed under state laws and has a legal identity distinct from its owners, the shareholders. Unlike in a proprietorship or partnership, the shareholders have no personal liability for the corporation's liabilities. The shareholders elect a board of directors who appoint officers to manage the organization.

Objective 2 - Analyze business activity with accounting concepts and principles.

The **Financial Accounting Standards Board** (FASB), the **Securities and Exchange Commission** (SEC) and the **American Institute of Certified Public Accountants** (AICPA) are three groups that influence the practice of accounting in the United States. **Generally Accepted Accounting Principles** (GAAP) are the rules governing accounting, which include five important standards: 1) the **entity concept**, 2) the **reliability (or objectivity) principle**, 3) the **cost principle**, 4) the **going-concern principle**, and 5) the **stable-monetary-unit concept**. (Helpful hint: review Exhibit 1-3 in your text.)

The **entity concept** states that the records of a business entity should be separate from the personal records of the owner. For example, if a business owner borrows money to remodel her home, the loan is a personal debt, not a debt to the business.

The **reliability (or objectivity) principle** states that accountants should attempt to provide reliable, accurate records and financial statements. All data that the accountant uses should be verifiable by an independent observer. Ideally, accounting records should be determined by objective evidence. For example, the most objective and reliable measure of the value of supplies is the price paid for the supplies. The objective evidence documenting the price is the bill from the supplier.

The **cost principle** states that the assets and services should be recorded at their actual (historical) cost. For example, if a firm pays $150,000 for land, then $150,000 is the value recorded in the books even if an independent appraiser states that the land is worth $200,000.

The **going-concern concept** holds that the entity will remain in operation for the foreseeable future. Therefore, the relevant measure of the entity's assets is historical cost. If the entity were going out of business, the relevant measure of its assets would be market value.

The **stable-monetary-unit concept** holds that the purchasing power of the dollar is relatively stable. Therefore, accountants may add and subtract dollar amounts as though each dollar had the same purchasing power.

Objective 3 - Use the accounting equation to describe an organization's financial position.

The **accounting equation** is expressed as

$$\text{ASSETS} = \text{LIABILITIES} + \text{OWNERS' EQUITY}$$

Assets are a firm's resources that are expected to provide future benefits. **Liabilities** are claims by outsiders (creditors) to those resources. Claims by insiders (owners) are called **owners' equity** or **capital**.

Examples of assets are cash, merchandise, supplies, land, and buildings. Merchandise inventory are the items a business sells to its customers. Long-lived assets, such as equipment, land, buildings, etc., are also called **plant assets**.

Examples of liabilities are accounts payable and notes payable, which arise when the business makes purchases on credit.

Owners' equity is what is left of the assets after subtracting the liabilities:

ASSETS - LIABILITIES = OWNERS' EQUITY

The owners' equity of a proprietorship and partnership is called **capital**. The owners' equity of a corporation is called **stockholders' equity** and is divided into two categories: **paid-in capital** and **retained earnings**. **Paid-in capital** is the amount invested in the corporation by its owners. **Common stock** is a basic component of paid-in capital. **Retained earnings** is the amount earned by the corporation to date that has not been paid out in dividends. Revenues increase retained earnings, whereas expenses decrease retained earnings. Net income results when revenues exceed expenses. A net loss results when expenses exceed revenues.

Dividends are proportional distributions of assets, usually cash, to the owners of the corporation (called stockholders.) (Helpful hint: review Exhibit 1-5 in your text to become familiar with concepts introduced in this section.)

Objective 4 - Evaluate a company's operating performance, financial position, and cash flows.

Accountants summarize the results of business activity in four primary financial statements: 1) the **income statement**, 2) the **statement of retained earnings**, 3) the **balance sheet**, and 4) the **statement of cash flows**.

The **income statement** presents a summary of the firm's revenues and expenses for some period of time, such as a month, and reports net income if total revenues exceed total expenses. A net loss occurs if total expenses are greater than total revenues.

The **statement of retained earnings** presents a summary of changes in retained earnings during the same period as the income statement. Retained earnings increase with income and decrease with dividends and net losses.

The **balance sheet** reports all assets, liabilities, and stockholders' equity as of a specific date. That date will be the same date as the last day of the period for which activities are summarized in the income statement and the statement of retained earnings. Assets are divided into two major categories—current and long term. Current assets are ones which will convert to cash or be consumed within one year or within the operating cycle if it is longer. A company's operating cycle is the time span between the expenditure of cash for goods or services, the sale of those goods and services to customers, and the collection of cash by the business for those goods and services. Liabilities are also divided into two categories—current and long term, using the same standard (one year). Note that the term balance sheet comes from the fact that the report balances; that is, total assets equal total liabilities plus total stockholders' equity.

The **statement of cash flows** shows the cash inflows and outflows, organized into three areas—operating activities, investing activities, and financing activities.

The major source of cash receipts from operating activities will be the cash received from customers, whereas the major source of cash payments will be to suppliers and employees. Investing activities include the acquisition and sale of long-term assets—things such as buildings and equipment. Financing activities include short-term and long-term debt, the sale or purchase of the company's stock, and the payment of dividends. These three sections each results in a net cash inflow or outflow, which are then summarized into a "net" cash increase or decrease for the period. This final "net" reconciles the difference between the beginning cash balance and the ending cash balance. Study carefully the financial statements for The Gap (Exhibits 1-7, 1-8, 1-9, and 1-10) in your text.

Objective 5 - Explain the relationships among financial statements.

All financial statements begin with three line headings as follows:

Company Name
Statement Name
Appropriate Date

The income statement is prepared first, listing the revenues and expenses for the period. The result is either net income (when revenues are greater than expenses) or net loss (when revenues are less than expenses). This result is carried forward to the next statement.

The statement of retained earnings is prepared after the income statement. It details the amounts and sources of changes in retained earnings during the period as follows:

	Beginning Retained Earnings
+	Net Income (or - Net Loss)
-	Dividends
=	Ending Retained Earnings

The result, listed as Ending Retained Earnings, is carried forward to the next financial statement.

The balance sheet is a formal listing of the accounting equation as of the last day in the financial period. The individual assets are added together to equal total assets. The liabilities are totaled and added to stockholders' equity.

The statement of cash flows reports cash receipts and payments for operating, investing, and financing activities. Each section results in a net cash inflow or outflow. These three sections are then summarized in one net amount for the period. This final figure is added (if a net inflow) to the beginning cash balance or deducted (if a net outflow) from the beginning cash balance to arrive at an ending cash balance. This ending cash balance is reported on the balance sheet. Review Exhibit 1-11 in your text to become more familiar with these relationships.

> **Study Tip**: The statement order is important to remember.
> 1. Income Statement
> 2. Retained Earnings Statement
> 3. Balance Sheet
> 4. Statement of Cash Flows
>
> Memorize the acronym IRBS to help you.

APPENDIX TO CHAPTER 1

Accounting's Role in Business

Accounting provides useful information to owners, managers, investors, and lenders. Owners rely on accounting to provide the records needed to make sound business decisions. Managers need information provided by accounting to plan future activities. Potential investors look to accounting for information about the company as a potential investment and current investors (the stockholders) rely on the accuracy of the company's statements to evaluate the company and decide whether to maintain (or sell) their ownership interest. Finally, lenders use accounting for information to assist in making decisions about the credit worthiness of the client. Once a bank has agreed to lend money, the bank will continue to rely on accounting information as it monitors the company's progress. The accounting information used by these various interest groups comes from either private accountants or public accountants.

Private Accounting

Private accountants are employees working for a single company. Both profit and non-profit organizations employ accountants. While the specific tasks completed by the accountant for the employer will vary greatly, the work of most private accountants includes budgeting, information systems design, cost accounting, and internal auditing. These functions require more skills than accounting, including communication skills (both written and oral), analytical skills, and 'people skills'—the ability to work successfully with individuals from a variety of other technical disciplines.

Public Accounting

Public accountants serve the general public in one of three areas: consulting, auditing, and tax accounting. Consulting services are designed to assist clients in operating efficiently, evaluating potential expansion opportunities, and analyzing organizational design options, among others. Auditors provide professional opinions regarding a company's financial statements, so other interested parties know they can rely on the information contained in those statements. Tax accountants assist clients in complying with the tax laws and minimizing the tax bill. Exhibit 1A-1 in your text lists the 10 largest U. S. accounting firms.

TEST YOURSELF

All the self-testing materials in this chapter focus on information and procedures that your instructor is likely to test in quizzes and examinations.

I. Matching *Match each numbered term with its lettered definition.*

_____ 1. AICPA
_____ 2. assets
_____ 3. corporation
_____ 4. expenses
_____ 5. FASB
_____ 6. GAAP
_____ 7. Income Statement
_____ 8. liabilities
_____ 9. common stock

_____ 10. partnership
_____ 11. sole proprietorship
_____ 12. revenues
_____ 13. SEC
_____ 14. Statement of Cash Flows
_____ 15. Statement of Retained Earnings
_____ 16. dividends
_____ 17. contributed capital

A. a summary of revenues and expenses for a period
B. a business owned by one person
C. a professional organization of Certified Public Accountants
D. a financial statement summarizing changes in retained earnings
E. a legal entity owned by stockholders, which conducts its business in its own name
F. the body that formulates GAAP
G. resources expected to provide future benefit
H. the "rules" of accounting
I. claims on assets by outsiders
J. increases in retained earnings from delivering goods and services to customers
K. a business co-owned by two or more individuals
L. a federal agency with the legal power to set and enforce accounting and auditing standards
M. decreases in retained earnings that result from operations
N. certificates representing ownership in a corporation
O. details the net change in cash from one period to the next
P. the amount invested in the corporation by the owners
Q. a distribution of assets to the owners of a corporation

II. Multiple Choice *Circle the best answer.*

1. An example of a liability is

   A. insurance expense
   B. equipment
   C. notes payable
   D. dividends

2. Which of the following appears on the income statement?

   A. cash receipts from customers
   B. revenues from customers
   C. cash paid to employees
   D. cash paid to suppliers

3. Which of the following does not appear on the statement of cash flows?

   A. dividends paid
   B. proceeds from short-term borrowing
   C. payments for new equipment
   D. accounts payable

4. The proper order for financial statements preparation is

   A. income statement, balance sheet, statement of cash flows, statement of retained earnings
   B. income statement, statement of cash flows, statement of retained earnings, balance sheet
   C. income statement, statement of retained earnings, balance sheet, statement of cash flows
   D. balance sheet, statement of cash flows, income statement, statement of retained earnings

5. If the date on a financial statement is August 31, 2001, then the financial statement must be

   A. the income statement
   B. the statement of retained earnings
   C. the balance sheet
   D. the statement of cash flows

6. If the financial statement is dated "For the Month Ended August 31, 2001," then the financial statement must be

   A. the income statement
   B. the statement of retained earnings
   C. the balance sheet
   D. either the income statement or the statement of retained earnings

7. Net income equals

   A. Assets - Liabilities
   B. Liabilities + Stockholders' Equity
   C. Revenues + Expenses
   D. Revenues - Expenses

8. If total assets equal four times liabilities, and stockholders' equity is $90,000, what are total assets?

   A. $140,000
   B. $120,000
   C. $100,000
   D. $80,000

9. If the beginning balance in retained earnings was $120, the ending balance is $115, and net income for the month was $86, how much were dividends during the period?

A. $206
B. $34
C. $91
D. $101

10. On January 1, 2002, Richard's Design Company had assets of $160,000 and stockholders' equity of $75,000. During the year, assets increased by $45,000 and stockholders' equity decreased by $22,000. What were the liabilities on December 31, 2002?

A. $85,000
B. $152,000
C. $53,000
D. $205,000

III. Completion   *Complete each of the following statements.*

1. The four primary financial statements are 1) _____, 2) _____, 3)_____, and 4) _____.
2. Keeping accounting records for a business separate from the owner's personal accounting records follows from the _____ concept.
3. Revenues are _____.
4. _____ are the costs incurred in operating a business.
5. Outsider claims against assets are called _____, and insider claims are called _____.
6. What is the accounting equation? _____.
7. When assets are purchased by a firm, they are recorded at _____.
8. _____is the clerical recording of the data used in an accounting system.
9. All financial statements begin with a three-line heading listing:

_____
_____
_____

10. Assuming the purchasing power of the dollar remains relatively stable over time underlies the _____ concept.
11. The statement of cash flows details cash inflows/outflows from three activities. These are _____, _____, and _____.
12. Which item appears on both the income statement and the retained earnings statement? _____
13. _____ appears on both the retained earnings statement and the balance sheet.
14. The payment of dividends appears in which section of the statement of cash flows? _____.
15. You would look to the _____ to determine if a company was profitable.

IV. True/False
For each of the following statements, circle T for true or F for false.

1.   T F   Net income is most closely associated with operating activities.
2.   T F   An example of an investing activity is purchasing outstanding common stock.
3.   T F   Operating activities are most closely associated with customers, suppliers, and employees.
4.   T F   The corporate form of business allows owners the most flexibility in running the business.
5.   T F   Stockholders in corporations have no personal liability for the corporation's obligations.
6.   T F   GAAP is a well-known clothing company.
7.   T F   The organization most closely associated with GAAP is the Financial Accounting Standards Board.
8.   T F   The terms "capital" and "creditor" are synonymous.
9.   T F   The income statement details activity for a specific period of time.
10.   T F   The excess of revenues over expenses is called a net loss.
11.   T F   Assets and expenses are listed on the balance sheet.
12.   T F   The balance sheet is a detailed expression of the accounting equation.
13.   T F   The income statement is prepared after the statement of retained earnings.
14.   T F   Stockholders' equity consists of paid-in capital and retained earnings.
15.   T F   On the statement of cash flows, financing activities refer to borrowing funds and repaying them and transactions involving the shareholders.

V. Exercises

1. Technik.com specializes in providing technical services to corporations in the St. Louis area. At the end of their first year of operation, they had the following cash flows:

   1. $866,000 was received from clients for services provided during the year.
   2. Employees were paid a total of $192,500.
   3. The company paid a total of $82,680 in interest charges during the year and received $1,275 in interest on a savings account.
   4. The outside consultants who provided the technical assistance were paid a total of $421,140 during the year.
   5. A total of $710 was paid in taxes during the year.

   In the space below, present the cash flows from operating activities for Technik.com.

_____
_____
_____
_____
_____
_____
_____
_____

2. Presented below are the balances in the assets, liabilities, and stockholders' equity for Jenny's Juice Bar, on January 31, 2002. The balance for common stock has been intentionally omitted.

Accounts Payable	$225
Accounts Receivable	180
Cash	108
Common Stock	?
Equipment	144
Retained Earnings	180
Supplies	63

Prepare a balance sheet for Jenny's Juice Bar, on January 31, 2002.

Jenny's Juice Bar
Balance Sheet
January 31, 2002

Assets:		Liabilities:	
Cash		Accounts payable	
Accounts receivable	_____	Total liabilities	_____
Supplies	_____	Stockholders' equity:	_____
Equipment	_____	Common stock	
	_____	Retained earnings	_____
		Total liabilities	_____
Total assets	_____	and stockholders' equity	_____

3. The following are the balances in the accounts of Larry's Landscaping, on August 31, 2002.

Accounts Receivable	$ 41
Accounts Payable	53
Advertising Expense	185
Common Stock	64
Dividends	42
Equipment	298
Fees Earned	456
Notes Receivable	100
Retained Earnings	92
Salary Payable	18
Salary Expense	70
Supplies	24
Supplies Expense	32
Truck Rental Expense	124
Utilities Expense	106

Prepare an income statement for Larry's Landscaping, for the month of August 2002.

Larry's Landscaping		
Income Statement		
For the Month Ended August 31, 2002		
		$
Revenues		
Expenses:		
	$	
Net income (loss)		$

VI. Critical Thinking

Can a profitable business (one where revenues consistently exceed expenses) become insolvent (unable to pay its bills)? Conversely, can an unprofitable business remain solvent?

_____

_____

_____

_____

_____

VII. Demonstration Problems

Demonstration Problem #1

The following list summarizes the cash transactions for Ramirez Refinishers, Inc., at the end of its most recent fiscal period:

1. Additional shares of common stock were sold for $275,000.
2. $20,000 was used to pay off some short-term notes payable.
3. A new building was acquired during the year—the total cost was $920,000. A cash down payment of $240,000 was made at the time the building was purchased.
4. Some old equipment was sold and replaced with newer, more sophisticated equipment. The old equipment was sold for $9,200. The new equipment cost $105,000, paid in cash.
5. At the beginning of the year, customers owed a total of $71,500. During the year invoices totaling $1,205,400 were sent to customers. At the end of the year, the total amount owed to Ramirez Refinishers was $116,770.
6. Dividends of $80,000 were paid to shareholders during the year.
7. The total amount paid to employees during the year was $362,500.
8. Ramirez Refinishers borrowed $150,000 from its bank, signing a two-year promissory note.
9. The business earned $2,452 in interest during the year.
10. Suppliers were paid $184,270 during the year.
11. The company purchased 10,000 shares of its outstanding common stock, paying $28.50 per share.
12. The company paid $52,290 for income taxes during the year.
13. $27,415 was paid in interest during the year.

Required

1. Classify each of the cash flows as operating, investing, or financing activities.

   1. _____   8. _____
   2. _____   9. _____
   3. _____   10. _____
   4. _____   11. _____
   5. _____   12. _____
   6. _____   13. _____
   7. _____

2. Using the following form, prepare a statement of cash flows for Ramirez Refinishers (check your answers to Requirement 1 with the solution before proceeding with the statement).

Ramirez Refinishers, Inc.		
Statement of Cash Flows		

Demonstration Problem #2

Jonathan Savy is a media consultant living in North Dakota. His business is called Savy Advice, Inc. From the following information, prepare an Income Statement, Statement of Retained Earnings, and Balance Sheet for Savy Advice, Inc., for the month of July 2002.

Accounts Payable	$ 700
Accounts Receivable	1,800
Advertising Expense	500
Building	55,000
Cash	8,200
Commissions Earned	12,000
Common Stock	50,000
Dividends	2,000
Equipment	6,600
Interest Expense	200
Interest Receivable	100
Notes Payable	14,000
Notes Receivable	1,000
Retained Earnings	9,325
Salaries Expense	1,750
Salaries Payable	250
Supplies	2,325
Supplies Expense	2,900
Utilities Expense	100
Vehicle	3,800

Income Statement

Statement of Retained Earnings

Balance Sheet

SOLUTIONS

I. Matching

1. C	4. M	7. A	10. K	13. L	16. Q
2. G	5. F	8. I	11. B	14. O	17. P
3. E	6. H	9. N	12. J	15. D	

II. Multiple Choice

1. C Of the choices given, only "Notes Payable" meets the definition of a liability. Insurance Expense is an expense, Equipment is an asset, and Dividends are reductions in equity.

2. B Cash receipts from customers, cash paid to employees, and cash paid to suppliers all appear on the statement of cash flows.

3. D Accounts payable are a liability and are listed on the balance sheet.

4. C

5. C The balance sheet lists all the assets, liabilities, and stockholders' equity as of a specific date. The income statement, statement of retained earnings, and statement of cash flows cover a specific time period.

6. D The income statement and statement of retained earnings cover a specific period of time. The balance sheet lists all the assets, liabilities, and stockholders' equity as of a specific date.

7. D Revenues minus expenses equals net income. Assets minus liabilities equals stockholders' equity. Liabilities plus stockholders' equity equals assets. Revenues plus expenses has no meaning.

8. B Let "L" stand for liabilities. Given that total assets equals 4L and that stockholders' equity equals $90,000, then according to the accounting equation:
    4L = L + $90,000, subtract L from both sides of the equation:
    3L = $90,000, therefore L = $30,000
    Total Assets = $30,000 + $90,000
    Total Assets = $120,000

    > **Study Tip**: Memorizing and understanding the basic accounting equation is important and will be helpful in future chapters.

9. C

Beginning balance in Retained Earnings	$ 120
+ Net Income	86
Subtotal	206
-Dividends	91
Ending balance in Retained	$115

10.   B   Assets   = Liabilities + Stockholders' Equity

$160,000 = $ 85,000	+	$ 75,000	Jan. 1
+45,000		- 22,000	
$205,000 = $152,000	+	$ 53,000	Dec. 31

III. Completion

1. Income Statement, Statement of Retained Earnings, Balance Sheet, and Statement of Cash Flows
2. entity (The most basic concept in accounting is that each entity has sharp boundaries between it and every other entity.)
3. amounts earned by delivering goods and services to customers
4. expenses
5. liabilities, owners' equity
6. Assets = Liabilities + Owners' equity
7. cost
8. Bookkeeping
9. company name, statement name, date
10. Stable-Monetary-Unit
11. operating, investing, financing
12. net income (loss)
13. ending retained earnings
14. financing activities
15. income statement

IV. True/False

1.   T
2.   F   Purchasing common stock is a financing activity.
3.   T
4.   F   The greatest flexibility for an owner is the sole proprietorship form of business. The owners of a corporation are the shareholders, and they have no direct involvement in "running" the business.
5.   T
6.   F   GAAP stands for Generally Accepted Accounting Principles.
7.   T
8.   F   The terms are similar in that both represent claims on the economic resources of the organization; however, capital represents the claims of owners, whereas creditors represent the claims of non-owners.
9.   T
10. F   The excess of revenues over expenses is called net income.
11. F   Assets are on the balance sheet, but expenses are on the income statement.
12. T

13.   F   The income statement is prepared first, before the statement of retained earnings, because you need net income from the income statement in order to complete the statement of retained earnings.

14.   T

15.   T

V. Exercises

1.

Cash received from clients	$866,000
Cash received from interest	1,275
Cash paid to suppliers/employees	(613,640)
Cash paid for interest	(82,680)
Cash paid for taxes	(710)
Cash flows from operating activities	$170,245

2.

Jenny's Juice Bar
Balance Sheet
January 31, 2002

Assets:		Liabilities:		
Cash	$108	Accounts payable	$225	
Accounts receivable	180	Total liabilities		225
Supplies	63	Stockholders' equity:		
Equipment	144	Common stock	90*	
		Retained earnings	180	270
		Total liabilities		
Total assets	$495	and Stockholders' equity		$495

* common stock = X. X = total asset – liabilities – retained earnings. X = 495 – 225 – 180; X = 90.

3.

Larry's Landscaping
Income Statement
For the Month Ended August 31, 2002

Revenues: Fees earned		$456
Expenses:		
Salaries	$ 70	
Truck rental	124	
Supplies	32	
Advertising	185	
Utilities	106	517
Net income (loss)		($61)

Study Tip: Net income results when revenues are greater than expenses. Net loss results when revenues are less than expenses.

VI. Critical Thinking

The answer to both questions is "yes." How is this possible? Profitability is presented on the Income Statement and occurs when revenues exceed expenses. Solvency is analyzed by examining the Balance Sheet and comparing assets (specifically cash and receivables) with liabilities. A business is solvent when there are sufficient assets on hand to pay the debt as the debt becomes due. Remember, however, there is a third financial statement—the Statement of Retained Earnings—which links the Income Statement to the Balance Sheet. A profitable business will become insolvent if, over time, the owners withdraw assets (dividends) in excess of net income. Conversely, an unprofitable business can remain solvent over time if the owner is able to contribute assets in excess of the net losses.

VII. Demonstration Problems

Demonstration Problem 1 Solved and Explained

Requirement 1
1. Financing activity
2. Financing activity
3. Investing activity
4. Investing activity
5. Operating activity
6. Financing activity
7. Operating activity
8. Financing activity
9. Operating activity
10. Operating activity
11. Financing activity
12. Operating activity
13. Operating activity

Remember, operating activities are those relating to the company's operations, i.e., why they are in business. Operating activities can be traced back to the income statement. Investing activities detail the acquisition and disposition of long-term assets. Financing activities refer to debt and stockholders' equity.

Requirement 2

Ramirez Refinishers, Inc.
Statement of Cash Flows

Cash flows from operating activities:	
Cash received from customers	$1,160,130 [1]
Cash received from interest	2,452
Cash paid to suppliers and employees	(546,770) [2]
Cash paid for interest	(27,415)
Cash paid for taxes	(52,290)
Net cash flows from operating activities	$536,107

Cash flows from investing activities:

Cash paid for new building	(240,000)[3]	
Proceeds from sale of equipment	9,200	
Cash paid for new equipment	(105,000)	
Net cash flows from investing activities		(335,800)

Cash flows from financing activities:

Cash paid for short-term debt	(20,000)	
Proceeds from long-term borrowing	150,000	
Proceeds from sale of common stock	275,000	
Purchase of treasury stock	(285,000)[4]	
Payment of dividends	(80,000)	
Net cash flows from investing activities		40,000

Net increase (decrease) in cash		$240,307

[1] Remember the Study Tip given to you earlier: Beginning balance + additions - deductions = ending balance.

[2] $184,270 (suppliers) + $362,500 (employees) = $546,770.

[3] While the building cost $920,000, only $240,000 in cash was used; therefore, only $240,000 appears on the statement of cash flows.

[4] 10,000 shares × $28.50 =$285,000

Demonstration Problem 2 Solved

Savy Advice, Inc.
Income Statement
Month Ended July 31, 2002

Commissions earned		$12,000
Less: Expenses		
Advertising	500	
Interest	200	
Salaries	1750	
Supplies	2900	
Utilities	100	
Total expenses		5,450
Net income		$ 6,550

Savy Advice, Inc.
Statement of Retained Earnings
Month Ended July 31, 2002

Retained earnings 7/1/02		$ 9,325
Add: Net income	6,550	
Less: Dividends	2,000	4,550
Retained earnings 7/31/02		$13,875

Savy Advice, Inc.
Balance Sheet
July 31, 2002

ASSETS		**LIABILITIES**		
Cash	$ 8,200	Accounts payable	$ 700	
Accounts receivable	1,800	Notes payable	14,000	
Notes receivable	1,000	Salaries payable	250	
Interest receivable	100	Total liabilities		14,950
Supplies	2,325			
Equipment	6,600	**STOCKHOLDERS' EQUITY**		
Vehicle	3,800	Common stock	50,000	
Building	55,000	Retained earnings	13,875	
		Total stockholders' equity		63,875
		Total liabilities and stockholders' equity		
Total assets	$78,825			$78,825

CHAPTER 2—PROCESSING ACCOUNTING INFORMATION

CHAPTER OVERVIEW

Chapter 2 uses the foundation established in the previous chapter and introduces you to the recording process for business transactions. A thorough understanding of this process is vital to your success in mastering topics in future chapters. The specific learning objectives for this chapter are to

1. Use key accounting terms
2. Analyze business transactions
3. Understand how double-entry accounting works
4. Record business transactions
5. Prepare and use a trial balance
6. Analyze transactions for quick decisions

CHAPTER REVIEW

Objective 1 - Use key accounting terms

The terms used in accounting sometimes have meanings that differ from ordinary usage. Therefore, you must learn the accounting meaning of terms. Key terms to remember are: account, assets, liabilities, stockholders' (owners') equity, common stock, retained earnings, dividends, revenues, and expenses.

An **account** is the basic summary device used to record changes that occur in a particular asset, liability, or stockholders' equity.

Assets are those economic resources that will benefit the business in the future. Examples of asset accounts are Cash, Accounts Receivable, Inventory, Notes Receivable, Prepaid Expenses, Land, Buildings, Equipment, Furniture, and Fixtures.

Liabilities are obligations that a business owes. Examples of liability accounts include Notes Payable, Accounts Payable, and Accrued Liabilities.

Stockholders' equity is the claim that the stockholders have on the assets of the business. Examples of stockholders' equity accounts are Common Stock, Retained Earnings, and Dividends; revenues, such as Service Revenue; and expenses such as Rent Expense.

Common stock represents owners' (stockholders') investment in the business. When individuals invest in a corporation, they receive a stock certificate for the number of shares purchased.

Retained earnings represents the cumulative net incomes of the corporation less any dividends and less any net losses.

Dividends are distributions of assets by the corporation to the shareholders. Dividends decrease stockholders' equity.

Revenues represent the goods or services provided to customers. The Gap earns revenues when it sells merchandise (inventory) to customers, while a transportation company earns revenues when it provides a service to its customers. Revenues increase stockholders' equity.

Expenses are the costs of operating a business. Some examples of expenses are rent, cost of sales, insurance, supplies, and salaries. Expenses decrease stockholders' equity.

> **Study Tip:** When revenues are greater than expenses, the difference is net income. When revenues are less than expenses, the difference is net loss.

Objective 2 - Analyze business transactions.

Every transaction will have a dual effect on the accounting equation. Therefore, the equation always remains in balance. Study carefully the eleven business transactions analyzed in the text, and reinforce your understanding by following the demonstration problems and explanations in this chapter of the Study Guide. You must have a thorough knowledge of how transactions affect the accounting equation in order to proceed further in this course.

See Exhibit 2-1 in the text. Transactions affecting stockholders' equity result in changes to either Common Stock or Retained Earnings. Common stock is affected when a corporation issues stock certificates to shareholders and receives assets in return (usually cash). Retained earnings are affected when the corporation records revenues, expenses, or authorizes the payment of dividends to the stockholders. Revenues increase retained earnings by bringing cash or other assets into the business in the form of earnings made by delivering goods or services to customers. Expenses are decreases in retained earnings that occur in the course of earning revenue.

After the transactions have been analyzed and recorded, the financial statements are used to summarize the business events. Recall the following from Chapter 1:
1. The statement of cash flows summarizes the cash inflows and outflows and groups these cash flows into three categories.
2. The income statement summarizes the revenues and expenses and results in either net income or net loss.
3. The retained earnings statement summarizes the source and amounts of changes in retained earnings.
4. The balance sheet lists the details of the three elements in the accounting equation (assets, liabilities, stockholders' equity)

Exhibit 2-2 presents the financial statements using the transaction summary from Exhibit 2-1.

Objective 3 - Understand how double-entry accounting works.

Accounting is based on a **double-entry** system. Each transaction affects at least two accounts. **T-accounts** illustrate the dual effects of a transaction. The left side of the T-account is the **debit** side. The right side is the **credit** side.

> **Study Tip**: Remember: debit = left side and credit = right side, nothing more.

The account type determines how debits and credits are recorded. A debit increases the balance of an asset, and a credit decreases the balance. A credit increases the balance of a liability or stockholders' equity, and a debit decreases the balance.

Assets		=	Liabilities		+	Stockholders' Equity	
debit for increase	credit for decrease		debit for decrease	credit for increase		debit for decrease	credit for increase

To illustrate, suppose that Clinton Corporation buys on credit office furniture of $35,000 for a consulting business. What debits and credits should be recorded? Debit Office Furniture, an asset, for $35,000. (Assets are increased by a debit.) Credit a liability, for $35,000. (Liabilities are increased by a credit.)

> **Study Tip**: Refer to the basic accounting equation to understand the debit/credit rules. Increases in items on the *left side* of the equation are placed on the *left side* (debit) of the account. Increases in the items on the *right side* of the equation are placed on the *right side* (credit) of the account.

Exhibit 2-6 in your text summarizes the debit/credit rules for the expanded accounting equation.

Objective 4 - Record business transactions.

A **journal** is a chronological record of a corporation's transactions. It is the first place where a transaction is recorded. To record a transaction in the journal, follow these five steps:

1. Identify the transaction from the source documents.
2. Specify each account affected by the transaction and classify it by type (asset, stockholders' equity, revenue, or expense).
3. Determine whether each account balance is increased or decreased.
4. Determine whether to debit or credit the account.
5. Enter the transaction in the journal: first the debit, then the credit, and finally a brief explanation.

To illustrate, suppose that Gore Corporation borrows $150,000 from the bank to expand the business. What is the journal entry for this transaction?

Step 1 The source documents are a deposit slip for $150,000 and a loan agreement with the bank, both of which are dated March 20, 2002.
Step 2 The accounts affected are Cash (an asset) and Notes Payable (a liability).
Step 3 Both accounts will increase by $150,000.
Step 4 Debit Cash for $150,000 to increase Cash, and Credit Notes Payable for $150,000 to increase Notes Payable.
Step 5 Record the journal entry:

Date		Debit	Credit
Mar. 20	Cash	150,000	
	Notes Payable		150,000
	Bank loan for business expansion.		

> **Study Tip**: If one of the accounts affected is Cash, first determine whether Cash increases or decreases.

Examples of some typical journal entries are:

Cash	25,000	
Common Stock		25,000
Issued shares of stock.		
Prepaid Insurance	3,000	
Cash		3,000
Purchased a 3-year insurance policy.		
Supplies	1,500	
Accounts Payable		1,500
Purchased supplies on account.		
Accounts Receivable	2,200	
Commissions Earned		2,200
Billed clients for services rendered.		
Salary Expense	800	
Cash		800
Paid salaries.		
Cash	1,400	
Accounts Receivable		1,400
Received payments from clients previously billed.		

Posting means transferring amounts from the journal to the appropriate accounts in the ledger. The journal entry for the bank loan in the previous example would be posted this way:

Cash		Notes Payable	
150,000			150,000

Review Exhibit 2-8 in your text for an illustration of journalizing and posting.

> **Study Tip**: Still having difficulty remembering how to increase a specific account? Memorize this acronym—DEAD CRLS (pronounced "dead curls"). Debits increase Expenses, Assets, and Dividends (DEAD) while Credits increase Revenues, Liabilities, and Stockholders' equity (CRLS).

Objective 5 - Prepare and use a trial balance.

The **trial balance** is a list of all accounts with their balances. It tests whether the total debits equal the total credits. If total debits do not equal the total credits, an error has been made. However, some errors may not be detected by a trial balance. One example is the posting of a transaction to the wrong account. Another is a transaction recorded at the wrong amount.

A **chart of accounts** consists of a list of all the accounts used in the business. Each account is assigned a unique number (this account number is used as a reference in the posting process). The order of the accounts in this list parallels the accounting equation. In other words, assets are listed first, followed by liability accounts and, lastly, stockholders' equity. Stockholders' equity is subdivided into common stock, retained earnings, dividends, revenue, and expense accounts. The numbers are assigned in ascending order so assets are assigned the lowest numbers while expenses carry the highest numbers.

The term **normal balance** refers to the type of balance (debit or credit) the account usually carries. The normal balance for any account is always the side of the account where increases are recorded. Therefore, the normal balances are

Account	Normal Balance
Assets	debit
Liabilities	credit
Common Stock	credit
Retained Earnings	credit
Dividends	debit
Revenues	credit
Expenses	debit

Study Tip: Spend some time reading and thinking about the Decision Guidelines in your text. These should help you place the recording process in the proper context.

Objective 6 - Analyze transactions for quick decisions.

In general, the ledger is more useful than the journal in providing an overall model of a business. Therefore, when time is of the essence, accountants skip the journal and go directly to the ledger in order to compress transaction analysis, journalizing, and posting into a single step. This informal analysis permits decision makers to arrive at their decisions more quickly.

TEST YOURSELF

All the self-testing materials in this chapter focus on information and procedures that your instructor is likely to test in quizzes and examinations.

I. Matching   *Match each numbered term with its lettered definition.*

_____ 1. account
_____ 2. stockholders' equity
_____ 3. chart of accounts
_____ 4. transaction
_____ 5. credit
_____ 6. debit
_____ 7. double-entry system
_____ 8. journal

_____ 9. ledger
_____ 10. normal balance
_____ 11. posting
_____ 12. post reference
_____ 13. prepaid expenses
_____ 14. trial balance
_____ 15. dividends

A. detailed record of changes in a particular asset, liability, or stockholders' equity during a period of time
B. costs recorded before being used
C. a way of tracing amounts between the journal and ledger
D. left side of an account
E. list of all the accounts and their account numbers
F. transferring information from the journal to the ledger
G. a list of all the accounts with their balances which tests whether total debits equals total credits
H. the book of accounts
I. right side of an account
J. chronological record of an entity's transactions
K. the type of balance an account usually carries
L. the shareholders' claim to the business assets
M. payments of assets to shareholders
N. any event that both affects the financial position of a business entity and can be reliably recorded
O. recording the dual effects of transactions

II. Multiple Choice   *Circle the best answer.*

1. When cash is received on an accounts receivable

   A. total assets increase
   B. total assets decrease
   C. total assets are unchanged
   D. cannot be determined

2. A receivable is recorded when a business makes

   A. sales on account
   B. purchases on account
   C. sales for cash
   D. purchases for cash

3. An investment of equipment by a stockholder will result in

   A. an increase in both assets and liabilities
   B. an increase in both liabilities and stockholders' equity
   C. an increase in both assets and stockholders' equity
   D. no change in assets or stockholders' equity

4. A lawyer performs services for which he receives cash. The correct entry for this transaction is

   A. debit Legal Fees Revenue and credit Accounts Payable
   B. debit Legal Fees Revenue and credit Cash
   C. debit Accounts Receivable and credit Legal Fees Revenue
   D. debit Cash and credit Legal Fees Revenue

5. An accountant debited Insurance Expense $10,600 and credited Cash $10,600 in error. The correct entry should have been to debit Prepaid Insurance for $10,600 and credit Cash for $10,600. As a result of this error

   A. assets are overstated by $10,600
   B. expenses are understated by $10,600
   C. the trial balance will not balance
   D. expenses are overstated by $10,600

6. Accounts Receivable had total debits for the month of $2,500 and total credits for the month of $1,700. If the beginning balance in Accounts Receivable was $2,200, what was the net change in Accounts Receivable?

   A. a decrease of $800
   B. an increase of $3,200
   C. an increase of $800
   D. a decrease of $3,200

7. Accounts Payable had a balance of $5,000 on April 1. During April, $750 of supplies was purchased on account. The April 30 balance was a credit of $2,850. How much were payments on Accounts Payable during April?

   A. $2,200
   B. $2,250
   C. $2,900
   D. $8,600

8. Balance sheet accounts are

   A. assets and liabilities
   B. revenues and dividends
   C. revenues and expenses
   D. assets and expenses

9. The posting reference in the ledger tells

   A. the page of the ledger that the account is on
   B. the explanation of the transaction
   C. whether it is a debit or a credit entry
   D. the page of the journal where the entry can be found

10. The list of accounts and their account numbers is called the

    A. chart of accounts
    B. trial balance
    C. ledger
    D. accountants reference

11. When the business pays cash to stockholders, the journal entry should include a

    A. debit to Accounts Payable
    B. credit to Capital
    C. debit to Cash
    D. debit to Dividends

12. When cash was received in payment for services rendered on account, the accountant debited Cash and credited Service Revenue. As a result there was

    A. an overstatement of Cash and understatement of Service Revenue
    B. an understatement of assets and overstatement of revenues
    C. an overstatement of assets and liabilities
    D. an overstatement of assets and an overstatement of revenues

III. Completion   *Complete each of the following.*

1. Put the following in proper sequence by numbering them from 1 to 4.

   _____ A.   Journal entry
   _____ B.   Post to ledger
   _____ C.   Source document
   _____ D.   Trial balance

2. Indicate whether debits increase or decrease each of the following accounts.

	Increase	Decrease
A. Cash	_____	_____
B. Accounts payable	_____	_____
C. Prepaid insurance	_____	_____
D. Notes receivable	_____	_____
E. Commissions Earned	_____	_____
F. Rent Expense	_____	_____

3. Indicate the normal balance for each of the following.

	Debit	Credit
A. Accounts Receivable	_____	_____
B. Accounts Payable	_____	_____
C. Prepaid Rent	_____	_____
D. Vehicles	_____	_____
E. Common Stock	_____	_____
F. Notes Receivable	_____	_____
G. Salaries Expense	_____	_____
H. Fees Earned	_____	_____
I. Equipment	_____	_____
J. Dividends	_____	_____

IV. True/False   *For each of the following statements, circle* T *for true or* F *for false.*

1. T F   Liabilities are the costs of doing business that decrease stockholders' equity.
2. T F   The trial balance proves that no errors exist in the accounting records.
3. T F   When the business records the receipt of cash from a customer paying an invoice, revenues will increase.
4. T F   When revenues exceed dividends, net income results.
5. T F   A chart of accounts would list assets first, followed by liabilities and stockholders' equity.
6. T F   When a corporation buys equipment and pays cash, total assets will increase by the cost of the new equipment.
7. T F   Expenses carry normal debit balances.
8. T F   Debit means left, credit means right.
9. T F   Liability accounts are increased with credits.
10. T F   Assets, expenses, and dividends are subdivisions of stockholders' equity.
11. T F   The basic accounting equation will increase when the business borrows money from a bank.
12. T F   When a client is billed for services rendered, both assets and stockholders' equity increase.
13. T F   If a corporation pays dividends to the shareholders, the business records a cost.
14. T F   The effect of paying a creditor is to record an expense.
15. T F   Inventory is one type of asset account.

V. Exercises

1. Open Your Locks, Inc., operates an emergency unlocking service for automobiles. During the first month of operation the following events occurred:

   A. Sold 5,000 shares of common stock for $50,000.
   B. Paid rent of $2,250
   C. Purchased $12,000 of equipment on account.
   D. Purchased $610 of supplies for cash.
   E. Performed services on account, $1,875.
   F. Paid $2,600 on the equipment purchased in C.
   G. Received $900 from customers on account.

Prepare an analysis of transactions showing the effects of each event on the accounting equation.

		ASSETS					LIABILITIES	+	STOCKHOLDERS' EQUITY		
Cash	+	Accounts Receivable	+	Supplies	+	Equipment	=	Accounts Payable	+	Common Stock	+	Retained Earnings
A.											
B.											
C.											
D.											
E.											
F.											
G.											

2. Van Tran Thuy, Inc., began business as a concept and design consulting corporation on May 1, 2002. During the first month of operations, the following transactions occurred:

5/1   Sold 5,000 shares of stock for $40,000.
5/2   Purchased office furniture for $28,000. Made a $7,000 cash down payment and gave the seller a note payable due in 120 days.
5/3   Paid $9,100 for a month's rent.
5/10 Collected $19,000 in cash for services rendered during the first 10 days of May.
5/19 Purchased $1,030 of supplies on account.
5/19 Paid the phone bill for the month, $412.
5/20 Billed clients for $17,800
5/21 Received but did not pay the $282 utility bill for October.
5/25 Paid secretary a salary of $3,300.
5/28 Paid for the supplies purchased on 5/19.
5/31 Performed $1,400 in services for the last third of May. Clients paid for $1,400 of these services.
5/31 Paid $24,200 dividends to stockholders.

Prepare the journal entries for each of these transactions. (Omit explanations.)

Date	Accounts	PR	Debit	Credit

3. The following are normal balances for the accounts of Larry's Limo Service, Inc., on July 31, 2002.

Accounts payable	$2,250
Accounts receivable	3,075
Advertising expense	115
Cash	3,380
Common stock	3,625
Fuel expense	975
Insurance expense	640
Prepaid rent	90
Salary expense	2,755
Salaries payable	215
Service revenue	5,545
Uniform cleaning expense	605

Prepare a trial balance based on the account balances above.

	Debit	Credit
Cash	_____	_____
Accounts receivable	_____	_____
Prepaid rent	_____	_____
Accounts payable	_____	_____
Salaries payable	_____	_____
Common stock	_____	_____
Service revenue	_____	_____
Advertising expense	_____	_____
Insurance expense	_____	_____
Fuel expense	_____	_____
Salary expense	_____	_____
Uniform cleaning expense	_____	_____
Total	=========	=========

4. Harlan's Horse Hire Corporation had the following trial balance on June 30, 2002.

Cash	$ 56,000	
Accounts receivable	18,000	
Notes receivable	6,000	
Land	70,000	
Accounts payable		$ 8,400
Common stock		120,000
Delivery revenue		24,000
Salary expense		7,000
Insurance expense	3,000	
	$153,000	$ 159,400

The following errors caused the trial balance not to balance:

A. All accounts have a normal balance.
B. Recorded a $2,000 note payable as a note receivable.
C. Posted a $4,000 credit to Accounts Payable as $400.
D. Recorded Prepaid Insurance of $3,000 as Insurance Expense.
E. Recorded a cash revenue transaction by debiting Cash for $6,000 and crediting Accounts Receivable for $6,000.

Prepare a corrected trial balance as of June 30, 2002.

Harlan's Horse Hire Corporation
Trial Balance
June 30, 2002

Cash	_____	_____
Accounts receivable	_____	_____
Notes receivable	_____	_____
Prepaid insurance	_____	_____
Land	_____	_____
Accounts payable	_____	_____
Notes payable	_____	_____
Common stock	_____	_____
Delivery revenue	_____	_____
Salary expense	_____	_____
Insurance expense	_____	_____
Total	=========	=========

VI. Critical Thinking

The following errors occurred in posting transactions from the journal to the ledger.

1. A payment of $170 for advertising was posted as a $170 debit to Advertising Expense and a $710 credit to Cash.
2. The receipt of $300 from a customer on account was posted as a $300 debit to Cash and a $300 credit to Fees Earned.
3. The purchase of supplies on account for $140 was posted twice as a debit to Supplies and once as a credit to Accounts Payable.
4. The payment of $220 to a creditor on account was posted as a credit to Accounts Payable for $220 and a credit to Cash for $220.

For each of these errors, determine the following:
   A. Is the trial balance out of balance?
   B. If out of balance, what is the difference between the column totals?
   C. Which column total is larger?
   D. Which column total is correct?

Error	Out of balance?	Column total difference	Larger column total	Correct column total
1.				
2.				
3.				
4.				

VII. Demonstration Problems

Demonstration Problem #1

Livingston Leisure Services Corporation organizes and leads small group tours to Antarctica. During the month of January 2002 (the first month of operation), the following transactions occurred.

1/1   Sold 1,000 shares of common stock for $35,000.
1/1   An office was located in town and rent of $2,000 was paid for the first month.
1/3   Office supplies were purchased for cash at a cost of $400.
1/5   A computer and a laser printer to be used in the business were purchased on account for $3,200.
1/8   Additional office supplies costing $1,200 were purchased on account.
1/10 Commissions of $4,250 were billed on account to clients.
1/15 Additional fees totaling $1,800 collected from clients during the first 15 days of the month were deposited in the business checking account.
1/16 Cash of $2,300 was received from clients billed on 1/10.
1/18 Paid for the office supplies purchased on 1/8.
1/21 Dividends of $1,500 were paid.
1/31 Commissions totaling $3,100 were collected from clients during the second half of the month. These fees were deposited in the business checking account.

Required

1. Prepare an analysis of transactions of Livingston Leisure Services Corporation. Use Exhibit 2-1 of the text as a guide and the format on the next page for your answers.

2. Prepare the income statement, statement of retained earnings, balance sheet, and statement of cash flows for the business after recording the January transactions.

Requirement 1 (Analysis of transactions)

		ASSETS				LIABILITIES	+	STOCKHOLDERS' EQUITY		
Cash	+	Accounts Receivable	+ Supplies	+ Equipment	=	Accounts Payable	+	Common Stock	+	Retained Earnings

Requirement 2 (Income Statement, Statement of Retained Earnings, Balance Sheet, and Statement of Cash Flows)

Demonstration Problem #2

The trial balance of River Rafting, Inc., on May 1, 2002, lists the entity's assets, liabilities, and stockholders' equity.

	Balance	
Account Title	Debit	Credit
Cash	$ 8,000	
Equipment	24,000	
Accounts Payable		$ 5,000
Common Stock		27,000

During May, the business performed transactions *a* through *i* :
a. In anticipation of expanding the business in the near future, the company borrowed $65,000 from a local bank. A note payable was signed.
b. A small parcel of land was acquired for $25,000 cash. The land is expected to be used as the future location of the business.
c. Rafting trips were provided for clients. Cash totaling $4,000 was received for these trips.
d. Supplies costing $800 to be used in the business were purchased on account.
e. Rafting trips were provided for clients. Earned revenue on account totaled $4,500.
f. The following expenses were paid in cash:
   1. Salary expense, $3,000
   2. Rent expense, $1,400
   3. Advertising expense, $1,150
   4. Interest expense, $650
g. Paid dividends of $2,200.
h. Paid $3,600 owed on account.
i. Received $3,100 cash on account for services previously rendered.

Required:

1. Using the T-account format, open the following ledger accounts for River Rafting, Inc., with the balances as indicated.

   ASSETS
   Cash , $8,000
   Accounts receivable, no balance
   Supplies, no balance
   Equipment, $24,000
   Land, no balance

   LIABILITIES
   Accounts payable, $5,000
   Notes payable, no balance

   STOCKHOLDERS' EQUITY
   Common stock, $27,000
   Dividends, no balance

   REVENUE
   Rafting revenue, no balance

   EXPENSES
   Salary expense, no balance
   Rent expense, no balance
   Interest expense, no balance
   Advertising expense, no balance

2. Journalize the transactions. Key each journal entry by its transaction letter.
3. Post to the T-accounts. Key all amounts by letter and compute a balance for each account.
4. Prepare the trial balance as of May 31, 2002.
5. Prepare the income statement, statement of retained earnings, and balance sheet.

Requirements 1 and 3: (Open ledger accounts and post journal entries)

ASSETS

LIABILITIES

STOCKHOLDERS' EQUITY

REVENUE

EXPENSES

Requirement 2 (Journal entries)

Date	Accounts and Explanation	PR	Debit	Credit

Requirement 4 (Trial Balance)

ACCOUNTS	DEBITS	CREDITS
Cash		
Accounts receivable		
Supplies		
Equipment		
Land		
Accounts payable		
Notes payable		
Common stock		
Dividends		
Rafting revenue		
Salary expense		
Rent expense		
Interest expense		
Advertising expense		

Requirement 5

_____
_____
_____

_____
_____
_____

_____
_____
_____

SOLUTIONS

I. Matching

1. A	4. N	7. O	10. K	13. B
2. L	5. I	8. J	11. F	14. G
3. E	6. D	9. H	12. C	15. M

II. Multiple Choice

1. C When cash is received on an account receivable, two assets are affected: cash is increased and accounts receivable is decreased. Since the increase in cash is equal to the decrease in accounts receivable, total assets are unchanged.

2. A Only sales on account cause a receivable to be recorded. Purchases on account cause a payable to be recorded; sales for cash and purchases for cash do not affect receivables.

3. C The sale of common stock causes an increase in the assets of the business. Since the owners have claim to those assets they invested in the business, there is also an increase in stockholders' equity.

4. D The receipt of cash, an asset, for the performance of services causes an increase in equity. This increase in equity from providing services is called revenue. Cash is increased with a debit and revenue is increased with a credit.

5. D The recorded entry incorrectly increased expenses by $10,600. Accordingly, expenses are overstated. Since the entry should have debited Prepaid Insurance, but did not, assets are *understated*. Even though the entry is erroneous, it included both a debit and credit and the trial balance will balance.

6. C The $2,500 of debits to Accounts Receivable increased the balance, while the $1,700 of credits to Accounts Receivable decreased the balance. The net effect of the debits and the credits is $2,500 - $1,700 = $800 increase.

7. C The following equation is used to solve this problem:

Beginning balance
+ increase   (new accounts)
- decrease   (payments)
= ending balance

Rearranged to solve for payments the equation is:

Payments = beginning balance + new accounts - ending balance
Payments = $5,000 + 750 - $2,850 = $2,900

8. A Of the combinations of accounts listed, only "Assets and Liabilities" are balance sheet accounts. All other responses include at least one income statement account.

9.   D   The posting reference provides a "trail" through the accounting records for future reference.

10.   A   A list of accounts and account numbers is called the chart of accounts.

11.   D   Dividends decrease the Cash account balance and increase the balance in the Dividends account. To decrease the cash balance it is necessary to credit the Cash account; to increase the dividends account balance it is necessary to debit the Dividends account.

12.   D   The journal entry made incorrectly credited (increased) the Service Revenue account balance. The correct entry should have been to credit (decrease) Accounts Receivable. As a result, assets (Accounts Receivable) are overstated and revenue (Service Revenue) is overstated.

III. Completion

1. A. 2.   B. 3.   C. 1   D. 4
(Source documents provide the information necessary to prepare journal entries. Journal entries are posted to the ledger. The trial balance is prepared from ledger balances.)

2. A. increase   B. decrease   C. increase   D. increase   E. decrease   F. increase
(Debits increase accounts with a normal debit balance and decrease accounts with a normal credit balance. Assets, dividends, and expenses have normal debit balances, while liabilities, stockholders' equity, and revenue have normal credit balances.)

| **Study Tip**: Remember DEAD CRLS, the study tip given earlier? |

3. A. debit   B. credit   C. debit   D. debit   E. credit   F. debit   G. debit   H. credit
   I. debit   J. debit
(Assets, expenses, and dividends have normal debit balances. Liabilities, stockholders' equity, and revenue have normal credit balances.)

IV. True/False

1.   F   Liabilities are obligations of the business; expenses are the costs of doing business.
2.   F   The trial balance only proves the equality of debits and credits in the ledger; it does not prove that no errors were made.
3.   F   Revenues will increase at the time the customer is sent the invoice, not at the time the invoice is paid by the customer.
4.   F   Net income is the excess of revenues over expenses. Dividends have no effect on net income.
5.   T
6.   F   Because the amount of increase in equipment is equal to the amount of decrease in cash, total assets will not change.
7.   T
8.   T
9.   T
10.   F   Expenses and dividends are subdivisions of stockholders' equity (along with common stock, retained earnings and revenues); assets are the economic resources available for future use.
11.   T

12. T
13. F Dividends are not a cost of doing business; they are the distribution of assets to shareholders.
14. F When paying a creditor, both assets (cash) and liabilities (accounts payable) decrease. Expenses are not affected.
15. T

V. Exercises

	Cash	+	Accounts Receivable	+	Supplies	+	Equipment	=	Accounts Payable	+	Common Stock	+	Retained Earnings
A.	$50,000							=			$50,000		
B.	-2,250							=					$-2,250
	$47,750							=			$50,000		$-2,250
C.							$12,000	=	$12,000				
	$47,750					+	$12,000	=	$12,000	+	$50,000		$-2,250
D.	-610			+	$ 610			=					
	$47,140			+	$ 610	+	$12,000	=	$12,000	+	$50,000		$-2,250
E.			$ 1,875					=					$ 1,875
	$47,140	+	$ 1,875	+	$ 610	+	$12,000	=	$12,000	+	$50,000		$-375
F.	-2,600							=	- 2,600				
	$44,540	+	$ 1,875	+	$ 610	+	$12,000	=	$9,400	+	$50,000		$-375
G.	900		-900					=					
	$45,440	+	$ 975	+	$ 610	+	$12,000	=	$9,400	+	$50,000		$-375

2.

Date	Account	PR	Debit	Credit
5/1	Cash		40,000	
	Common Stock			40,000
5/2	Furniture		28,000	
	Cash			7,000
	Notes Payable			21,000
5/3	Rent Expense		9,100	
	Cash			9,100
5/10	Cash		19,000	
	Consulting Revenues			19,000
5/19	Supplies		1,030	
	Accounts Payable			1,030

			Debit	Credit
5/19	Telephone Expense		412	
	Cash			412
5/20	Accounts Receivable		17,800	
	Consulting Revenues			17,800
5/21	Utility Expense		282	
	Utilities Payable (or Accounts Payable)			282
5/25	Salary Expense		3,300	
	Cash			3,300
5/28	Accounts Payable		1,030	
	Cash			1,030
5/31	Cash		14,000	
	Accounts Receivable		10,200	
	Consulting Revenues			24,200
5/31	Dividends		1,400	
	Cash			1,400

3.

Larry's Limo Service, Inc.
Trial Balance
July 31, 2002

	Debit	Credit
Cash	$ 3,380	
Accounts receivable	3,075	
Prepaid rent	90	
Accounts payable		$ 2,250
Salaries payable		215
Common stock		3,625
Service revenue		5,545
Advertising expense	115	
Insurance expense	640	
Fuel expense	975	
Salary expense	2,755	
Uniform cleaning expense	605	
Total	$11,635	$11,635

4.

Harlan's Horse Hire Corporation
Trial Balance
June 30, 2002

	Debit	Credit
Cash	$ 56,000	
Accounts receivable	24,000	
Notes receivable	4,000	
Prepaid insurance	3,000	
Land	70,000	
Accounts payable		$ 12,000
Notes payable		2,000
Common stock		120,000
Delivery revenue		30,000
Salary expense	7,000	
Insurance expense	0	
Total	$164,000	$164,000

VI. Critical Thinking

Error	Out of balance?	Column total difference	Larger column total	Correct column total
1.	yes	$540	credit	credit
2.	no			
3.	yes	$140	debit	credit
4.	yes	$440	credit	debit

VII. Demonstration Problems

Demonstration Problem #1 Solved and Explained

1/1   The sale of common stock for $35,000 increased equity in the business by the same amount. Thus:

Assets	=	Liabilities	+	Stockholders' Equity
Cash +35,000		no change		Common Stock +35,000

1/1   Monthly rent of $2,000 was paid, so Cash decreased by $2,000. In return for the rent, the business received the right to use the office space. However, the corporation still owns no part of the office; its right to use the office cannot be considered an asset. Since it has paid $2,000 cash but has not received an asset in return, nor paid a liability, the equity in the business has decreased by $2,000.

Assets	=	Liabilities	+	Stockholders' Equity
Cash -2,000		no change		Retained Earnings -2,000

1/3 $400 was paid for office supplies. In return for the cash, the business received ownership of the office supplies. When a business owns a resource to be used in the business, that resource is an asset. Since the $400 cash was exchanged for $400 worth of assets, stockholders' equity was not affected. Remember: When cash is exchanged for an asset, stockholders' equity is unaffected.

Assets		=	Liabilities	+	Stockholders' Equity
Cash	Office Supplies				
-400	+400		no change		no change

1/5   A computer and laser printer were purchased for $3,200 on account. The business now owns the equipment, which is an asset. However, payment was not made, but promised. The promise of payment is a debt, a liability. By promising the computer sales company $3,200, the business has added $3,200 to its liabilities, which until this point were zero.

Assets	=	Liabilities	+	Stockholders' Equity
Equipment				
+3,200		+3,200		no change

1/8   Office supplies costing $1,200 were purchased on account. As we saw in the 1/5 debt transaction, when a business incurs a debt in exchange for an asset, the business has added the asset but it has also added a corresponding liability.

Assets	=	Liabilities	+	Stockholders' Equity
Supplies		Accounts Payable		
+1,200		+1,200		no change

1/10 Commissions of $4,250 were provided on account to clients. When a client promises to pay for services rendered, the promise represents an asset to the business. A business earns revenue when it performs a service, whether it receives cash immediately or expects to collect the cash later. Revenue transactions cause the business to grow, as shown by the increase in total assets and equities. Note that both the assets and the stockholders' equity in the business have increased.

Assets	=	Liabilities	+	Stockholders' Equity
Accounts Receivable				Retained Earnings
+4,250		no change		+4,250

1/15   Fees totaling $1,800 were earned and collected. When services are rendered and cash is collected, the asset Cash increases by the amount collected and the retained earnings of the business increase as well.

Assets	=	Liabilities	+	Stockholders' Equity
Cash				Retained Earnings
+1,800		no change		+1,800

1/16   Collected $2,300 cash on the account receivable created on 1/10. The asset Cash is increased and the asset Accounts Receivable is decreased by the same amount. Note that revenue is unaffected by the actual receipt of the cash since the firm has already recorded the revenue when it was earned on 1/10.

Assets		=	Liabilities	+	Stockholders' Equity
Cash	Accounts Receivable				
+2,300	-2,300		no change		no change

1/18   Paid for the supplies purchased on 1/8. The payment of cash on account does not affect the asset Office Supplies because the payment does not increase or decrease the supplies available to the business. The effect on the accounting equation is a decrease in the asset Cash and a decrease in the liability Accounts Payable.

Assets	=	Liabilities	+	Stockholders' Equity
Cash		Accounts Payable		
-1,200		-1,200		no change

1/21   Dividends of $1,500 were paid. The cash dividends decrease the asset Cash and reduce the stockholders' equity in the business. Note that the dividends do not represent a business expense.

Assets	=	Liabilities	+	Stockholders' Equity
Cash				Retained Earnings
-1,500		no change		-1,500

1/31   Fees totaling $3,100 were collected. When services are rendered and immediately collected, the asset Cash increases by the amount received, and the retained earnings of the business increase as well.

Assets	=	Liabilities	+	Stockholders' Equity
Cash				Retained Earnings
+3,100		no change		+3,100

LIVINGSTON LEISURE SERVICES, INC.

	ASSETS			=	LIABILITIES +		STOCKHOLDERS' EQUITY	
	Cash +	Office Supplies +	Accounts Receivable +	Equipment =	Accounts Payable +	Common Stock +	Retained Earnings	Type of stockholders' equity transaction
1/1	+35,000					+35,000		Investment by stockholders
1/1	-2,000						-2,000	Rent expense
1/3	-400	+400						
1/5				+3,200	+3,200			
1/8		+1,200			+1,200			
1/10			+4,250				+4,250	Service income
1/15	+1,800						+1,800	Service income
1/16	+2,300		-2,300					
1/18	-1,200				-1,200			
1/21	-1,500						-1,500	Dividends
1/31	+3,100						+3,100	Service income
	$37,100	$1,600	$1,950	$3,200	$3,200	$35,000	$5,650	
			$43,850				$43,850	

Requirement 2 (Income Statement, Statement of Retained Earnings, Balance Sheet, and Statement of Cash Flows)

Livingston Leisure Services, Inc.
Income Statement
For the Month Ended January 31, 2002

Commissions earned	$9,150
Less: Expenses	
Rent	2,000
Net income	$7,150

Livingston Leisure Services, Inc.
Statement of Retained Earnings
For the Month Ended January 31, 2002

Retained earnings 1/1/02		-0-
Add: Net income	$7,150	
Less: Dividends	1,500	5,650
Retained earnings 1/31/02		$5,650

Livingston Leisure Services, Inc.
Balance Sheet
January 31, 2002

ASSETS			LIABILITIES		
Cash	$37,100		Accounts payable		$ 3,200
Accounts receivable	1,950				
Office supplies	1,600				
Equipment	3,200		**STOCKHOLDERS' EQUITY**		
			Common stock	35,000	
			Retained earnings	5,650	40,650
Total assets	$43,850		Total liabilities & stockholders' equity		$43,850

Livingston Leisure Services, Inc.
Statement of Cash Flows
For the Month Ended January 31, 2002

Cash Flows from operating activities:		
Cash received from customers	$7,200*	
Cash paid to suppliers	(3,600)	
Net cash flows from operating activities		$ 3,600
Cash flows from financing activities:		
Proceeds from sale of stock	35,000	
Cash paid for dividends	(1,500)	
Net cash flows from financing activities		33,500
Net cash increase during the month		37,100
Add: beginning cash balance		0
Cash balance, 1/31/02		$37,100

* The business earned commissions of $9,150; however, only $7,200 was received in cash. Note the ending Accounts Receivable balance of $1,950.

Demonstration Problem #2 Solved

Requirement 1 (Open ledger accounts)

ASSETS

Cash
Bal. 8,000

Accounts Receivable

Supplies

Equipment
Bal. 24,000

Land

LIABILITIES

Accounts Payable
Bal. 5,000

Notes Payable

STOCKHOLDERS' EQUITY

Common Stock
Bal. 27,000

Dividends

REVENUE

	Rafting Revenue	

EXPENSES

	Salary Expense			Rent Expense	

	Interest Expense			Advertising Expense	

Requirement 2 (Journal entries)

Date	Accounts and Explanation	PR	Debit	Credit
a.	Cash		65,000	
	Notes Payable			65,000
	Borrowed cash and signed note payable.			
b.	Land		25,000	
	Cash			25,000
	Purchased land for future office location.			
c.	Cash		4,000	
	Rafting Revenue			4,000
	Revenue earned and collected.			
d.	Supplies		800	
	Accounts Payable			800
	Purchased supplies on account.			
e.	Accounts Receivable		4,500	
	Rafting Revenue			4,500
	Performed services on account.			
f.	Salary Expense		3,000	
	Rent Expense		1,400	
	Advertising Expense		1,150	
	Interest Expense		650	
	Cash			6,200
	Paid cash expenses.			
g.	Dividends		2,200	
	Cash			2,200
	Paid dividends.			

h.	Accounts Payable		3,600	
	Cash			3,600
	Paid on account.			
i.	Cash		3,100	
	Accounts Receivable.			3,100
	Received on account.			

Requirement 3 (Posting)

ASSETS

Cash

Bal. 8,000	
(a) 65,000	(b) 25,000
(c) 4,000	(f) 6,200
(i) 3,100	(g) 2,200
	(h) 3,600
Bal. 43,100	

Accounts Receivable

(e) 4,500	(i) 3,100
Bal. 1,400	

Supplies

(d) 800	
Bal. 800	

Equipment

Bal. 24,000	
Bal. 24,000	

Land

(b) 25,000	
Bal. 25,000	

LIABILITIES

Accounts Payable

	Bal. 5,000
(h) 3,600	(d) 800
	Bal. 2,200

Notes Payable

	(a) 65,000
	Bal. 65,000

STOCKHOLDERS' EQUITY

Common Stock

	Bal. 27,000
	Bal. 27,000

Dividends

(g) 2,200	
Bal. 2,200	

REVENUE

Rafting Revenue

	(c) 4,000
	(e) 4,500
	Bal. 8,500

EXPENSES

Salary Expense	
(f) 3,000	
Bal. 3,000	

Rent Expense	
(f) 1,400	
Bal. 1,400	

Interest Expense	
(f) 650	
Bal. 650	

Advertising Expense	
(f) 1,150	
Bal. 1,150	

Requirement 4 (Trial Balance)

Account	Debits	Credits
Cash	$43,100	
Accounts receivable	1,400	
Supplies	800	
Equipment	24,000	
Land	25,000	
Accounts payable		$2,200
Notes payable		65,000
Common stock		27,000
Dividends	2,200	
Rafting revenue		8,500
Salary expense	3,000	
Rent expense	1,400	
Interest expense	650	
Advertising expense	1,150	
Total	$102,700	$102,700

Total debits = total credits. The accounts appear to be in balance. If the trial balance did not balance, we would look for an error in recording or posting.

Requirement 5

River Rafting, Inc
Income Statement
May 2002

Revenues: Rafting revenue		$8,500
Less: Expenses		
Salary expense	$3,000	
Rent expense	1,400	
Interest expense	650	
Advertising expense	1,150	
Total expenses		6,200
Net income		$2,300

River Rafting, Inc.
Statement of Retained Earnings
May 2002

Retained earnings 5/1/02		$ 0
Add: Net income	$2,300	
Less: Dividends	2,200	
Net increase in retained earnings		100
Retained earnings 5/31/02		$100

River Rafting, Inc.
Balance Sheet
May 31, 2002

ASSETS		LIABILITIES		
Cash	$43,100	Accounts payable	$ 2,200	
Accounts receivable	1,400	Notes payable	65,000	
Supplies	800	Total liabilities		$67,200
Equipment	24,000	**STOCKHOLDERS' EQUITY**		
Land	25,000	Common stock	$27,000	
		Retained earnings	100	27,100
Total assets	$94,300	Total liabilities & stockholders' equity		$94,300

CHAPTER 3—ACCRUAL ACCOUNTING AND THE FINANCIAL STATEMENTS

CHAPTER OVERVIEW

Chapter 3 continues the discussion begun in Chapter 2 concerning the recording of business transactions using debit and credit analysis. Therefore, you should feel comfortable with the debit and credit rules when you begin. In this chapter, you will learn about the adjusting process which takes place prior to the preparation of the financial statements. In addition, you are introduced to the closing process. The specific learning objectives for this chapter are to

1. Link cash flows with accrual-basis accounting
2. Apply the revenue and matching principles
3. Adjust the accounts to update the financial statements
4. Prepare the financial statements
5. Understand what closing the books means
6. Use the current ratio and the debt ratio to evaluate a business

CHAPTER REVIEW

Objective 1 - Link cash flows with accrual-basis accounting.

In **cash-basis accounting**, transactions are recorded only when cash is received or paid. In **accrual-basis accounting**, a business records transactions as they occur, without regard to when cash changes hands. GAAP requires that businesses use the accrual basis so that financial statements will not be misleading. Revenues are considered earned when services have been performed or merchandise is sold because the provider has a legal right to receive payment. Expenses are considered incurred when merchandise or services have been used. Financial statements would understate revenue if they did not include all revenues earned during the accounting period and would understate expenses if they did not include all expenses incurred during the accounting period.

Accountants prepare financial statements at specific intervals called accounting periods. The basic interval is a year, and nearly all businesses prepare annual financial statements. Usually, however, businesses need financial statements more frequently at quarterly or monthly intervals. Statements prepared at intervals other than the one-year interval are called **interim statements**.

Whether financial statements are prepared on an annual basis or on an interim basis, the **time-period concept** ensures that accounting information is prepared at regular intervals. The cutoff date is the last day of the time interval for which financial statements are prepared. All transactions that occur up to the cutoff date should be included in the accounts. Thus, if financial statements are prepared for January, all transactions occurring on or before January 31 should be recorded. Review Exhibit 3-2 in your text.

Objective 2 - Apply the revenue and matching principles.

The **revenue principle** guides the accountant as to 1) when to record revenue and 2) the amount of revenue to record. Revenue is recorded when it is earned, that is, when a business has delivered a completed good or service. The amount of revenue to record is generally the cash value of the goods delivered or the services performed. See Exhibit 3-3 in your text.

The **matching principle** guides the accountant in recording expenses. The objectives of the matching principle are 1) to identify the expenses that have been incurred in an accounting period; 2) to measure the expenses and 3) to match them against revenues earned during the same period. There is a natural association between revenues and some types of expenses. If a business pays its salespeople commissions based on amounts sold, there is a relationship between sales revenue and commission expense. Other expenses, such as rent, do not have a strong association with revenues. These types of expenses are generally associated with a period of time, such as a month or a year. Review Exhibit 3-4 in your text.

Objective 3 - Adjust the accounts to update the financial statements.

Accrual-basis accounting requires adjustments at the end of the accounting period. Accountants use adjusting entries to obtain an accurate measure of the period's income, to bring the accounts up to date for the preparation of financial statements, and to properly record the effect of transactions which span more than one accounting period. End-of-period processing begins with the preparation of a trial balance, which is sometimes referred to as an unadjusted trial balance.

Adjusting entries fall into three basic categories: 1) **deferrals**, 2) **depreciation**, and 3) **accruals.** Deferrals adjust asset or liability accounts. Frequently, a business will pay for goods and services in advance. Examples are supplies, insurance, and rent. Because these have been paid before being used they are recorded as assets. As time passes, these are used and the asset needs to be adjusted to reflect an accurate balance on the financial statements. The adjustment transfers an amount from the asset account to an expense account. The amount transferred represents the amount of the asset consumed. Many businesses receive payments from customers before the service has been provided (or the goods sold.) For example, in order to fly to visit a relative you need a ticket. To get the ticket you have to pay the airline (or travel agent) in advance. At the time you purchase your ticket the airline receives the cash but has not yet provided the service to earn the cash received. This is another example of deferral. Because the airline has accepted your money they have a liability (an obligation) to provide you with a service in the future. Once the service has been provided, the airline needs to transfer an amount from a liability account to a revenue account. These two examples illustrate the more common types of deferral adjustments-- prepaid expenses and unearned revenues.

Depreciation is a process which systematically allocates the cost of a plant asset to an expense account over the useful life of the plant asset. All plant assets (except land) are subject to depreciation. The effect of adjusting for depreciation is to reduce the value (called book value) of the plant asset over its life. This reduction in value also affects the income statement because depreciation expense is an additional cost to the business.

In a sense, accruals are the opposite of deferrals. Accruals refer to expenses and revenues that are not recorded in advance. Rather, they are recorded when the cash has been paid (for an expense) or received (for revenues.) The most common example of an accrued expense is salary because most employees receive their wages some time after they have performed the work. An example of accrued revenue is interest earned on the savings account. Although the interest is being earned as each day passes it is only recorded when received.

1) **Prepaid expenses** are expenses that are paid in advance. They are assets because the future benefits are expected to extend beyond the present accounting period. If we pay insurance premiums of $24,000 ($2,000 per month for the next twelve months) on December 31, then on December 31 we will have Prepaid Insurance of $24,000. None of the $24,000 payment is an expense during December because the payment benefits future periods. Insurance expense will be recorded each month as a portion of the $24,000 payment expires. Remember that the amount of a prepaid asset which has expired is an expense. Other examples of prepaid expenses are supplies, rent, and sometimes advertising.

Study Tip: Adjustments will be easier if you become familiar with the natural relationships that exist for each type of adjustment. For instance, the adjusting entry for a prepaid expense always affects an asset account and an expense account.

2) **Depreciation** is recorded to account for the fact that plant assets decline in usefulness as time passes. Examples of plant assets include buildings, office equipment, and vehicles. One distinguishing feature of plant assets, compared with prepaid expenses, is that plant assets are usually useful for longer periods. Land is the only plant asset that does not depreciate.

The reduction in the usefulness of plant assets is recorded in a contra account called **Accumulated Depreciation**. **Contra accounts** always have companion accounts and have account balances opposite from the account balances of the companion accounts. For accumulated depreciation, the companion account is a plant asset account. The plant asset account has a debit balance, and the contra account, Accumulated Depreciation, has a credit balance. The difference between these two amounts is called the asset's **book value**.

Study Tip: The adjusting entry for depreciation always debits Depreciation Expense and credits an Accumulated Depreciation account.

3) An **accrued expense** is an expense that a business has incurred but has not yet paid. Therefore, an accrued expense is also a liability. Accrued expenses include salary expense for employees. If you have worked a summer job, then you know that there may be an interval of several days or even a week between the end of your pay period and the date that you receive your paycheck. If an accounting period ends during such an interval, then your employer's salary expense would be accrued for the salary that you have earned but have not yet been paid. Other examples of accrued expenses are interest and sales commissions.

Study Tip: The adjusting entry for an accrued expense always debits an expense and credits a liability (payable) account.

4) **Accrued revenues** have been earned, but payment in cash has not been received nor has the client been billed. If a corporation earns $750 of revenue on January 28 but does not bill the client until February 3, then accrued revenue of $750 would be recorded on January 31.

Study Tip: The adjusting entry for accrued revenue always debits an asset (receivable) account and credits a revenue account.

5) **Unearned revenues** occur when cash is received from a customer before work is performed. Suppose that on March 15 you pay $80 for two tickets to a concert scheduled for April 7. The concert hall will not earn the $80 until April 7. Therefore, on March 15, the concert hall will debit Cash and credit Unearned Revenue. Unearned revenue is a liability account. In April, when the concert occurs, the concert hall earns the revenue and will debit Unearned Revenue and credit Revenue.

Study Tip: The adjusting entry for unearned revenue always involves a liability (unearned) account and a revenue account.

Note that each type of adjusting entry affects at least one income statement account and at least one balance sheet account. Also note that none of the adjusting entries has an effect on Cash. Adjusting entries are noncash transactions required by accrual accounting.

(Review Exhibits 3-10 and 3-11 in your text for a concise summary of these adjustments.)

The adjusted trial balance lists all the accounts and balances after the adjustments have been prepared. The general sequence for preparing an adjusted trial balance is

1) Prepare an unadjusted trial balance.
2) Assemble the information for adjusting entries.
3) Journalize and post adjusting entries.
4) Compute the adjusted account balances.

Study Exhibit 3-14 in your text to become familiar with the adjusted trial balance.

Objective 4 - Prepare the financial statements.

The **adjusted trial balance** provides the data needed to prepare the financial statements. The financial statements should always be prepared in the following order:

1) Income Statement
2) Statement of Retained Earnings
3) Balance Sheet

The reason for this order is quite simple: The income statement computes the amount of net income. Net income is needed for the statement of retained earnings. The statement of retained earnings computes the amount of ending retained earnings. Ending retained earnings are needed for the balance sheet. Exhibits 3-15, 3-16, and 3-17 in your text illustrate the flow of data from the income statement.

The income statement starts with revenues for the period and subtracts total expenses for the period. A positive result is net income; a negative result is net loss.

The statement of retained earnings starts with the amount of retained earnings at the beginning of the period, adds net income or subtracts net loss, and subtracts dividends. The result is the ending retained earnings balance.

The balance sheet uses the asset and liability balances from the adjusted trial balance and the retained earnings balance from the statement of retained earnings.

Note that none of the financial statements will balance back to the total debits and total credits on the adjusted trial balance. This is because the financial statements group accounts differently from the debit and credit totals listed on the adjusted trial balance. For example, the new balance for retained earnings on the balance sheet is a summary of the beginning retained earnings balance, the revenue and expense accounts used to obtain net income, and dividends paid during the period.

Objective 5 – Understand what closing the books means.

Closing the accounts refers to the process of preparing the accounts for the next accounting period. Closing involves journalizing and posting the **closing entries**. Closing the accounts sets the balances of revenues, expenses, and dividends to zero. Remember that when the balance sheet is prepared, the retained earnings balance includes the summary effect of the revenue, expense, and dividend accounts. These accounts are temporary accounts—they measure the effect on shareholders' equity for a single accounting period. This is in contrast to balance sheet accounts which are permanent accounts—they do not affect retained earnings.

The closing process uses a special holding account called **Income Summary**. The steps taken to close the accounts of an entity are

1. Transfer the credit balances from the revenue accounts to the Income Summary account. This is accomplished by debiting the accounts for the amount of their credit balances and crediting the Income Summary account for the total amount of the debits.

2. Transfer the debit balances from the expense accounts to the Income Summary account. This is accomplished by crediting the expense accounts for the amount of their debit balances and debiting the Income Summary account for the total amount of the credits.

   After these first two closing entries have been journalized and posted, all the revenue and expense accounts should have zero balances, and the Income Summary account should have two amounts (one debit amount and one credit amount) which summarize all the debit and credit balances in the individual revenue and expense accounts.

3. Transfer the balance from the Income Summary account to the Retained Earnings account. If the Income Summary account has a credit balance, the balance is net income. If the Income Summary account has a debit balance, the balance is net loss.

> **Study Tip:** The amount of the third closing entry must always agree with the amount of net income (or loss) reported on the income statement.

4. Transfer the balance in the Dividends account to Retained Earnings. This is accomplished by crediting the Dividends account for the amount of its debit balance and debiting Retained Earnings.

Exhibit 3-18 in your text illustrates the closing process. Note that when the closing entries are posted, the balance in Retained Earnings should be the same as the amount reported on the balance sheet.

Assets and liabilities are classified according to their liquidity. **Liquidity** is a measure of how quickly an item can be converted into cash. The balance sheet lists assets and liabilities in the order of their relative liquidity, with Cash as the most liquid asset listed first.

Current assets are those assets which are expected to be converted into cash, sold, or consumed within one year or within the business normal operating cycle if longer than a year. Current assets include: 1) Cash, 2) Accounts Receivable, 3) Notes Receivable, 4) Inventory, and 5) Prepaid Expenses.

Long-term assets are all assets which are not current assets. Long-term assets include plant assets such as: 1) Land, 2) Buildings, and 3) Equipment.

Current liabilities are obligations due within one year or one operating cycle if the cycle is longer than one year. Current liabilities include: 1) Accounts Payable, 2) Notes Payable due within one year, 3) Salary Payable, 4) Unearned Revenue, and 5) Interest Payable.

Long-term liabilities are obligations due in future years. Long-term liabilities include: 1) Notes Payable due at least partly in more than one year, 2) Bonds Payable, and 3) Mortgages Payable.

Objective 6 - Use the current ratio and the debt ratio to evaluate a business.

Before a loan is made, creditors like to be able to predict whether a borrower can repay the loan. Ratios of various items drawn from a company's financial statements can help creditors assess the likelihood that a loan can be repaid.

The **current ratio** measures the ability of a company to pay current liabilities (short-term debt) with current assets.

$$\text{Current ratio} = \frac{\text{Total current assets}}{\text{Total current liabilities}}$$

The debt ratio measures the relationship between total liabilities and total assets. The debt ratio is an indication of a company's ability to pay both current and long-term debt.

$$\text{Debt ratio} = \frac{\text{Total liabilities}}{\text{Total assets}}$$

TEST YOURSELF

All the self-testing materials in this chapter focus on information and procedures that your instructor is likely to test in quizzes and examinations.

I. Matching   *Match each numbered term with its lettered definition.*

_____ 1. contra asset
_____ 2. matching principle
_____ 3. prepaid expenses
_____ 4. unearned revenue
_____ 5. depreciation
_____ 6. plant asset
_____ 7. revenue principle
_____ 8. book value
_____ 9. deferrals
_____ 10. accruals
_____ 11. accumulated depreciation
_____ 12. valuation account

_____ 13. accrued expenses
_____ 14. liquidation
_____ 15. accrued revenues
_____ 16. closing the accounts
_____ 17. current liability
_____ 18. liquidity
_____ 19. long-term asset
_____ 20. closing entries
_____ 21. Income Summary
_____ 22. long-term liability
_____ 23. permanent accounts
_____ 24. temporary accounts

A. a category of miscellaneous assets that typically expire in the near future
B. a liability created when a business collects cash from customers in advance of doing work for the customer
C. an asset account with a credit balance and a companion account
D. expense associated with spreading (allocating) the cost of a plant asset over its useful life
E. long-lived assets, such as land, buildings, and equipment, that are used in the operations of the business
F. the basis for recording revenues that tells accountants when to record revenues and the amount of revenue to record
G. the basis for recording expenses that directs accountants to identify all expenses incurred during the period, to measure the expenses, and to match them against the revenues earned during that same period
H. a process of discontinuing operations and going out of business
I. revenues that have been earned but not recorded
J. an account used to determine the value of a related account
K. a collective term for accrued expenses and accrued revenues
L. expenses that have been incurred but not yet recorded
M. a balance sheet account credited when adjusting for depreciation
N. the difference between a plant asset account balance and its companion account balance
O. a collective term for prepaid expenses and unearned revenues
P. a debt due to be paid within one year or within one of the entity's operating cycles if the cycle is longer than a year
Q. a liability other than a current liability
R. a measure of how quickly an item may be converted to cash
S. a temporary holding account into which revenues and expenses are transferred prior to their final transfer to the stockholders' equity account
T. accounts that are not closed at the end of the accounting period
U. an asset other than a current asset
V. entries that transfer the revenue, expense, and dividend balances from these accounts to the stockholders' equity account

W. revenue accounts, expense accounts, and dividends

X. step in the accounting cycle that prepares the accounts for recording the transactions of the next period

II. Multiple Choice   *Circle the best answer.*

1. An accountant who does not necessarily recognize the impact of a business event as it occurs is probably using

   A. accrual-basis accounting
   B. cash-basis accounting
   C. income tax accounting
   D. actual-basis accounting

2. An example of accrual-basis accounting is

   A. recording the purchase of land for cash
   B. recording utility expense when the bill is paid
   C. recording revenue when merchandise is sold on account
   D. recording salary expense when wages are paid

3. Which of the following is considered an adjusting entry category?

   A. accruals
   B. deferrals
   C. depreciation
   D. all of the above

4. All of the following have normal credit balances *except*

   A. Accumulated Depreciation
   B. Salaries Payable
   C. Prepaid Rent
   D. Unearned Fees

5. The first financial statement prepared from the adjusted trial balance is the

   A. income statement
   B. balance sheet
   C. statement of retained earnings
   D. order does not matter

6. Which of the following statements regarding the link between the financial statements is correct?

   A. Net income from the income statement goes to the balance sheet.
   B. Stockholders' equity from the balance sheet goes to the statement of retained earnings.
   C. Net income from the balance sheet goes to the income statement.
   D. Retained earnings from the statement of retained earnings goes to the balance sheet.

7. Sowers Co. paid 12 months' insurance on January 1 and appropriately debited Prepaid Insurance for $30,000. On January 31, Sowers should

   A. credit Prepaid Insurance for $27,500
   B. debit Insurance Expense for $2,500
   C. debit Prepaid Insurance for $27,500
   D. credit Cash for $27,500

8. A company has a beginning balance in Supplies of $2,100. It purchases $2,200 of supplies during the period and uses $1,800 of supplies. If the accountant does not make an adjusting entry for supplies at the end of the period, then

   A. assets will be understated by $2,500
   B. assets will be overstated by $1,800
   C. expenses will be overstated by $1,800
   D. expenses will be understated by $2,500

9. During May, a company received $10,000 cash for services rendered. It also performed $4,500 of services on account and received $5,600 cash for services to be performed in June. The amount of revenue to be included on the May income statement is

   A. $13,600
   B. $14,500
   C. $10,100
   D. $18,100

10. A company correctly made an adjusting entry on December 31, 2002, and credited Prepaid Advertising for $900. During 2002 it paid $2,250 for advertising. The December 31, 2002, balance in Prepaid Advertising was $1,500. What was the balance in the Prepaid Advertising account on January 1, 2002?

    A. $3,500
    B. $ 150
    C. $4,650
    D. $2,400

11. Which of the following accounts will appear on the retained earnings statement?

    A. Supplies
    B. Salary Expense
    C. Interest earned
    D. Dividends

12. Which of the following is a permanent account?

    A. Supplies Expense
    B. Commissions Earned
    C. Advertising Expense
    D. Retained Earnings

13. Suppose a company has posted its closing entries to the Income Summary account. The account now has a debit balance. This means that the company had

    A. net income
    B. a net loss
    C. net income only if there were no dividends
    D. a net loss only if there were no dividends

14. Dividends has a balance of $8,000 before closing. What is the correct entry to close the Dividends account?

    A. debit Retained Earnings and credit Dividends, $8,000
    B. debit Dividends and credit Income Summary, $8,000
    C. debit Dividends and credit Retained Earnings, $8,000
    D. debit Income Summary and credit Dividends, $8,000

15. Which of the following accounts would not be classified as a current asset?

    A. Supplies
    B. Accounts Receivable
    C. Prepaid Insurance
    D. Vehicles

16. The current ratio compares

    A. current assets to long-term assets
    B. current assets to current liabilities
    C. current liabilities to long-term liabilities
    D. total liabilities to total assets

III. Completion   *Complete each of the following statements.*

1. _____basis accounting recognizes revenue when it is earned and expenses when they are incurred.
2. Adjusting entry categories include _____ , _____ , _____ , _____ , and _____ .
3. The end-of-period process of updating the accounts is called _____ .
4. Accumulated Depreciation is an example of a(n) _____ account.
5. The revenue principle provides guidance to accountants as to _____ and _____ .
6. The objectives of the matching principle are: _____ , _____ , and _____ .
7. Financial statements should be prepared in the following order: 1)_____ , 2)_____ , and 3)_____ .
8. The basic interval for financial statements is _____ , while statements prepared at other times and for shorter intervals of time are called _____ .
9. Revenue and expense accounts are _____ accounts.
10. The accounts that are never closed at the end of an accounting period are called _____ accounts.

11. The Dividends account is closed to _____.
12. _____ refers to how quickly an asset can be converted into cash.
13. The two types of deferrals are _____ and _____.
14. The debt ratio compares _____ to _____.
15. The _____ is a measure of short-term liquidity.

IV. True/False *For each of the following statements, circle* T *for true or* F *for false.*

1. T F The revenue principle ensures that accounting information is reported at regular intervals.
2. T F Adjusting entries affect both the income statement and the balance sheet.
3. T F An example of a deferral is prepaid advertising.
4. T F The adjustment for supplies transfers part of the account balance to a liability account.
5. T F Book value is the difference between cost and depreciation expense.
6. T F When an expense accrues, a liability is also accruing.
7. T F When adjusting for accrued revenue, a liability is being increased.
8. T F The amounts appearing on an adjusted trial balance are the same amounts that will appear on the income statement.
9. T F The amounts appearing on an adjusted trial balance are the same amounts that will appear on the balance sheet.
10. T F Revenue, Expense, and the Dividends accounts are all nominal accounts.
11. T F The Income Summary account will carry a debit balance if there has been net income for the period.
12. T F The balance in the Dividends account is closed to the Income Summary account.
13. T F The Retained Earnings account is closed to the Income Summary account.
14. T F To calculate the current ratio, current assets are divided by long-term assets.
15. T F After the closing process is complete, all real accounts will have zero balances.

V. Exercises

1. The accounting records of Andrew's Adjustments include the following unadjusted normal balances on April 30:

Accounts Receivable	$ 1,800
Supplies	610
Salary Payable	0
Unearned Revenue	900
Salary Expense	1,225
Service Revenue	5,100
Supplies Expense	0
Depreciation Expense	0
Accumulated Depreciation	1,100

The following information is available for the September 30 adjusting entries:

a. Supplies on hand, $260
b. Salaries owed to employees, $470
c. Service revenue earned but not billed, $405
d. Services performed which had been paid for in advance, $245
e. Depreciation, $550

Required:

1. Open the T-accounts. See the format below.
2. Record the adjustments directly to the T-accounts. (Key each entry by letter.)
3. Compute the adjusted balance for each account.

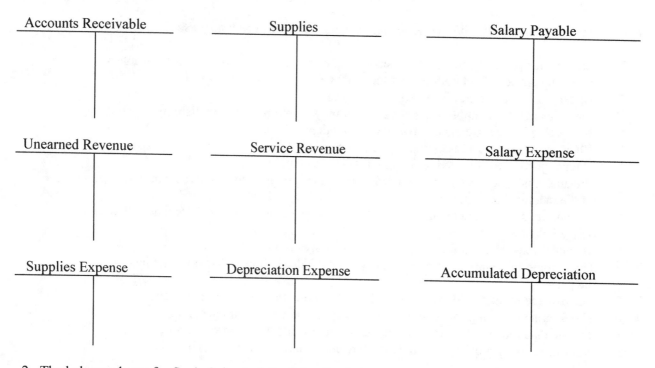

| Accounts Receivable | Supplies | Salary Payable |

| Unearned Revenue | Service Revenue | Salary Expense |

| Supplies Expense | Depreciation Expense | Accumulated Depreciation |

2. The balance sheets for Sue's Salon had the following balances after adjusting entries:

	2002	2003
Supplies	$2,700	$1,075
Prepaid insurance	3,400	800
Taxes payable	2,100	200
Unearned revenue	4,150	4,100

Cash payments and receipts for 2003 included

Payments for supplies	$3,500
Payments for insurance	4,000
Payments of taxes	2,400
Receipts from customers	82,000

How much supplies expense, insurance expense, salary expense, and revenue were reported on the 2003 income statement?

3. Record the December 31 adjusting entries in the space provided.

   A. On 1/1, the Prepaid Rent account has a balance of $12,000 representing 6 months' rent through 6/30. On 6/30 a 2-year lease was signed for a total cost of $60,000 and a check issued for that amount.
   B. On 12/31, the balance in the Unearned Subscriptions account was $11,700, which represented advance payments from customers for annual subscriptions to a newsletter. As of 12/31, 22 issues of the newsletter had been published.
   C. The company had a $12,000 note receivable on the books at year end. The 6-month note was dated 11/1 and carried a 9% interest rate.
   D. A total of $9,150 wages and salaries had accrued on 12/31.

A.   GENERAL JOURNAL

Date	Accounts and Explanation	PR	Debit	Credit

B.   GENERAL JOURNAL

Date	Accounts and Explanation	PR	Debit	Credit

C.   GENERAL JOURNAL

Date	Accounts and Explanation	PR	Debit	Credit

D.   GENERAL JOURNAL

Date	Accounts and Explanation	PR	Debit	Credit

4.

Williams Inc.
Trial Balance
December 31, 2002

Cash	$ 19,000	
Accounts receivable	8,000	
Prepaid advertising	3,600	
Supplies	4,200	
Notes payable		$11,400
Unearned revenue		5,400
Common stock		10,000
Retained earnings		2,200
Dividends	900	
Fees earned		18,000
Salary expense	6,600	
Rent expense	3,000	
Utilities expense	1,700	
	$47,000	$47,000

Additional information:

A. Supplies at year end totaled $1,900.
B. $1,700 of the prepaid advertising was expired at year end.

Required:

1. Prepare the appropriate adjusting entries.
2. Prepare closing entries.
3. Compute Williams' ending retained earnings balance.

Requirement 1 (Adjusting entries)

GENERAL JOURNAL

Date	Accounts and Explanation	PR	Debit	Credit

Requirement 2 (Closing entries)

GENERAL JOURNAL

Date	Accounts and Explanation	PR	Debit	Credit

Requirement 3 (Ending Retained Earnings balance)

Beginning Retained Earnings	$
Plus: Net Income	
Less: Dividends	
Ending Retained Earnings	$

VI. Critical Thinking

If a business is using cash-basis accounting, what is the amount listed on the Balance Sheet for Accounts Receivable, assuming clients have been billed $118,500 during the year and sent in payments totaling $93,000 by the end of the year?

_____

_____

_____

_____

_____

_____

VII. Demonstration Problems

Demonstration Problem #1

Videos Forever, Inc., is in the business of renting videos. The trial balance for Videos Forever, Inc., at December 31, 2002, and the data needed for year-end adjustments are as follows:

Trial Balance
December 31, 2002

Cash	$19,415	
Accounts receivable	90	
Prepaid rent	1,200	
Supplies	400	
Rental tape library	24,000	
Accumulated depreciation—tape library		$12,000
Furniture	9,500	
Accumulated depreciation—furniture		3,800
Accounts payable		1,450
Salary payable		
Unearned tape rental revenue		1,300
Common stock		15,000
Retained earnings		7,150
Dividends	3,000	
Tape rental revenue		43,365
Salary expense	14,400	
Rent expense	6,600	
Utilities expense	2,800	
Depreciation expense—tape library		
Depreciation expense—furniture		
Advertising expense	2,660	
Supplies expense		
Total	$84,065	$84,065

Adjustment data:

a. Depreciation for the year:
   - on the rental tape library, $6,000
   - on the furniture, $1,900
b. Accrued salary expense at December 31, $120.
c. Prepaid rent expired, $600.
d. Unearned tape rental revenues which remain unearned as of December 31, $625.
e. Supplies on hand at December 31, $230
f. Accrued advertising expense at December 31, $115. (Credit Accounts Payable)

Required:

1. Prepare T-accounts for those accounts listed on the trial balance that are affected by the adjusting entries. Enter their December 31 unadjusted balances, then prepare and post the adjusting journal entries in the accounts. Key adjustment amounts by letter as shown in the text.

2. Using the form provided, enter the adjusting entries in the Adjustment columns, and prepare an adjusted trial balance, as shown in Exhibit 3-10 of the text. Be sure that each account balance affected by an adjusting entry agrees with the adjusted T-account balances as calculated in Requirement 1.

Requirement 1 (T-accounts; adjusting journal entries; posting to ledger)

a.

Date	Accounts	PR	Debit	Credit
Dec. 31				

b.

Date	Accounts	PR	Debit	Credit
Dec. 31				

c.

Date	Accounts	PR	Debit	Credit
Dec. 31				

d.

Date	Accounts	PR	Debit	Credit
Dec. 31				

e.

Date	Accounts	PR	Debit	Credit
Dec. 31				

f.

Date	Accounts	PR	Debit	Credit
Dec. 31				

Requirement 2 (Adjusted trial balance)

Videos Forever, Inc.
Preparation of Adjusted Trial Balance
For the Year Ended December 31, 2002

Accounts	Trial Balance		Adjustments		Adjusted Trial Balance	
	Debit	Credit	Debit	Credit	Debit	Credit
Cash	$19,415					
Accounts receivable	90					
Prepaid rent	1,200					
Supplies	400					
Rental tape library	24,000					
Accumulated depreciation—tape library		$12,000				
Furniture	9,500					
Accumulated depreciation—furniture		3,800				
Accounts payable		1,450				
Salary payable						
Unearned tape rental revenue		1,300				
Common stock		15,000				
Retained earnings		7,150				
Dividends	3,000					
Tape rental revenue		43,365				
Salary expense	14,400					
Rent expense	6,600					
Utilities expense	2,800					
Depreciation expense—tape library						
Depreciation expense—furniture						
Advertising expense	2,660					
Supplies expense						
	$84,065	$84,065				

Demonstration Problem #2

Refer to the adjusted trial balance in Demonstration Problem #1 and complete the following:

1. An income statement
2. A statement of retained earnings
3. A balance sheet
4. The necessary closing entries

Income Statement

Statement of Retained Earnings

Balance Sheet

Closing Entries

Date	Accounts	PR	Debit	Credit

SOLUTIONS

I. Matching

1. C	6. E	11. M	16. X	21. S
2. G	7. F	12. J	17. P	22. Q
3. A	8. N	13. L	18. R	23. T
4. B	9. O	14. H	19. U	24. W
5. D	10. K	15. I	20. V	

II. Multiple Choice

1.   B   In cash-basis accounting, the accountant does not record a transaction until cash is received or paid. In accrual-basis accounting, the accountant records a transaction when it occurs. Income tax accounting is appropriate for the preparation of income tax returns, and actual-basis accounting has no meaning.

2.   C   Recording revenue when the merchandise is sold is the only event listed that does not involve the receipt or payment of cash. Accordingly, it would not be recorded using cash-basis accounting and is the only item that would be recorded under accrual-basis accounting.

3.   D   Adjusting entries assign revenues to the period in which they are earned and expenses to the period in which they are incurred. The categories of adjusting entries are 1) deferrals, 2) depreciation, 3) and accruals.

4.   C   Prepaid rent is an asset account with a normal debit balance. The other items listed have normal credit balances.

5.   A   Since net income is required to prepare the statement of retained earnings, the income statement should be prepared first.

6.   D   The correct sequence is
1) Net income from the income statement goes to the statement of retained earnings.
2) Retained earnings from the statement of retained earnings goes to the balance sheet.

7.   B   One month of insurance will expire during January. Therefore, $1/12 \times \$30,000$ (or $2,500) will be expensed by the following journal entry:

Insurance Expense	2,500	
Prepaid Insurance		2,500

8.   B   The entry that should be made is:

Supplies Expense	1,800	
Supplies		1,800

Failure to credit the Supplies account for $1,800 means that assets will be overstated by $1,800.

9.   B   With accrual accounting, total revenues in May will be $10,000 of revenues received in cash plus $4,500 of revenues that have been billed but not received.

10. B This problem requires you to work backward to find the solution.

Adjusted balance (given)	$1,500
Adjustment (given)	900
Unadjusted balance	$2,400

The unadjusted trial balance amount of $2,400 consists of the beginning balance and purchases made during the year. Since the purchases were $2,250 (given), the beginning balance must have been $150.

> **Study Tip**: Once again, remember this important formula:
> Beginning balance + Additions - Reductions = Ending balance

11. D The retained earnings statement includes retained earnings, net income (or loss), and dividends.

12. D Revenue, Expenses, and Dividends are temporary accounts. They are closed at the end of each accounting period. Retained Earnings is a permanent account.

13. B Closing has the effect of transferring all revenues to the credit side of Income Summary and all expenses to the debit side. If revenues are larger than expenses, Income Summary will have a credit balance which reflects net income. If expenses are greater than revenue, Income Summary will have a debit balance which reflects a net loss.

14. A The entry to close dividends is

Retained Earnings	XX	
Dividends		XX

Note that Dividends is closed directly to Retained Earnings and is not closed through Income Summary.

15. D Current assets are assets that are expected to be converted to cash, sold, or consumed during the next 12 months or within the business's normal operating cycle if longer than a year. Vehicles would not fit this description, while the other accounts listed would.

16. B The current ratio is current assets ÷ current liabilities.

III. Completion

1. Accrual
2. prepaid expenses, depreciation, accrued expenses, unearned revenue, accrued revenues (order not important)
3. adjusting the accounts
4. contra asset

> **Study Tip**: A contra account has two distinguishing characteristics: (1) it always has a companion account, and (2) its normal balance is opposite that of the companion account. Accumulated Depreciation's companion account is Property, Plant, and Equipment.

5. when to record revenue, the amount of revenue to record
6. to identify expenses which have been incurred, to measure the expenses, to match the expenses with revenues earned during the same time period
7. income statement, statement of retained earnings, balance sheet (order is important)

8. one year, interim statements
9. temporary (Revenue, Expenses, and Dividends are temporary accounts. They are closed at the end of each accounting period.)
10. permanent (Permanent accounts, i.e., assets, liabilities and stockholders' equity, are not used to measure income for a period and are not closed at the end of the period.)
11. Retained Earnings (The entry to close dividends is always:

Retained Earnings   XX

    Dividends   XX

Note that Dividends is closed directly to Retained Earnings and is *not* closed through Income Summary.)
12. Liquidity (Balance Sheets list assets and liabilities in the order of their relative liquidity.)
13. Prepaid expenses and unearned revenues
14. total liabilities, total assets
15. current ratio (current assets ÷ current liabilities)

IV. True/False

1.	F	The time-period concept ensures that accounting information is reported at regular intervals.
2.	T	
3.	T	
4.	F	When adjusting for supplies (a prepaid expense), an expense account and an asset account are affected.
5.	F	Book value is the difference between cost and accumulated depreciation.
6	T	
7.	F	The adjustment for accrued revenue increases both a revenue account and an asset (receivable) account.
8.	T	
9.	F	The balance in retained earnings on the adjusted trial balance will not be the same as the amount reported on the balance sheet because the ending retained earnings balance carried forward from the retained earnings statement has been updated to include net income (or loss) and dividends.
10.	T	
11.	F	A debit balance in the income summary account represents a net loss.
12.	F	The Dividends account is closed to Retained Earnings.
13.	F	The Retained Earnings account is a permanent account, not a temporary account; therefore, it is not closed at the end of the accounting period.
14.	F	The current ratio is calculated by dividing current assets by current liabilities.
15.	F	After closing, the temporary accounts have zero balances. The real (permanent) accounts are not closed out at the end of the accounting period.

IV. Exercises

1.

Accounts Receivable		Supplies			Salary Payable	
Bal. 1,800		Bal. 610				
(c) 405			(a) 350			(b) 470
Bal. 2,205		Bal. 260				Bal. 470

Unearned Revenue			Service Revenue			Salary Expense	
	Bal. 900			Bal. 5,100		Bal. 1,225	
(d) 245				(c) 405		(b) 470	
	Bal. 655			(d) 245		Bal. 1,695	
				Bal. 5,750			

Supplies Expense			Depreciation Expense			Accumulated Depreciation	
							Bal. 1,100
(a) 350			(e) 550				(e) 550
Bal. 350			Bal. 550				Bal. 1,650

2. Remember that Beginning balance + Additions - Reductions = Ending balance

For Supplies:

	Beginning balance	+	Supplies purchased for cash	-	Supplies expense	=	Ending balance
	$2,700	+	$3,500	-	?	=	$1,075

Supplies expense = $5,125

For Insurance:

	Beginning balance	+	Insurance Paid	-	Insurance expense	=	Ending balance
	$3,400	+	$4,000	-	?	=	$800

Insurance expense = $6,600

For Taxes payable:

	Beginning balance	+	Taxes expense	-	Cash paid for taxes	=	Ending balance
	$2,100	+	?	-	$2,400	=	$200

Interest expense = $500

For Unearned revenue:

	Beginning balance	+	Receipts from customers	-	Revenue earned	=	Ending balance
	$4,150	+	$82,000	-	?	=	$4,100

Revenue = $82,050

3.

Date	Accounts and Explanation	PR	Debit	Credit
A.	Rent Expense		27,000	
	Prepaid Rent			27,000
	($12,000 + 6 months at $2,500 per month)			
B.	Unearned Subscriptions		4,950	
	Subscriptions Revenue			4,950
	($11,700 / 52 = $225 × 22 = $4,950)			

C.	Interest Receivable		180	
	Interest Earned			180
	($12,000 × .09 × 2 / 12)			
D.	Wage and Salary Expense		9,150	
	Wage and Salary Payable			9,150

4.

Requirement 1

Date	Accounts and Explanation	PR	Debit	Credit
A.	Supplies Expense		2,300	
	Supplies			2,300
	If ending supplies are $1,900, then $2,300 of supplies were used.			
B.	Advertising Expense		1,700	
	Prepaid Advertising			1,700
	To record expired advertising.			

Requirement 2

Date	Accounts and Explanation	PR	Debit	Credit
	Fees Earned		18,000	
	Income Summary			18,000
	Income Summary		15,300	
	Salary Expense			6,600
	Rent Expense			3,000
	Utilities Expense			1,700
	Supplies Expense			2,300
	Advertising Expense			1,700
	Supplies Expense and Advertising Expense from Requirement 1 must be included.			
	Income Summary		2,700	
	Retained Earnings			2,700
	Income Summary had a credit balance of $2,700 before this entry ($18,000 credit - $15,300 debit).			
	Retained Earnings		900	
	Dividends			900

Requirement 3

Beginning Retained Earnings	$2,200
Plus: Net Income	2,700
	4,900
Less: Dividends	900
Ending Retained Earnings	$4,000

VI. Critical Thinking

The answer is 0. Why? Because cash-basis accounting does not record revenue when a client is billed, only when the business receives payment. Therefore, while the business may send bills to clients, they are not recorded.

VII. Demonstration Problems

Demonstration Problem #1 Solved and Explained

Requirement 1 (T-accounts; adjusting entries; posting to ledger)

a.

Depreciation Expense—Tape Library	
(a) 6,000	
Bal. 6,000	

Accumulated Depreciation—Tape Library	
	Bal. 12,000
	(a) 6,000
	Bal. 18,000

Depreciation Expense—Furniture	
(a) 1,900	
Bal. 1,900	

Accumulated Depreciation—Furniture	
	Bal. 3,800
	(a) 1,900
	Bal. 5,700

Date	Accounts	PR	Debit	Credit
Dec. 31	Depreciation Expense—Tape Library		6,000	
	Accumulated Depreciation—Tape Library			6,000
	To record depreciation expense on tape library			
	Depreciation Expense—Furniture		1,900	
	Accumulated Depreciation—Furniture			1,900
	To record depreciation expense on furniture			

Explanation of Adjustment (a)

As a long-lived plant asset (such as building, furniture, machinery, equipment) becomes less useful, its cost is gradually transferred from the asset account to a depreciation expense account. The recording of depreciation expense for Videos Forever, Inc., requires a debit of $7,900 ($6,000 on the rental tape library and $1,900 on furniture) to Depreciation Expense (expenses are increased with debits) and credits to the contra accounts of $6,000 to Accumulated Depreciation—Tape Library and $1,900 to Accumulated Depreciation —Furniture (assets are decreased with credits). Note that the original cost of the asset remains unchanged on the books of Videos Forever, Inc. The reduction in book value of each asset is accomplished by increasing the asset's accumulated depreciation account.

Example: Change in book value of furniture.

Plant Assets	Before Adjustment	Change	After Adjustment
Furniture	$9,500	0	$9,500
Less accumulated depreciation	3,800	+1,900	5,700
Book value	$5,700	-$1,900	$3,800

b.

Salary Expense		Salary Payable	
Bal. 14,400			(b) 120
(b) 120			
Bal. 14,520			Bal. 120

Date	Accounts	PR	Debit	Credit
Dec. 31	Salary Expense		120	
	Salary Payable			120
	To accrue salary expense			

Explanation of Adjustment (b)

Amounts owed employees for salary and wages unpaid as of the close of an accounting period must be accrued. The facts indicate that $120 must be accrued to record salary expense and the related liability. As a result, Salary Expense is debited $120 (expenses are increased by debits), and Salary Payable is credited $120 (liabilities are increased by credits).

c.

Rent Expense		Prepaid Rent	
Bal. 6,600		Bal. 1,200	(c) 600
(c) 600			
Bal. 7,200		Bal. 600	

Date	Accounts	PR	Debit	Credit
Dec. 31	Rent Expense		600	
	Prepaid Rent			600
	To record rent expense			

Explanation of Adjustment (c)

Videos Forever, Inc., paid two months' rent in advance early in December. This prepayment created an asset (Prepaid Rent) for Videos Forever, Inc., in the form of a purchased future right to use the rental space. At the end of the year, the prepaid asset account must be adjusted for the amount of the prepayment that has expired. During December, one month's worth of the prepayment was used up. As a result, one month's prepaid rent of $600 is transferred to expense by crediting (assets are reduced by credits) the Prepaid Rent account and debiting (expenses are recorded as debits) the Rent Expense account. Note that one month's rent remains in the Prepaid Rent account.

d.

Tape Rental Revenue		Unearned Revenue	
	Bal. 43,365		Bal. 1,300
	(d) 675	(d) 675	
	Bal. 44,040		Bal. 625

Date	Accounts	PR	Debit	Credit
Dec. 31	Unearned Rent Revenue		675	
	Tape Rental Revenue			675
	To record revenue collected in advance.			

Explanation of Adjustment (d)

When cash is collected from customers before the agreed-upon product or service is provided, a liability is created. If $625 of the $1,300 of unearned rental revenue remains unearned, then $675 has become earned revenue. The liability account Unearned Rental Revenue should be debited (a liability is reduced by a debit) and Tape Rental Revenue should be credited (a revenue is increased by a credit).

e.

Supplies Expense		Supplies		
(e) 170		Bal. 400	(e)	170
Bal. 170		Bal. 230		

Date	Accounts	PR	Debit	Credit
Dec. 31	Supplies Expense		170	
	Supplies			170
	To record supplies expense.			

Explanation of Adjustment (e)

Supplies purchased for business use represent an asset until they are used. The Supplies account must be adjusted periodically to reflect supplies no longer on hand. Supplies of $230 remain on hand at December 31. Since $400 of supplies were on hand initially, it is clear that $170 of supplies have been used up ($400 - $230 = $170). Reduce the Supplies account by crediting it $170 (assets are decreased by credits) and record the $170 supplies expense by debiting Supplies Expense (expenses are recorded by debits).

f.

Advertising Expense		
Bal.	2,660	
(f)	115	
Bal.	2,775	

Accounts Payable		
	Bal.	1,450
	(f)	115
	Bal.	1,565

Date	Accounts	PR	Debit	Credit
Dec. 31	Advertising Expense		115	
	Accounts Payable			115
	To record accrued advertising expense.			

Explanation of Adjustment (f)

The rationale for this entry is similar to that for the adjusting entry which accrued salary expense. Advertising Expense is increased by debiting the account (expenses are recorded by debits) and Accounts Payable is credited (liabilities are recorded by credits) to reflect the debt owed by Videos Forever, Inc.

Requirement 2 (Adjusted trial balance)

Videos Forever, Inc.
Preparation of Adjusted Trial Balance
For the Year Ended December 31, 2002

Accounts	Trial Balance Debit	Trial Balance Credit	Adjustments Debit	Adjustments Credit	Adjusted Trial Balance Debit	Adjusted Trial Balance Credit
Cash	$19,415				$19,415	
Accounts receivable	90				90	
Prepaid rent	1,200			(c) 600	600	
Supplies	400			(e) 170	230	
Rental tape library	24,000				24,000	
Accumulated depreciation— tape library		$12,000		(a) 6,000		$18,000
Furniture	9,500				9,500	
Accumulated depreciation— furniture		3,800		(a) 1,900		5,700
Accounts payable		1,450		(f) 115		1,565
Salary payable				(b) 120		120
Unearned tape rental revenue		1,300	(d) 675			625
Common stock		15,000				15,000
Retained earnings		7,150				7,150
Dividends	3,000				3,000	
Tape rental revenue		43,365		(d) 675		44,040
Salary expense	14,400		(b) 120		14,520	
Rent expense	6,600		(c) 600		7,200	
Utilities expense	2,800				2,800	
Depreciation expense—tape library			(a) 6,000		6,000	
Depreciation expense— furniture			(a) 1,900		1,900	
Advertising expense	2,660		(f) 115		2,775	
Supplies expense			(e) 170		170	
	$84,065	$84,065	$9,580	$9,580	$92,200	$92,200

Demonstration Problem #2 Solved

Requirement 1

Videos Forever, Inc.
Income Statement
For the Year Ended December 31, 2002

Revenues:		
Tape rental revenue		$44,040
Expenses:		
Salary expense	14,520	
Rent expense	7,200	
Utilities expense	2,800	
Depreciation expense	7,900	
Advertising expense	2,775	
Supplies expense	170	
Total expenses		35,365
Net income		$ 8,675

Requirement 2

Videos Forever, Inc.
Statement of Retained Earnings
For the Year Ended December 31, 2002

Retained earnings 1/1/02	$ 7,150
Add: Net Income	8,675
	15,825
Less: Dividends	3,000
Retained earnings 12/31/02	$12,825

Requirement 3

Videos Forever, Inc.
Balance Sheet
December 31, 2002

ASSETS			LIABILITIES		
Cash		$19,415	Accounts payable		$ 1,565
Accounts receivable		90	Salary payable		120
Prepaid rent		600	Unearned tape rental		
Supplies		230	Revenue		625
Tape rental library	24,000		Total liabilities		2,310
Less: Acc. dep.—library	18,000	6,000			
Furniture	9,500		**STOCKHOLDERS' EQUITY**		
Less: Acc. dep.—furniture	5,700	3,800	Common stock	15,000	
			Retained earnings	12,825	
			Total stockholders' equity		27,825
			Total liabilities and		
Total assets		$30,135	stockholders' equity		$30,135

Requirement 4

Date	Accounts	PR	Debit	Credit
Dec. 31	Tape Rental Revenue		44,040	
	Income Summary			44,040
Dec. 31	Income Summary		35,365	
	Salary Expense			14,520
	Rent Expense			7,200
	Utilities Expense			2,800
	Depreciation Expense—Tape Library			6,000
	Depreciation Expense—Furniture			1,900
	Advertising Expense			2,775
	Supplies Expense			170
Dec. 31	Income Summary		8,675	
	Retained Earnings			8,675
Dec. 31	Retained Earnings		3,000	
	Dividends			3,000

CHAPTER 4—INTERNAL CONTROL AND MANAGING CASH

CHAPTER OVERVIEW

This chapter introduces you to internal control and the processes a business follows to control the organization's assets. As cash is the most liquid asset, this chapter applies internal control concepts to cash. However, internal control applies to all assets—topics covered in upcoming chapters. The specific learning objectives for this chapter are to

1. Describe an effective system of internal control
2. Use a bank reconciliation as a control device
3. Manage and account for cash
4. Apply internal controls to cash receipts
5. Apply internal controls to cash payments
6. Use a budget to manage cash
7. Weigh ethical judgments in business

CHAPTER REVIEW

Internal control is the organizational plan and all related measures designed to safeguard assets, ensure reliable accounting records, promote efficiency, and encourage adherence to company policies.

Objective 1 – Describe an effective system of internal control.

An effective system of internal control has four characteristics:
1. **Competent, reliable, and ethical personnel**. Paying competitive salaries, training people thoroughly, and providing adequate supervision help to promote competence.
2. **Assignment of responsibilities**. All duties to be performed must be identified, and responsibility for the performance of those duties must be assigned to appropriate people.
3. **Proper authorization**. An organization generally has a written set of rules that outlines approved procedures. Proper authorization must be obtained for deviations from standard policies.
4. **Separation of duties**. Separation of duties is designed to limit the possibility of fraud or theft in the handling of assets. The company must have
   a) separation of operations from accounting
   b) separation of the custody of assets from accounting
   c) separation of the authorization of transactions from the custody of related assets
   d) separation of duties within the accounting function

Auditors evaluate the system of internal control to estimate the reliability of the accounting system. Auditors also help to spot areas where improvements in internal control can be made. **Internal auditors** are employees of the company. **External auditors** are employed by public accounting firms and are hired by a business to audit its books.

Business documents and records are designed according to each company's needs. Source documents and records include sales invoices, purchase orders, and special journals. Good internal control requires documents to be prenumbered. A gap in the numbered sequence will call attention to a missing document.

Additional controls include electronic sensors (for inventory), fireproof vaults (for cash), point-of-sale terminals (also for cash), fidelity bonds (for employee theft), and electronic data processing auditors (for computer systems).

The limitations of an internal control system are determined by the opportunities available for collusion and the resources that management devotes to the system. Collusion between two or more people working together to defraud the firm may go undetected by the system of internal control. Internal control must be designed and judged in light of the costs and the benefits.

Using a bank account promotes internal control over cash. For accounting purposes, cash includes currency, coins, checks, money orders, and bank accounts. Banks safeguard cash and provide detailed records of transactions. Cash is the most common means of exchange, and it is also the most tempting asset for theft.

Documents used to control bank accounts include signature cards, deposit tickets, checks, and bank statements. Banks usually send monthly statements to depositors. The bank statement shows the beginning balance in the account, all transactions recorded during the month, and the ending balance. The bank also returns canceled checks with the statement.

Electronic Funds Transfer (EFT) is a system that relies on electronic impulses to account for cash transactions. EFT systems reduce the cost of processing cash transactions by reducing the documentary evidence of transactions. This lack of documentation poses a challenge to managers and auditors to enforce the internal control system.

Bank reconciliations are necessary because there are usually differences between the time that transactions are recorded on a business's books and the time that those transactions are recorded by the bank. For example, if you mail a check to a supplier on the last day of the month, you will record it on that day. However, the check will not clear your bank until the supplier has received it and deposited it in his bank several days later.

Objective 2 - Use a bank reconciliation as a control device.

The general format for a bank reconciliation is:

BANK		BOOKS
	Balance, last day of month	Balance, last day of month (trial balance of general ledger)
+	Deposits in transit	
-	Outstanding checks	+ Bank collections
±	Correction of bank errors	+ Interest paid on deposits
		- Service charge
		± Correction of book errors
	Adjusted bank balance	= Adjusted book balance

Adjustments to the bank balance never require preparation of journal entries. Adjustments to the bank balance include the following items:

1. Deposits in transit have been recorded by the company, but not by the bank. There is often a time lag of a day or two until the deposit is sent to the bank and posted by the bank.
2. Outstanding checks are checks issued by the company and recorded on its books but which have not yet been paid by the bank. There is a time lag of several days until the checks are cashed or deposited by the payee and sent to the business's bank to be paid.
3. Corrections of bank errors are the responsibility of the bank. The bank should be notified and the corrections should appear on the next statement.

Adjustments to the books always require preparation of journal entries. Adjustments to the book balance include the following items:

1. The bank collects money on behalf of depositors. Examples are a lock-box system where customers pay directly to the bank accounts. A bank may also collect on a note receivable for the depositor. The bank will notify the depositor of these collections on the bank statement. The journal entry for the collection of a note receivable and the related interest is

Cash	XXX	
Note Receivable		XX
Interest Revenue (if applicable)		X

2. Interest revenue is sometimes paid on the checking account. The journal entry to record the interest is

Cash	XX	
Interest Revenue		XX

3. Service charges are the bank's fees for processing transactions. The journal entry for a service charge is

Miscellaneous Expense	X	
Cash		X

4. Nonsufficient funds (NSF) checks are customer checks that have been returned by the customer's bank because the customer's account did not have sufficient funds in the account to cover the amount of the check. Checks may also be returned if the maker's account has closed, the date is stale, the signature is not authorized, the check has been altered, or the check form is improper. The amount of returned checks is subtracted from the book balance and the following journal entry is made:

Accounts Receivable	XX	
Cash		XX

5. The cost of printing checks is handled like a service charge. The journal entry is

Miscellaneous Expense	XX	
Cash		XX

6. Errors on the books must be handled on a case-by-case basis. If checks are recorded on the books for the wrong amount, then an entry must be prepared to correct the original entry.

Study Exhibit 4-7 carefully. Be sure you understand the components of a bank reconciliation and the journal entries needed to correct the Cash account balance.

Objective 3 - Manage and account for cash.

Study Exhibit 4-8 which illustrates the **operating cycle**. In order for companies to maximize earnings, they need to keep their cash circulating. When a company records credit sales, the seller needs detailed information about each customer. For this reason, companies use a subsidiary accounts receivable ledger. The subsidiary ledger provides information about each customer's account balance, including payments received and invoices sent. To encourage customers to pay invoices before the due date, many companies offer **sales discounts**. These discounts are expressed as percentages (usually small ones) that can represent considerable savings to the customer. For example, the term "1/15, n/60" means the customer can take a one percent reduction from the amount of the credit sale if the invoice is paid within 15 days from the sale date. Should the customer fail to take advantage of the discount the entire amount is due by the 60th day following the date of the sale. When the seller receives the cash early, the business is able to use the cash to replace inventory and/or pay other bills. When the customer takes the discount, the purchaser pays less for the goods received. The seller records the discount in the Sales Discount account, which is classified as a **contra-revenue** account.

> **Study Tip**: You were first introduced to *contra* accounts in Chapter 3, specifically Accumulated Depreciation. Remember, a contra account is one whose balance is deducted from a companion account. For Accumulated Depreciation, the companion account was the related Property, Plant or Equipment account. The companion account for Sales Discounts is the Sales Revenue account.

Objective 4 - Apply internal controls to cash receipts.

The objective of internal control over cash receipts is to ensure that all cash is deposited in the bank and recorded correctly in the company's accounting record.

A point-of-sale terminal is a good device for management control over cash received in a store. Positioning the machine so that customers see the amounts rung up discourages cashiers from overcharging customers and pocketing the excess over actual prices. Issuing receipts requires cashiers to record the sale. Comparing actual receipts to control tapes maintained by the terminal discourages theft.

For payments received from customers by mail, separation of duties among different people promotes good internal control. The mailroom clerk should open all mail and record incoming payments. The mailroom should deliver checks to the cashier for deposit and send remittance advices to the accounting department for posting. Comparison of mailroom totals, cashier totals, and accounting totals should be made daily.

Some companies use a lock-box system as another means of internal control. Customers mail payments to an address which is actually the company's bank. This also increases efficiency because the funds can be put to use immediately.

(Helpful hint: Review Exhibit 4-10 in your text.)

Objective 5 - Apply internal controls to cash payments.

Payment by check is a good control over cash disbursements. However, before a check can be issued, additional control procedures have occurred. For instance, companies require approved purchase orders before goods and/or services can be acquired, receiving reports verifying that goods received conform to the purchase order, an invoice which agrees with both the purchase order and receiving report, and, finally, an authorized check in payment of the invoice. Additionally, many companies require two signatures before a check can be sent.

(See Exhibits 4-11, 4-12, and 4-13 in your text.)

Businesses keep a **petty cash** account to have cash on hand for minor expenses which do not warrant preparing a check. Such expenses include taxi fares, local delivery costs, and small amounts of office supplies.

Suppose a petty cash fund of $200 is established. The cash is placed under the control of a custodian and the following entry is made:

Petty Cash	200	
Cash		200

This type of entry is also used to increase the amount in the fund, say from $200 to $300:

Petty Cash	100	
Cash		100

> **Study Tip**: Note that once the fund is established, no entry is made to the Petty Cash account except to change the total amount in the fund.

Petty cash is disbursed using petty cash tickets, which document the disbursements. Cash on hand plus the total of the petty cash tickets should always equal the fund balance. This is referred to as an **imprest fund**.

A petty cash fund must be periodically replenished, particularly on the balance sheet date. A check is drawn for the amount of the replenishment. An entry is made as follows:

Various accounts listed on petty cash tickets	XX	
Cash		XX

Note that the expenses on the petty cash tickets are recorded in the general journal when the fund is replenished.

Objective 6 - Use a budget to manage cash.

A **budget** is a quantitative expression of a plan that helps managers coordinate the organization. Cash budgeting, therefore, is a way to manage cash. This is accomplished by developing a plan for future cash receipts and disbursements. The cash budget starts with the amount of cash on hand at the beginning of the period. To this is added the budgeted cash receipts. Sources of cash receipts will include revenue transactions, the sale of assets, and proceeds from borrowing money and/or selling shares of stock. Budgeted cash disbursements will include expenditures for operating activities, acquisition of assets, dividends, and payments of debt. Once these budgeted receipts and disbursements have been determined, they can be compared with the expected receipts and disbursements. If the results of the expected cash activity exceed the budgeted activity, the managers will have the opportunity to invest the excess and generate additional revenue (the interest earned on the invested cash). If the budgeted activity exceeds the expected activity, the company will need to arrange financing in order to maintain the desired amount of cash. Exhibit 4-15 illustrates a typical format for a cash budget.

When reported on the balance sheet, most companies list "Cash and equivalents"—this includes cash and other items similar enough to be included with cash (such as petty cash, short-term time deposits, and certificates of deposit).

Objective 7 - Weigh ethical judgments in business.

Most businesses have codes of ethics to which their employees are expected to conform. In addition, the accounting profession has the AICPA Code of Professional Conduct and the Standards of Ethical Conduct for Management Accountants. In many situations, the ethical course of action is clear. However, when this is not the case, the following questions and guidelines may prove helpful:

Questions	Decision Guidelines
1. What are the facts?	Determine the facts.
2. What are the ethical issues, if any?	Identify the ethical issues.
3. What are the options?	Specify the alternatives.
4. Who is involved in the situation?	Identify the people involved.
5. What are the possible consequences?	Assess the possible outcomes.
6. What shall I do?	Make the decisions.

TEST YOURSELF

All the self-testing materials in this chapter focus on information and procedures that your instructor is likely to test in quizzes and examinations.

I. Matching   *Match each numbered term with its lettered definition.*

_____ 1. external auditors
_____ 2. lock-box system
_____ 3. bank statement
_____ 4. operating cycle
_____ 5. electronic funds transfer
_____ 6. nonsufficient funds check
_____ 7. outstanding check
_____ 8. service charge
_____ 9. sales discounts

_____ 10. discount period
_____ 11. bank reconciliation
_____ 12. check
_____ 13. deposit in transit
_____ 14. credit period
_____ 15. internal control
_____ 16. petty cash
_____ 17. contra-revenue
_____ 18. budget

A. a deposit recorded by the company but not by its bank
B. a check for which the payer's bank account has insufficient money to pay the check
C. a check issued by a company and recorded on its books but not yet paid by its bank
D. an account related to and deducted from a revenue account
E. a document for a particular bank account that shows its beginning and ending balances and lists the month's transactions that affect the account
F. a document that instructs the bank to pay a designated person or business a specified amount of money
G. a fund containing a small amount of cash that is used to pay minor expenditures
H. the length of time between the expenditure of cash for goods and services that are sold to customers who then pay the business in cash
I. a method to encourage customers to pay bills early
J. a system that accounts for cash transactions by electronic impulses rather than paper documents
K. the length of time a customer is given to pay the invoice
L. the quantitative expression of a plan that helps managers coordinate the organization
M. bank's fees for processing depositor's transactions
N. the number of days a customer has to qualify for a reduction in the amount due
O. employed by public accounting firms; hired to audit a client's books
P. a method of internal control over cash receipts where customers send payments directly to the company's bank
Q. process of explaining the reasons for the difference between a depositor's records and the bank's records of the depositor's bank account
R. the organizational plan and all related measures adopted by an entity to safeguard assets, ensure accurate and reliable accounting records, promote operational efficiency, and encourage adherence to company policies

II. Multiple Choice *Circle the best answer.*

1. Lupe Rodriguez handles cash receipts and has the authority to write off accounts receivable. This violates separation of

    A. custody of assets from accounting
    B. operations from accounting
    C. duties within the accounting function
    D. authorization of transactions from custody of related assets

2. Celeste Stewart records both cash receipts and cash disbursements. This violates separation of

    A. custody of assets from accounting
    B. operations from accounting
    C. duties within the accounting function
    D. authorization of transactions from custody of related assets

3. Which of the following items does not require a journal entry?

    A. interest paid on checking account
    B. deposits in transit
    C. collection by bank of note receivable
    D. bank service charge

4. The journal entry to record an NSF check returned by the bank is

    A. debit Cash, credit Accounts Receivable
    B. debit Accounts Payable, credit Cash
    C. debit Accounts Receivable, credit Cash
    D. debit Miscellaneous Expense, credit Cash

5. Which of the following is not an internal control procedure for cash receipts?

    A. comparing actual cash to cash register tape totals
    B. pricing merchandise at uneven amounts
    C. paying bills by check
    D. enabling customers to see amounts entered on cash receipts

6. If you discover a bank error while completing a reconciliation, you

    A. debit Cash if the error is in your favor
    B. credit Cash if the error is in the bank's favor
    C. debit (or credit) Bank Expense for the amount of the error
    D. none of the above

7. Which of the following documents is prepared first?

   A. purchase requisition
   B. receiving report
   C. purchase order
   D. check

8. Which of the following documents is prepared last?

   A. purchase requisition
   B. receiving report
   C. purchase order
   D. check

9. The sales discount term "1/15, n/30" equates to which of the following annual rates?

   A. 3%
   B. 18%
   C. 24%
   D. 72%

10. Which of the following is NOT an internal control for cash?

    A. fidelity bonds
    B. point-of-sale terminal
    C. electronic sensors
    D. fireproof vault

III. Completion   *Complete each of the following.*

1. _____ is a measure of making small cash disbursements quickly.

2. _____ auditors are regular employees of a business; _____ auditors are independent of the business.

3. In a good internal control system, the following functions are separated:

   a)_____

   b)_____

   c)_____

   d)_____

4. _____ is usually the first asset listed on the balance sheet.

5. Indicate how each of the following items is treated in a bank reconciliation. Use: AB for additions to the bank balance; AF for additions to the firm's balance; DB for deductions from the bank balance; and DF for deductions from the firm's balance.

   _____ A.   A deposit for $143 was not recorded in the books

   _____ B.   A check for $34 was entered in the books as $43

   _____ C.   Bank collection of a note receivable

   _____ D.   Bank service charges

   _____ E.   A deposit was credited by the bank to the firm's account in error

   _____ F.   Deposits in transit

_____ G. Interest earned on checking account

_____ H. Outstanding checks

_____ I. NSF checks

6. What account is debited for 5F above? _____

7. What will be the amount of the adjustment in 5B above? _____

8. What account(s) is (are) debited when Petty Cash is replenished? _____

9. _____ insure a company against theft by an employee.

10. Cash, petty cash, short-term time deposits, and certificates of deposits are referred to collectively as

    _____.

11. Sales Discount is a _____ account whose companion account is _____.

12. The purpose of an audit is to _____.

13. _____ are one means a company uses to encourage customers to pay their bills early.

14. The length of time between the expenditure of cash for inventory and the receipt of cash from a customer is
    called the _____.

15. The quantitative expression of a plan that helps managers coordinate the entity's activities is called a

    _____.

16. A _____ helps a company manage its cash by developing a plan for _____ and

    _____.

IV. True/False   *For each of the following statements, circle* T *for true or* F *for false.*

1.   T F   NSF checks are reconciled by deducting them from the balance per bank.
2.   T F   The vice president for accounting is the chief accounting officer in a corporation.
3.   T F   Internal auditors are employees of the corporation.
4.   T F   The most liquid asset is inventory.
5.   T F   When preparing a bank reconciliation, outstanding checks are deducted from the balance
            per book.
6.   T F   The bank reconciliation is one method of internal control.
7.   T F   The longer the operating cycle, the quicker the cash flow.
8.   T F   Subsidiary ledgers provide detail to a general ledger account.
9.   T F   Discounts offered to customers are a method for improving cash flow.
10. T F   Credit period and discount period refer to the same length of time.
11. T F   The Sales Discounts account is a contra-asset account.
12. T F   The purchase requisition precedes a purchase order.
13. T F   The Petty Cash account is a revenue account and carries a normal credit balance.
14. T F   Certificates of deposit are classified as cash equivalents.
15. T F   A cash budget and the statement of cash flows present the same information, just in
            different formats.

V. Exercises

1. Sidney's bank statement gave an ending balance of $518.00. Reconciling items include: deposit in transit,
   $225.00; service charge, $9.00; outstanding checks, $189.00; and interest earned on her checking account,
   $1.50. What is the adjusted bank balance after the bank reconciliation is prepared?

2. Using the information in Exercise 1 above, what was the unadjusted ending balance in Sidney's checking
   account?

3. During the month of April, J & J's Services, had the following transactions in its Petty Cash fund.

4/1	Established petty cash fund, $300
4/6	Paid postage, $29
4/8	Paid freight charges on supplies purchased, $43
4/11	Purchased office supplies, $31
4/22	Paid miscellaneous expenses, $28
4/30	Replenished the petty cash fund ($167 was in the fund)

Prepare the journal entries required by each of the above transactions.

Date	Accounts and Explanation	PR	Debit	Credit

4. Analyze each of the following and calculate the correct amount of the payment.

	Invoice Amount	Invoice Date	Discount	Payment Date	Payment Amount
1.	$4,250	Aug. 20	2/20, N/45	Sept. 7	_____
2.	$1,200	March 2	1/10, N/30	March 30	_____
3.	$3,150	Aug. 24	3/15, N/60	Sept. 9	_____
4.	$736	Oct. 4	N/7	Oct. 11	_____

5. From the following information, present a Cash Budget for the year ended September 30, 2002.

Proceeds from note receivable	$150,000
Purchases for inventory	110,000
Receipts from customers	285,000
Payments for dividends	55,000
Proceeds from sale of equipment	21,500
Payments for interest and taxes	108,000
Cash required for operating expenses	92,250
Debt payments	81,700

The cash balance as of October 1, 2001, is $95,500. The budgeted cash balance for September 30, 2002, is $100,000.

Cash Budget
For the Year Ended September 30, 2002

VI. Critical Thinking

At the Fat Lady Sings Opera House, you notice that there is a box office at the entrance where the cashier receives cash from customers and, with a press of a button, a machine ejects serially numbered tickets. To enter the opera house, a customer must present his or her ticket to the door attendant. The attendant tears the ticket in half and returns the stub to the customer. The other half of the ticket is dropped into a locked box.

1. What internal controls are present in this scenario?
2. What should management do to make these controls more effective?
3. How can these controls be rendered ineffective?

_____

_____

_____

_____

_____

_____

_____

VII. Demonstration Problems

Demonstration Problem #1

The following petty cash transactions occurred in July:

7/1	Management decided to establish a petty cash fund. A check for $200 was written and cashed with the proceeds given to Cheryl Haynes, who was designated custodian of the fund.
7/1	The president of the business immediately took $25 for lunch money.
7/4	$12.95 was disbursed to reimburse an employee for an air-express package paid for with personal funds.
7/6	COD freight charges on supplies were paid, $22.00.
7/9	$29 was spent on postage stamps while the postage meter was being repaired.
7/11	The president "borrowed" another $35 from the fund.
7/12	COD freight charges on supplies were paid, $31.
7/13	Because the fund was running low, Ms. Haynes requested a check to replenish it for the disbursements made. As there was $45.05 on hand, Ms. Haynes requested a check for $154.95. However, her supervisor authorized a check for $354.95 so sufficient funds would be on hand and only require monthly replenishment.
7/16	The monthly charge for the office newspaper was paid, $18.
7/19	COD charges on supplies were paid, $47.
7/20	The president took $55 from the fund.
7/22	Ms. Haynes took $12 from the fund to purchase coffee and supplies for the office coffee room.
7/25	The president's spouse arrived by taxi. The fare of $19 plus a $3 tip was paid from the petty cash fund.
7/26	$35 was paid from the fund to have the front windows washed.
7/28	A coworker did not have lunch money. Ms. Haynes gave the coworker $15 from the fund and took a postdated check for that amount.
7/31	The company decided to replenish the fund on the last working day each month. There was $196.00 left in the fund.

Required:

1. Record the appropriate transactions in the General Journal.
2. Post any entries to the Petty Cash account.

Requirement 1 (General Journal entries)

GENERAL JOURNAL

Date	Accounts and Explanation	PR	Debit	Credit

Requirement 2 (Post entries to Petty Cash Fund)

Petty Cash Fund

_____|_____
                   |
                   |
                   |
                   |

Demonstration Problem #2

The cash account for Bill's Bargains shows the following information on August 31, 2002:

Cash			
Balance	$5,682	8/2	$ 232
8/3	242	8/5	2,114
8/7	701	8/9	445
8/12	408	8/14	756
8/14	900	8/15	905
8/24	2,715	8/18	105
8/31	382	8/22	781
		8/29	828
Balance	$4,864		

Bill's Bargains received the following bank statement on August 31, 2002.

Bank Statement for Bill's Bargains

Beginning balance			$5,682
Deposits and other credits:			
Aug. 4	242		
8	701		
11	1,830	BC	
13	408		
15	900		
25	2,715		
31	16	INT	
			6,812
Checks and other debits:			
Aug. 3	$725		
7	223		
11	2,114		
12	445		
15	756		
20	175	NSF	
24	905		
30	781		
31	14	SC	
			6,138
Ending balance:			$6,356

Legend:
BC = Bank Collection   NSF = Nonsufficient Funds Check
SC = Service Charge   INT = Interest Earned

Additional data for the bank reconciliation:

1. The $1,830 bank collection on Aug. 11 includes $130 interest revenue. The balance was attributable to the collection of a note receivable.
2. The correct amount of the Aug. 2 transaction is $223, a payment on account. The bookkeeper mistakenly recorded the check as $232.
3. The NSF check was received from Joy's Jewelry.
4. The bank statement includes a $725 deduction for a check drawn by Gil Co. The bank has been notified of its error.
5. The service charge consists of two charges: $4 for the monthly account charge and $10 for the NSF check.

Required:

1. Prepare the bank reconciliation of Bill's Bargains on August 31, 2002. Use the form below.
2. Record the entries based on the bank reconciliation. Include explanations. Use the form on the next page.

Requirement 1 (Bank reconciliation)

Bill's Bargains
Bank Reconciliation
August 31, 2002

Requirement 2 (Entries based on bank reconciliation)

Date	Accounts and Explanation	PR	Debit	Credit

SOLUTIONS

I. Matching

1. O	5. J	9. I	13. A	17. D
2. P	6. B	10. N	14. K	18. L
3. E	7. C	11. Q	15. R	
4. H	8. M	12. F	16. G	

II. Multiple Choice

1.   D   Handling cash receipts and having authority to write off accounts receivable puts the person in a position to illegitimately write off an account on which payment has been received. This is a violation of separation of the authorization of transactions from custody of related assets.

2.   C   Independent performance of various phases of accounting helps to minimize errors and the opportunities for fraud.

3.   B   Deposits in transit are cash receipts that have been recorded in the journal of the business but have not yet been recorded by the bank. The other items listed are items that will be reflected in the bank's records but have not yet been recorded on the books of the business.

4.   C   An NSF check represents a previously recorded cash receipt that has no substance and, accordingly, must be reversed; reduce Cash (credit) and reestablish the receivable (debit).

5.   C   Paying bills by check is an internal control procedure for cash disbursements, not cash receipts. The other items listed are internal control procedures for cash receipts.

6.   D   Bank errors are not recorded in the company's records. They are reported to the bank.

7.   A   The purchasing process starts when the sales department identifies need for merchandise and prepares a purchase requisition. The purchase order, receiving report, and check follow in that order.

8.   D   Of the items listed, the check is prepared last and is supported by the purchase order, receiving report, and invoice.

9.   C   There are 15 days from the end of the discount period to the end of the credit period, with a one-percent reduction offered for early payment. There are twenty-four 15-day periods in a year (365/15), therefore $24 \times 1\% = 24\%$ on an annual basis.

10.   C   Electronic sensors attempt to control inventory, not cash.

III. Completion

1. Petty Cash fund
2. Internal; external (Internal auditors report directly to the company's president or audit committee of the board of directors. External auditors audit the entity as a whole and usually report to the stockholders.)

3. custody of assets from accounting, authorization of transactions from custody of related assets, operations from accounting, duties within the accounting function
4. Cash (Assets are listed in order of relative liquidity; cash is listed first because it is the most liquid.)
5. A) AF   B) AF   C) AF   D) DF   E) DB   F) AB   G) AF   H) DB   I) DF

6. None—the business has already recorded them.
7. $9, the difference between $34 and $43
8. Various expense accounts (Note that the Petty Cash account is debited or credited only when the amount of the fund is changed.)
9. fidelity bonds
10. Cash and equivalents
11. contra-revenue; Sales Revenues
12. examine financial statements, accounting systems, and controls
13. Sales discount
14. operating cycle
15. budget
16. cash budget; cash receipts; cash disbursements

IV. True/False

1.	F	The bank has already deducted the NSF check. The NSF check is deducted from the balance per books.
2.	F	The controller is the chief accounting officer in the corporation.
3.	T	
4.	F	Cash is the most liquid asset.
5.	F	Outstanding checks have already been deducted from the books. When preparing the bank reconciliation they are deducted from the balance per bank.
6.	T	
7.	F	With a longer operating cycle, the cash flows are slower.
8.	T	
9.	T	
10.	F	The credit period determines when the entire invoice must be paid. The discount period refers to the number of days within which the bill can be paid at a lesser amount.
11.	F	Sales Discounts is a contra-revenue account.
12.	T	
13.	F	Petty Cash is an asset account and carries a debit balance.
14.	T	
15.	F	A cash budget looks to the future whereas the statement of cash flows reflects the past.

V. Exercises

1.

Balance per bank statement	$518
Add:	
Deposit in transit	225
	743
Deduct:	
Outstanding checks	189
Adjusted bank balance	$554

2. This requires you to work backwards. Start by setting up what is known and then solve for the unknown balance. Remember that the adjusted balance in the checkbook will equal the adjusted bank balance on the bank reconciliation.

Balance per checkbook	?
Add:	
Interest earned	1.50
	?
Deduct:	
Service charge	9.00
Adjusted bank balance	$554

Book balance + $1.50 - $9.00 = $554
Book balance = $561.50

3.

Date	Accounts and Explanation	PR	Debit	Credit
4/1	Petty Cash		300	
	Cash			300
4/30	Miscellaneous Expense		28	
	Postage Expense		29	
	Supplies		74	
	Cash Short and Over		2	
	Cash			133

Note that you make an entry to record the various expenses only when the Petty Cash fund is replenished.

4.
1) $4,165 ($4,250 less $85)
2) $1,200. The discount period ended on March 12; therefore, no discount was allowed.
3) $3,150. The discount period ended on Sept. 8; therefore, the entire amount was due on Sept. 9.
4) $736. N/7 means no discount is being offered. N/7 is a typical credit term in the shipping industry.

5.

Cash Budget
For the Year Ended September 30, 2002

Cash balance, 10/1/01		$ 95,500
Estimated cash receipts		
Receipts from customers	$285,000	
Proceeds from sale of equipment	21,500	
Proceeds from note receivable	150,000	456,500
Estimated cash disbursements		
Purchases of inventory	110,000	
Payments for dividends	55,000	
Payments for interest and taxes	108,000	
Operating expenses	92,250	
Payments for debt	81,700	446,950
Cash available (needed) before new financing		105,050
Budgeted cash balance, 9/30/02		100,000
Cash available for additional investments		$ 5,050

VI. Critical Thinking

1. Notice that there is separation of duties—one person issues the ticket and collects the money and the other person oversees the admission to the opera house. Thus, a ticket is necessary to gain entrance.

   The tickets are serially numbered. Management can determine the amount of cash that should be in the drawer by multiplying the price of each ticket by the number of tickets issued.

2. To make the controls effective, management should 1) record the serial number of the first and last ticket sold on each cashier's shift, 2) maintain control over the unsold tickets, and 3) count the cash at the beginning and end of each shift.

3. The controls are ineffective if there is collusion by the cashier and the door attendant. The door attendant may choose to keep the entire ticket instead of tearing it in half. The ticket is then given to the cashier to be sold again. The cashier can then pocket the cash received for the "used" tickets. Remember, internal controls are ineffective if everyone colludes.

VII. Demonstration Problems

Demonstration Problem #1 Solved and Explained

Requirement 1

Only three entries were required in this problem! Remember, the purpose of a petty cash fund is to make small disbursements while avoiding the time and cost of writing checks. Therefore, entries are only recorded when a fund is established, when the fund balance is changed, and when the fund is replenished.

7/1	Petty Cash Fund	200	
	Cash		200
7/13	Accounts Receivable (President)	60.00	
	Postage	41.95	
	Supplies	53.00	
	Petty Cash Fund	200.00	
	Cash		354.95

Freight charges on assets are debited to the asset account because they represent an additional cost incurred to acquire the asset. The amounts taken by the president are debited to accounts receivable because they represent an amount the president owes the fund. However, the purpose of a petty cash fund is NOT to provide "pocket money" for an officer of the corporation. This practice should not continue.

7/31	Supplies	47	
	Accounts Receivable (President)	77	
	Accounts Receivable (Employee)	15	
	Miscellaneous Expense	65	
	Cash		204

The newspaper, coffee money, and window washing were all charged to Miscellaneous Expense although they could be debited to separate accounts. The postdated check is charged to Accounts Receivable because it represents an amount the employee owes the business. Allowing an employee to "borrow" from the petty cash fund violates effective internal control procedures and should be stopped immediately. If permitted to continue, the petty cash fund will contain nothing but a stack of postdated checks!

Requirement 2

Petty Cash Fund			
7/1	200		
7/13	200		
Bal.	400		

Assuming the company is correct in its estimates that a $400 balance is sufficient for the petty cash fund, the general ledger account (Petty Cash Fund) will remain as presented above with the $400 balance undisturbed.

Demonstration Problem #2 Solved and Explained

Requirement 1

Bill's Bargains
Bank Reconciliation
August 31, 2002

BANK:		
Balance 8/31		$6,356
Add:		
Deposit in transit of 8/31		382
Correction of bank error		725
		7,463
Less:		
Outstanding checks		
8/18 Check	105	
8/29 Check	828	933
Adjusted bank balance 8/31		$6,530
BOOKS:		
Balance 8/31		$4,864
Add:		
Bank collection of note receivable,		
including interest of $130		1,830
Interest earned on bank balance		16
Error—8/2 Check		9
		6,719
Less:		
Service charge		14
NSF check		175
Adjusted bank balance 8/31		$6,530

Explanation: bank reconciliation

1. A bank reconciliation prepared on a timely basis provides good internal control over a company's cash accounts. Comparing the cash balance in the general ledger with the cash balance maintained by the bank makes errors easy to detect.

2. The month-end balance shown in the general ledger rarely agrees with the month-end balance shown on the bank statement. The difference generally occurs for one of two reasons:

    1. Timing differences: These occur because of the time lag that occurs when one record keeper records a transaction before the other. Typical timing differences include

        - Deposits in transit (the bank has yet to record)
        - Outstanding checks (the bank has yet to record)
        - Bank service charges (the company has yet to record)
        - Notes collected by the bank (the company has yet to record)

- Interest earned on account (the company has yet to record)
- NSF checks (the company has yet to record)

2. Errors: An error must result in an adjustment by the record keeping party that made the error. If the error is made by the company, a general journal entry is made. The correcting entry will include an increase or decrease to the Cash account. Note that if the bank has made the error, the proper procedure is to notify the bank promptly. Since the company's records are accurate, no journal entry is needed.

Requirement 2

Date	Accounts and Explanation	PR	Debit	Credit
a.	Cash		1,830	
	Note Receivable			1,700
	Interest Revenue			130
	Note Receivable collected by the bank.			
b.	Cash		16	
	Interest Revenue			16
	Interest earned on bank balance.			
c.	Miscellaneous Expense		4	
	Cash			4
	Bank service charge.			
d.	Accounts Receivable – Joy's Jewelry		185	
	Cash			185
	NSF check returned by bank plus service charge.			
e.	Cash		9	
	Accounts Payable			9
	To correct error in recording Check #115.			

Explanations: Journal Entries

Entries (a) and (b) are necessary to record the increase in the cash account attributable to 1) the collection of interest and principal on the note receivable, and 2) interest earned on the account paid by the depository bank. These are timing differences which occur because of the time lag between the recording of an item on the bank's books and the books of the company. The bank has already recorded these items in its records (as evidenced by the bank statement), and the company must do so when it learns of the transaction(s).

Entries (c) and (d), which are similar to entries a and b, reduce cash on the company's books. These timing differences have already been recorded by the bank. Entry (c) reduces cash for checking account (or other) service charges for the monthly period and brings the account up to date. The entry for the NSF check is necessary to establish an account receivable for Joy's Jewelry. They had paid the company with a check that was deposited in the Cash account. Because the check was returned unpaid for nonsufficient funds, the company must pursue collection of the debt and record on its books that $185 is still owed.

Entry (e) represents the correction of an error when check #669 was recorded as a reduction to Cash of $233 instead of $223.

Note: No entry is required for the bank error. Once notified, the bank needs to correct their books.

CHAPTER 5—RECEIVABLES AND SHORT-TERM INVESTMENTS

CHAPTER OVERVIEW

In Chapter 4, you learned about the importance of internal control and the application of internal control procedures to cash. Chapter 5 expands this discussion to include other current assets, specifically short-term investments and receivables. The learning objectives for this chapter are to

1. Understand short-term investments
2. Apply internal controls to receivables
3. Use the allowance method for uncollectible receivables
4. Account for notes receivable
5. Evaluate financial position with the acid-test ratio and days' sales in receivables
6. Report receivables and investment transactions on the statement of cash flows

CHAPTER REVIEW

<u>Study Tip</u>: Much of the discussion in this chapter will be easier to understand if you become conversant with the following terms: creditor, debt instrument, debtor, equity securities, maturity, and term.

Objective 1 – Understand short-term investments.

The three most liquid assets companies have are cash and cash equivalents, short-term investments, and accounts receivables. **Short-term investments** (also called marketable securities) are investments that the company plans to hold for one year or less. Short-term investments fall into three groups: held-to-maturity securities, trading securities, and available-for-sale securities. **Held-to-maturity securities**, on which the company earns interest, are those the company intends to keep until they mature. **Trading securities** are those being held to earn profit on short-term price movements. **Available-for-sale securities** are defined by exception: if the short-term investment is neither a trading security nor a held-to-maturity security, it is classified as an available-for-sale security. Remember, however, that these three groups refer only to short-term investments.

Short-term held-to-maturity securities (examples are T-bills, short-term commercial paper) earn interest which accrues over time. When acquired, held-to-maturity securities are recorded at cost. At the end of the accounting period, an adjusting entry is required to accrue the interest on the security, as follows:

Short-term Investment	XX	
Interest Revenue		XX

Note that the debit is to the Investment account, not Interest Receivable. By increasing the Investment account to reflect the accrued interest, the amortized cost of the held-to-maturity security can be listed on the balance sheet. **Amortized cost** is simply original cost plus accrued interest.

Short-term trading securities can be either equity securities or debt instruments. The **market-value method** is used to account for trading securities. When acquired, trading securities are recorded at cost. As dividends (on equity securities) or interest (on debt securities) are received, they are credited to the appropriate revenue account. At the end of the accounting period, the amount at which the trading securities are reported on the balance sheet should reflect their current market value, not original cost. The current market value is established in the account as the result of an adjusting entry. If the market value is greater than the balance in the trading security account, the following adjusting entry is required:

Short-term Investment	XX	
Unrealized Gain on Investment		XX

The amount of the entry will be the difference between the balance in the Short-term Investment account and the investment's current market value. If the market value was less than the balance in the account, the adjusting entry would be:

Unrealized Loss on Investment	XX	
Short-term Investment		XX

Unrealized gains and losses are reported on the income statement as "other revenues and expenses." This category is listed after operating income. When a trading security is sold, a gain (or loss) will result if the net sales price is different from the carrying amount of the security. This gain (or loss) is a realized gain (or loss) because it results from a transaction. **Realized gains and losses** are also reported on the income statement, after operating income, as "other revenues and expenses."

The treatment for available-for-sale securities is similar to the treatment for trading securities except unrealized gains and losses are reported on the balance sheet as part of stockholder's equity. Available-for-sale securities are covered in more detail in Chapter 10.

Accounts and Notes Receivable

Receivables arise when goods or services are sold on credit. The basic types of receivables are **accounts receivable** and **notes receivable**.

Accounts receivable are amounts that customers owe a business for purchases made on credit. They should be collectible according to a firm's normal terms of sale, such as net 30 days. Accounts receivable are sometimes called **trade receivables**, and are current assets.

Notes receivable occur when customers sign formal agreements to pay for their purchases. These agreements are called **promissory notes**, and usually extend for periods of 60 days or longer. The portion of notes receivable scheduled to be collected within a year is a current asset; the remaining amount is a long-term asset.

Other receivables includes miscellaneous items such as loans to employees and subsidiary companies.

Objective 2 - Apply internal controls to receivables.

The main issues in controlling and managing the collection of receivables are:

1. extending credit only to creditworthy customers
2. separating cash-handling, credit, and accounting duties
3. pursuing collection from customers to maximize cash flow

It is imperative that cash-handling and cash accounting duties be separated; otherwise, too many opportunities exist for employees to steal cash from the company. This is true in both the receivables department and the credit department.

The main issues in accounting for receivables are:

1. measuring and reporting receivables at the net realizable value (the amount we expect to collect)
2. measuring and reporting the expense associated with uncollectible accounts

Extending credit to customers involves the risk that some customers will not pay their obligations. Uncollectible-Account Expense (also called Doubtful-Account Expense or Bad-Debt Expense) occurs when a business is unable to collect from some credit customers. This expense is a cost of doing business, and should be measured, recorded, and reported. Two methods used by accountants are the **allowance method** and the **direct write-off method**.

The **allowance method** is the preferred way to account for Uncollectible-Account Expense (it is better for matching the expense with revenue earned). This method estimates and records collection losses before specific uncollectible accounts are identified.

Allowance for Uncollectible-Accounts is a contra account to Accounts Receivable. Remember, contra accounts are subtracted from a related account. Examples from earlier chapters are Accumulated Depreciation (which is subtracted from a related plant asset) and Sales Discounts (which is subtracted from Sales Revenue).

The allowance method records estimated Uncollectible-Account Expense. The entry to the contra account has the effect of reducing the net balance in Accounts Receivable:

> Accounts Receivable
> - Allowance for Uncollectible-Accounts
> = Net Accounts Receivable (also called **net realizable value**)

Recording estimated bad debts has the effect of reducing net Accounts Receivable and matching Uncollectible-Account Expense with its related Sales Revenue.

Objective 3 - Use the allowance method for uncollectible receivables.

Using the allowance method requires an estimate of uncollectible accounts.

The **percentage-of-sales method** (also called the **income statement approach**) estimates uncollectible accounts as a percentage of sales, using past experience to set the percentage. The amount of the journal entry is equal to credit sales times the bad debt percentage, and is recorded as:

Uncollectible-Account Expense   XX
    Allowance for Uncollectible-Accounts   XX

Aging-of-accounts receivable (also called the **balance-sheet approach)** involves grouping accounts receivable according to the length of time they have been outstanding. Accounts are usually grouped into 30-day increments, such as 1-30, 31-60, 61-90, and over 90 days. Different percentages of the total receivables in each group are estimated to be uncollectible. The amount for each group is equal to the total receivables in that group times the estimated uncollectible percentage for that group.

The amount of the journal entry will be what is needed to bring the Allowance account to the estimated amount calculated using the aging method. Therefore, if the existing balance in the Allowance for Uncollectible-Accounts is a credit, the amount of the journal entry will be less than the estimate. If the existing balance in the Allowance for Uncollectible-Accounts is a debit, the amount of the journal entry will be greater than the estimate.

The expense is recorded as:

Uncollectible-Account Expense   XX
     Allowance Uncollectible-Accounts   XX

Study Tip: When using an estimate based on sales, adjust *for* the estimate; when using an estimate based on accounts receivable, adjust *to* the estimate.

(Review Exhibit 5-5 in your text.)

When using the allowance method, specific accounts receivable are written off when the credit department determines that the receivable is not collectible. Specific accounts are written off with this journal entry:

Allowance for Uncollectible-Accounts   XX
     Accounts Receivable   XX

Note that this entry does not affect expense because the estimated expense has already been recorded.

Using the **direct write-off method**, the company writes off an account receivable directly to an expense account. In other words, the Allowance account is not used.

The journal entry for a direct write-off is:

Uncollectible-Account Expense   XX
     Accounts Receivable   XX

The direct write-off method is easy to use; however, it suffers from two defects. First, it does not set up an allowance for uncollectibles account and therefore overstates the value of accounts receivable on the balance sheet. Secondly, it may not match the uncollectible-account expense with the revenue which generated the account receivable.

Objective 4 - Account for notes receivable.

Notes receivable are more formal than accounts receivable. Usually, the maker (debtor) will sign a promissory note and must pay the principal amount plus interest to the payee (creditor) on the maturity date. The maturity value is the sum of the principal amount plus the interest.

Review Exhibit 5-7 in your text to be certain you are familiar with the following terms:

Promissory note	Interest period (note period or note term)
Maker	Maturity date (due date)
Payee	Maturity value
Principal	Interest rate

The formula for computing interest is :

Principal × Interest Rate × Time = Interest Amount

Study the examples in the text. It is important to be able to compute interest based on years, months, and days.

Generally notes arise from two events, as follows:

| Notes Receivable | XX | |
| Sales | | XX |

Sold goods and received a promissory note.

| Notes Receivable | XX | |
| Accounts Receivable | | XX |

Receipt of a note from a customer is payment of the account.

Interest revenue is earned as time passes, and not just when cash is collected. If the interest period of the note extends beyond the current accounting period, then part of the interest revenue is earned in the current accounting period and part is earned in the next accounting period.

A note receivable is a negotiable instrument. Frequently, a business will sell a note receivable to a bank to raise cash. Selling a note receivable before its maturity date is called **discounting a note receivable**. The seller receives less than the maturity value (that is, gives up some of the interest revenue) in exchange for receiving cash. The discounted value, called the proceeds, is the amount the seller (business) receives from the purchaser (bank).

Factoring accounts receivables is another way companies use receivables to finance operations. Similar to discounting notes receivables, factoring refers to selling the accounts receivables to a financial institution (called a factor). The factor earns money by purchasing them at less than face value and collecting them at the total amount due. The difference between the selling price of the receivable and the face value is recorded as interest expense on the books of the seller.

A **contingent liability** is a potential liability—one that may or may not occur. If the maker of the note fails to pay the maturity value to the new payee (bank), the seller (business) must pay the new payee (bank). Thus, the liability is potential. Contingent liabilities are not reported on the balance sheet, but are reported in the footnotes to the financial statements. Notes receivable that have been discounted represent contingent liabilities.

Objective 5 – Evaluate financial position with the acid-test ratio and days' sales in receivables.

The **acid-test (quick) ratio** measures the ability of a business to pay all of its current liabilities if they become due immediately.

$$\text{Acid-test Ratio} = \frac{\text{Cash} + \text{Short-term investments} + \text{Net current receivables}}{\text{Current Liabilities}}$$

Remember that inventory, supplies, and prepaid expenses are not used to compute the acid-test ratio.

Day's sales in receivables (also called the average collection period) measures the average days an account receivable is outstanding.

$$\text{One day's sales} = \frac{\text{Net Sales}}{365}$$

$$\text{Average Net Accounts Receivable} = \frac{\text{Beginning Accounts Receivable} + \text{Ending Accounts Receivable}}{2}$$

$$\text{Days' sales in average accounts receivable} = \frac{\text{Average Net Accounts Receivable}}{\text{One day's sales}}$$

Objective 6 - Report receivables and investment transactions on the statement of cash flows.

Because short-term investments and receivables affect cash, the statement of cash flows will report these effects. When cash is collected from accounts receivables, the amount is reflected in the operating activities section of the cash-flow statement. The purchase (or sale) of short-term investments is reported as an investing activity on the cash-flow statement. The collection of a note receivable would also be reported as an investing activity. However, the receipt of interest or dividend revenue from short-term investments is reported in the operating activities section of the cash-flow statement.

Review Exhibit 5-8 in your text.

TEST YOURSELF

All the self-testing materials in this chapter focus on information and procedures that your instructor is likely to test in quizzes and examinations.

I. Matching   Match each numbered term with its lettered definition.

_____ 1. aging of accounts receivable
_____ 2. short-term investments
_____ 3. contingent liability
_____ 4. direct write-off method
_____ 5. available for sale securities
_____ 6. term
_____ 7. maturity
_____ 8. payee
_____ 9. promissory note
_____ 10. Uncollectible-Account Expense

_____ 11. allowance method
_____ 12. securities
_____ 13. acid-test ratio
_____ 14. percentage of sales approach
_____ 15. equity securities
_____ 16. trading securities
_____ 17. debt instruments
_____ 18. principal
_____ 19. receivable
_____ 20. interest

A. a potential liability
B. notes payable or stock certificates that entitle the owner to the benefits of an investment
C. tells whether the entity could pay all its current liabilities if they came due immediately
D. a method of estimating uncollectible receivables as a percentage of net sales
E. a method of accounting for bad debts in which the company records uncollectible-account expense and credits the customer's account receivable when the credit department decides that a customer's account receivable is uncollectible
F. all investment securities not classified as held-to-maturity or trading securities
G. the length of time until a debt instrument matures
H. investments that are to be sold in the near future, with the intent of generating a profit on the sale
I. the date on which a debt instrument matures
J. the person who receives promised future payment on a note
K. the amount loaned out or borrowed
L. a written promise to pay a specified amount of money on a particular future date
M. a monetary claim against a business or an individual which is acquired by selling goods and services on credit or by lending money
N. a way to estimate bad debts by analyzing individual accounts receivable according to the length of time they have been due
O. investments that a company plans to hold for one year or less
P. a method of recording collection losses based on estimates made prior to determining that specific accounts are uncollectible
Q. the borrower's cost of renting money from a lender
R. stock certificates that represent the investor's ownership of shares of stock in a corporation
S. a payable, usually some form of note or bond payable
T. cost of extending credit that arises from the failure to collect from credit customers

II. Multiple Choice   *Circle the best answer.*

1. Using the allowance method, writing off a specific account receivable will

    A. increase net income
    B. decrease net income
    C. not affect net income
    D. affect net income in an undetermined manner

2. Uncollectible-Account Expense is

    A. a component of Cost of Goods Sold
    B. an operating expense
    C. a reduction to Sales
    D. an Other Expense

3. Which of the following will occur if Uncollectible-Account Expense is not recorded at the end of the year?

    A. Expenses will be overstated.
    B. Net Income will be understated.
    C. Liabilities will be understated.
    D. Assets will be overstated.

4. Net Accounts Receivable is equal to

    A. Accounts Receivable - Allowance for Uncollectible-Accounts
    B. Accounts Receivable + Allowance for Uncollectible-Accounts
    C. Accounts Receivable - Uncollectible-Account Expense
    D. Accounts Receivable + Uncollectible-Account Expense

5. Accounts Receivable has a debit balance of $8,500 and the Allowance for Uncollectible-Account has a credit balance of $350. A specific account of $150 is written off. What is the amount of net receivables after the write-off?

    A. $8,150
    B. $8,500
    C. $8,095
    D. $8,350

6. Allowance for Uncollectible-Accounts is

    A. an expense account
    B. a contra liability account
    C. a contra asset account
    D. a liability account

7. A three-month note receivable reported on the balance sheet is classified as a

   A. current asset
   B. long-term asset
   C. current liability
   D. long-term liability

8. Interest is equal to

   A. Principal × Rate
   B. Principal ÷ Rate ÷ Time
   C. Principal × Rate ÷ Time
   D. Principal × Rate × Time

9. Assets listed as Short-term Investments on the balance sheet are

   A. only liquid
   B. listed on the national stock exchange
   C. only intended to be converted to cash within one year
   D. liquid and intended to be converted to cash within one year

10. Trading securities are reported on the balance sheet at

    A. current cost
    B. historical cost
    C. lower of cost or market
    D. market value

11. Available-for-sale securities are

    A. stock investments only
    B. bond investments only
    C. the same as held-to-maturity investments
    D. those other than trading securities

12. An unrealized gain (or loss) results from

    A. available-for-sale securities
    B. trading securities
    C. held-to-maturity securities
    D. any of the above

13. All of the following current assets are included in the acid-test ratio *except*

    A. cash
    B. inventory
    C. short-term investments
    D. net current receivables

14. Short-term investments transactions are reported on the statement of cash flows as

    A. operating activities
    B. investing activities
    C. financing activities
    D. both operating and investing activities

15. Receivable transactions are reported on the statement of cash flows as

    A. operating activities
    B. investing activities
    C. financing activities
    D. none of the above

III. Completion   *Complete each of the following statements.*

1. _____ are investments that the company plans to hold for one year or less.

2. The three categories of short-term investments are _____, _____, and _____.

3. Debt instruments that pay interest are classified as _____.

4. Amortized cost equals _____ plus _____.

5. Trading securities are recorded at _____ when acquired but reported on the balance sheet at _____.

6. The difference between an Unrealized Loss and a Realized Loss is _____ _____.

7. The direct write-off method of accounting for bad debt violates the _____ principle.

8. The method of estimating bad debts that focuses on the balance sheet is the _____ _____ method.

9. The method of estimating bad debts that focuses on the income statement is the _____ _____ method.

10. A _____ liability will become an actual liability and require payment only if certain events occur in the future.

11. The _____ measures the ability of a business to pay all its current liabilities if they become due immediately.

12. To calculate the average days an account receivable is outstanding, average net accounts receivable is divided by _____.

IV. True/False   *For each of the following statements, circle* T *for true or* F *for false.*

1.   T F   Interest earned on short-term investments is reported in the investing activities section of the statement of cash flows.

2.   T F   Receipts from accounts receivables are reported as operating activities on the statement of cash flows.

3.   T F   Collections on notes receivables are reported as operating activities on the statement of cash flows.

4.   T F   Days' sales in receivables indicates how long, on average, it takes to collect accounts receivables.

5.   T F   When computing the acid-test ratio, inventory is included in the numerator.

6.   T F   Trading securities can be either equity securities or debt instruments.

7. T F Held-to-maturity securities can be either equity securities or debt instruments.
8. T F Held-to-maturity securities are reported on the balance sheet at their market value.
9. T F Trading securities are reported on the balance sheet at their market value.
10. T F Unrealized gains and losses on trading securities are reported on the income statement.
11. T F The maturity value of a note receivable is the sum of the principal and interest.
12. T F The direct write-off method violates the disclosure principle.
13. T F Net realizable value equals total accounts receivable less uncollectible-accounts expense.
14. T F When using the allowance method, the write-off on an uncollectible-account will reduce total assets by the amount of the account receivable written off.
15. T F Discounting notes receivables and factoring accounts receivables are two method of financing receivables.

V. Exercises

1. Sunshine Studios uses the Allowance method to account for bad debts. Indicate the effect that each of the following transactions will have on gross Accounts Receivable, the Allowance for Uncollectible-Accounts, net Accounts Receivable, and Uncollectible-Accounts Expense. Use + for increases and - for decreases, and 0 for no effect.

	Gross Accounts Receivable	Allowance for Uncollectible -Accounts	Net Accounts Receivable	Uncollec- tible- Accounts Expense
An account receivable is written off	_____	_____	_____	_____
An account receivable is reinstated	_____	_____	_____	_____
A customer pays his account receivable	_____	_____	_____	_____
1.5% of $950,000 in sales is estimated to be uncollectible	_____	_____	_____	_____
4% of $95,000 in accounts receivable is estimated to be uncollectible (the balance in the allowance account is a credit of $550)	_____	_____	_____	_____

2. Compute the missing amounts. Use a 360-day year.

	Principal	Interest rate	Duration	Interest	Maturity Value
A.	$9,000	8%	2 months	_____	_____
B.	$10,000	9%	120 days	_____	_____
C.	_____	12%	30 days	_____	$15,150
D.	$6,000	_____	10 months	$300	_____

3. Phillip's Fitness has a $185,000 balance in Accounts Receivable on December 31, 2002. The Allowance for Uncollectible-Accounts has a $200 credit balance. Credit sales totaled $825,000 for the year.

Part A.

a. If Phillip's Fitness uses the percentage-of-sales method and estimates that 1.0% of sales may be uncollectible, what is the Uncollectible-Account Expense for 2002?

b. What is the ending balance in the Allowance for Uncollectible-Accounts after adjustments?

c. Would your answers be different if the Allowance for Uncollectible-Accounts had a $200 debit balance?

Part B

a. If Phillip's Fitness uses the Aging-of-Accounts-Receivable method and has determined that $7,200 of Accounts Receivable is uncollectible, what is the Uncollectible-Account Expense for 2002?

b. What is the ending balance in the Allowance for Uncollectible-Accounts after adjustments?

c. Would your answers be different if the Allowance for Uncollectible-Accounts had a $200 debit balance?

4. Prepare journal entries for the following trading security transactions:

3/12   Purchased 250 shares of Scott Corporation at 47½. The commission was $62.50.
6/18   Received a $0.50 per share cash dividend.
8/28   Sold 100 shares of Scott Corporation for $60 per share. The commission was $35.
12/31 The market value of the shares is $59¼ as of today.

Date	Account and Explanation	Debit	Credit

5. On April 30, 2002, Solerno Corporation paid $400,000 for 8% commercial paper of Solis Inc., as a held-to-maturity investment. The commercial paper pays interest on April 30 and October 31.

Record Solerno's purchase of the commercial paper, the receipt of semiannual interest on October 31, and the accrual of interest revenue on December 31.

Date	Account and Explanation	Debit	Credit

VI. Critical Thinking

Examine the information in Exercise 4 above. Indicate what would change if:

1. the stock was acquired as an available-for-sale security
2. the stock was acquired as a hold-to-maturity security

_____
_____
_____
_____
_____
_____
_____
_____
_____
_____
_____
_____
_____
_____

VII. Demonstration Problems

Demonstration Problem #1

Huezo, Inc., manufactures machine parts. The company's year-end trial balance for 2002 reported the following:

Accounts Receivable	$5,125,200
Less: Allowance for Uncollectible-Accounts	51,770
	$5,073,430

Assume that net credit sales for 2002 amounted to $12,300,000 and Allowance for Uncollectible-Accounts has not yet been adjusted for 2002.

Required:

1. At the end of 2002, the following accounts receivable were deemed uncollectible:

Boyce Inc.	$ 9,150
Caster Corporation	8,007
Shaw Products	6,823
UST Wholesalers	13,090
Total	$37,070

Prepare the 2002 journal entry necessary to write off the above accounts.

2. Assume that the company uses the percentage-of-sales method to estimate Uncollectible-Account Expense. After analyzing industry averages and prior years' activity, Huezo's management has determined that Uncollectible-Account Expense for 2002 should be 1.5% of net credit sales. Prepare the journal entry to record and adjust Uncollectible-Account Expense.

3. Assume that the company uses the aging-of-accounts-receivable method. The aging schedule prepared by the company's credit manager indicated that an allowance of $202,000 for uncollectible-accounts is appropriate. Prepare the appropriate journal entry.

4. Calculate net realizable value of accounts receivable assuming (a) the percentage of sales method was used and (b) the aging-of-accounts-receivable method was used.

Requirement 1 (Write-off of uncollectible-accounts)

GENERAL JOURNAL

Date	Accounts and Explanation	PR	Debit	Credit

Requirement 2 (Adjustment to record Uncollectible-Account Expense using the percentage-of-sales method)

GENERAL JOURNAL

Date	Accounts and Explanation	PR	Debit	Credit

Requirement 3 (Adjustment to record Uncollectible-Account Expense using the aging-of-accounts-receivable)

GENERAL JOURNAL

Date	Accounts and Explanation	PR	Debit	Credit

Requirement 4

(a) $_____

(b) $_____

Demonstration Problem #2

At the beginning of the year, Bold Ventures, Inc., held the following short-term investments:

	Market Value
500 shares Atlas, Inc.	41 1/8 ea.
Money market funds	$45,000
1,200 shares EZ, Inc.	34 1/4 ea.
400 shares Valu.com	26 3/8 ea.
820 shares Wal-Way Corporation	104 3/4 ea.

During the current year, the following occurred:

On February 10 Bold Ventures received a 26¢/share dividend on the Atlas stock. Shortly thereafter, Atlas shares increased to $48½ so the security was sold on March 1, less a brokerage commission of $325.

The money market funds earned 0.5% interest monthly (6% annual interest), payable at the end of the month. Interest checks were received and used for other purposes.

Quarterly dividends of 17.5¢/share were received on the EZ stock on March 24 and June 24. On July 8 the shares were sold for 29½ per share, less a brokerage commission of $485.

On August 31, Bold Ventures, Inc., purchased a $100,000, 6-month Treasury note (T-bill). The T-bill earns 7.1% annual interest, payable at maturity.

The Valu.com shares remained in the portfolio throughout the year; no dividends were received during the year, and the stock was trading at $25 per share at year-end.

The Wal-Way shares also remained in the company's portfolio throughout the year. Quarterly dividends of $1.06 were received throughout the year. On December 31 the shares were trading at 121.

Required:
1. For each security, record journal entries to reflect interest/dividends received during the year.
2. Present journal entries to record the sale of the Atlas and EZ shares.
3. For the remaining securities (money market funds, T-bills, Valu.com, and Wal-Way), present year-end journal entries to record the unrealized gain or loss.

Requirement 1

Date	Accounts and Explanation	PR	Debit	Credit

Requirement 2

Date	Accounts and Explanation	PR	Debit	Credit

Requirement 3

Date	Accounts and Explanation	PR	Debit	Credit

SOLUTIONS

I. Matching

1. N	5. F	9. L	13. C	17. S
2. O	6. G	10. T	14. D	18. K
3. A	7. I	11. P	15. R	19. M
4. E	8. J	12. B	16. H	20. Q

II. Multiple Choice

1. **C** Writing off a specific account receivable using the allowance method takes the form of:

Allowance for Uncollectible-Accounts	XX
Accounts Receivable	XX

   Both accounts involved are balance sheet accounts; accordingly, net income is not affected.

2. **B** Uncollectible-Account Expense is estimated and recorded as sales are made. It is a function of the operations of the business and is an operating expense.

3. **D** Failing to record the Uncollectible-Accounts Expense also means that no increase in the Allowance for Uncollectible-Accounts (contra accounts receivable) was recorded. Accordingly, expenses are understated and assets are overstated.

4. **A** Net Accounts Receivable is the result of netting the Accounts Receivable balance against its contra account, Allowance for Uncollectible-Accounts.

5. **A** When Accounts Receivable and the Allowance are both reduced by $150, Net Accounts Receivable will be unchanged.
   [$8,500 - $350 = ($8,500 - $150) - ($350 - $150)]

6. **C** Allowance for Uncollectible-Accounts is a companion account to Accounts Receivable and has a normal credit balance while Accounts Receivable has a normal debit balance. A contra account has two distinguishing characteristics: 1) it always has a companion account, and 2) its normal balance is opposite that of the companion account.

7. **A** A note receivable is an asset. An asset that will be converted to cash within one year is a current asset.

8. **D** Interest is a function of the amount advanced to the borrower, the interest rate, and the term of the loan.

9. **D** Note that besides the determinable liquidity of the investment, the intent of management determines an investment's classification as a short-term investment.

10. **D** GAAP requires trading securities to be reported in the balance sheet at market value.

11. D Available-for-sale securities are stock investments other than trading securities and bond investments other than trading securities and held-to-maturity securities.

12. B Unrealized gains (or losses) are a result of the market value method applied to trading securities.

13. B Inventory is not included in the acid-test ratio because it may not be easy to sell the goods.

14. D The purchase and sale of short-term investments are investing activities, whereas the interest and dividends received on short-term investments are reported as operating activities.

15. A Collections from customers are cash receipts from operating activities.

III. Completion

1. Short-term investments (or marketable securities)
2. held-to-maturity securities, trading securities, available-for-sale securities (order not important)
3. held-to-maturity securities
4. cost, accrued interest (order not important)
5. cost, market value
6. unrealized losses are not the result of a sales transaction whereas realized losses do result from sales transactions
7. matching (The direct write-off fails to match the business's cost of extending credit to customers who do not pay with the revenue generating the expense.)
8. aging-of-accounts-receivable (Aging the accounts focuses on estimating the appropriate balance in the contra account receivable account, Allowance for Uncollectible-Accounts.)
9. percentage-of-sales (The percentage-of-sales method focuses on calculating the appropriate cost to match against sales in the current period as Uncollectible-Accounts Expense.)
10. contingent (Other liabilities are the result of past transactions and will definitely require payment in the future.)
11. acid-test (quick) ratio
12. one day's sales

IV. True/False

1. F Both interest revenue and dividend revenue are operating activities.
2. T
3. F Collections on notes receivables are investing activities, not operating activities.
4. T
5. F Generally, inventory does not convert to cash quickly enough and is therefore excluded from the acid-test ratio.
6. T
7. F Held-to-maturity securities are debt instruments.
8. F Held-to-maturity securities are reported at amortized cost (original cost plus accrued interest), not market value.
9. T
10. T Because they are short-term investments; however, if the investment is classified as available for sale, the unrealized gain (or loss) is reported on the balance sheet.
11. T
12. F Violates the matching principle, not the disclosure principle.

13. F Net realizable value equals total accounts receivable less allowance for uncollectible-accounts.

14. F One advantage of the allowance method is that the write-off of an account receivable does not affect the net realizable value of accounts receivables.

15. T

V. Exercises

1.

	Gross Accounts Receivable	Allowance for Uncollectible-Accounts	Net Accounts Receivable	Uncollec-tible-Accounts Expense
An account receivable is written off	-	-	0	0
An account receivable is reinstated	+	+	0	0
A customer pays his account receivable	-	0	-	0
1.5% of $950,000 in sales is estimated to be uncollectible	0	+	-	+
4% of $95,000 in accounts receivable is estimated to be uncollectible (the balance in the allowance account is a credit of $550)	0	+	-	+

2.
   A. interest = $9,000 × .08 × 2/12 = $120
      maturity value = $9,000 + $120 = $9,120

   B. interest = $10,000 × .09 × 120/360 = $300
      maturity value = $10,000 + $300 = $10,300

   C. maturity value = principal + interest
      interest = principal × rate × time
      $15,150 = P + (P × .12 × 30/360)
      P = $15,000
      interest = $150

D. interest = principal × rate × time
$300 = $6,000 × R × 10/12
R = 6%
maturity value = principal + interest
maturity value = $6,000 + $300 = $6,300

3. A. a. Uncollectible-Account Expense = .01 × $825,000 = $8,250
   b. Ending balance in Allowance for Uncollectible-Accounts = $200 + $8,250 = $8,450
   c. Yes. The amount of Uncollectible-Account Expense would be the same. However, the balance in the Allowance for Uncollectible-Accounts would be different ($8,250 - $200 = $8,050).

   B. a. The current balance in the Allowance account is $200 credit, and the desired balance in the Allowance account is $7,200 credit. The Uncollectible-Account Expense will be $7,200 - $200 = $7,000.
   b. The ending balance will be $7,200.
   c. Yes. It would require a credit of $7,400 to bring the balance in the Allowance account to a credit of $7,200; the corresponding debit is to the Uncollectible-Account Expense. The ending balance in the Allowance account will be the same, $7,200.

4.

3/12	Short-term Investment—Scott Corp.		11,937.50	
	Cash [(250 shares × $47.50) + $62.50]			11,937.50
	Per share cost = $47.75			
6/18	Cash		125	
	Dividend Revenue			125
8/28	Cash [(100 shares × $60) - $35]		5,965	
	Short-term Investment—Scott Corp. (100 shares × $47.75)			4,775
	Gain on Sale of Investment			1,190
12/31	Short-term Investment—Scott Corp.		1,725	
	Unrealized Gain on Short-term Investment			1,725

Before the 12/31 adjustment, the balance in the account is $7,162.50 ($11,937.50 - $4,775). The current market value is $8,887.50 (150 shares × $59.25). The unrealized gain is therefore $1,725 ($8,887.50 less $7,162.50).

5.

4/30	Short-term Investment—Solis Inc.		400,000	
	Cash			400,000
10/31	Cash		16,000	
	Interest Revenue			16,000
	($400,000 × .08 × 6/12 = $16,000)			

	12/31	Short-term Investment—Solis Inc.		5,333	
		Interest Revenue			5,333
		($400,000 × .08 × 2/12 = $5,333)			

VI. Critical Thinking

1. If the stock was acquired as an available-for-sale security, the journal entries would remain the same. *However*, the unrealized gain would be reported differently. Unrealized gains on trading securities are reported on the income statement (as "other revenues") whereas unrealized gains on available-for-sale securities are reported on the balance sheet in the stockholders' equity section.

2. The stock cannot be classified as a held-to-maturity short-term investment because stock is an equity security. Hold-to-maturity investments are only debt instruments.

VII. Demonstration Problems

Demonstration Problem #1 Solved and Explained

Requirement 1

GENERAL JOURNAL

Date	Accounts and Explanation	PR	Debit	Credit
12/31/X9	Allowance for Uncollectible-Accounts		37,070	
	Accounts Receivable—Boyce, Inc.			9,150
	Accounts Receivable—Caster Corporation			8,007
	Accounts Receivable—Shaw Products			6,823
	Accounts Receivable—UST Wholesalers			13,090
	To write off uncollectible accounts.			

Requirement 2

Uncollectible-Account Expense		184,500	
Allowance for Uncollectible-Accounts			184,500

Net credit sales of 2002 were $12,300,000. Uncollectible-Account Expense for 2002 is therefore $184,500 ($12,300,000 × 1.5% = $184,500). An examination of the activity to date in the Uncollectible-Account Expense and Allowance for Uncollectible-Accounts reveals the effect of the entries made in Requirements 1 and 2.

Uncollectible-Account Expense		Allowance for Uncollectible-Accounts		Accounts Receivable	
(2) 184,500		(1) 37,070	Bal. 51,770	Bal. 5,125,200	(1) 37,070
Bal. 184,500			(2) 184,500	Bal. 5,088,130	
			Bal. 199,200		

Note that the Allowance account started at $51,770. In Requirement 1, it was reduced by $37,070 when the uncollectible-accounts were written off against the Allowance account. Note that prior to the 2002 adjustment, the

Allowance was down to $14,700 ($51,770 - $37,070 = $14,700). The Allowance was then adjusted upward to $199,200 in Entry 2, when the company recorded 2002 Uncollectible-Account Expense of $184,500.

Requirement 3

Uncollectible-Account Expense	187,300	
Allowance for Uncollectible-Accounts		187,300

When the aging-of-accounts-receivable method is used, the adjustment brings Allowance for Uncollectible-Accounts to the balance indicated by the aging schedule. Before adjustment, the balance in the Allowance account was $14,700. The facts reveal that the desired balance in the Allowance account should be set at $202,000. The difference between the unadjusted balance and the desired balance ($202,000 - $14,700= $187,300) represents the amount of the adjustment and the amount of expense.

Study Tip: When using the percentage-of-sales method, adjust *for* the estimate. When using accounts receivable as a basis, adjust *to* the estimate (i.e., the estimate should be the balance in the Allowance account after the adjusting entry is posted).

Requirement 4

(a) 4,888,930
Net realizable value is the difference between total accounts receivable and the balance in the allowance account after adjustment. It represents the amount we expect to receive from those accounts. After adjustment in Requirement 2 above, the balance in Accounts Receivable is $5,088,130 and the balance in the Allowance account is $199,200.

(b) $4,886,130
After adjustment in Requirement 3 above, the balance in the Allowance account is $202,000. The balance in Accounts Receivable remains $5,088,130.

Study Tip: The two approaches to estimating uncollectible accounts will always result in different amounts for net realizable value. If each approach resulted in the same value, there wouldn't be any need for alternative approaches! Remember: the percentage-of-sales method emphasizes the revenue/expense relationship on the income statement, while the aging-of-accounts-receivable method emphasizes asset value on the balance sheet.

Demonstration Problem #2 Solved and Explained

Requirement 1

Atlas

2/10	Cash	130	
	Dividends Revenue		130
	(500 shares × $0.26 per share)		

Money Market

Cash	225	
Interest Revenues		225

($45,000 × 0.5%)

This entry would be recorded monthly. The annual amount of interest revenue would be $2,700 ($225 × 12).

EZ

3/24	Cash	210	
	Dividends Revenue		210

(1,200 shares × $0.175 per share)

6/24	Cash	210	
	Dividends Revenue		210

(as above)

T-Bill

No entry as interest is payable at maturity.

Valu.com

No entry—no dividends received.

Wal-Way

Cash	869.20	
Dividends Revenue		869.20

(820 shares × $1.06/share)

This entry would be recorded 4 times, for an annual total of $3,476.80 ($869.20 × 4).

Requirement 2

Atlas

3/1	Cash	23,925	
	Short-term Investment—Atlas		20,562.50
	Gain on Sale		3,362.50

($48.50 × 500 shares less $325 commission)

EZ

7/8	Cash	34,915	
	Loss on Sale	6,185	
	Short-term Investment—EZ		41,100

The security was valued at $41,100 (1,200 shares × $34.25/per share). It sold for $35,400 (1,200 shares × $29.50/per share) less a commission of $485, resulting in a loss of $6,185.

Requirement 3

Money market funds

No year-end entry required. Because interest was received throughout the year, the year-end amortized cost is the same as the carrying value, $45,000.

T-bill

12/31	Short-term Investment—T-bill	2,367	
	Interest Revenue		2,367
	($100,000 × 7.1% × 4/12)		

Because the T-bill is a hold-to-maturity security, the account needs to reflect the amortized cost of the investment at year-end. Amortized cost equals cost plus accrued interest.

Valu.com

12/31	Unrealized Loss	550	
	Short-term Investment—Valu.com		550
	($26 3/8 - $25) × 400 shares		

Valu.com is a trading security. As such, the account should reflect its market value as of the balance sheet date. The current market value is $1 3/8 less ($26 3/8 - $25) than last year.

Wal-Way

12/31	Short-term Investment—Wal-Way	13,325	
	Unrealized Gain		13,325
	($121.00 - $104.75) × 820 shares		

As with Valu.com, the trading security is reported at market value on the balance sheet.

Both realized and unrealized gains (and losses) on trading securities are reported in the income statement as additions (if a gain) or reductions (losses) to operating income.

CHAPTER 6—MERCHANDISE INVENTORY, COST OF GOODS SOLD, AND GROSS PROFIT

CHAPTER OVERVIEW

In Chapters 4 and 5, you learned more about current assets (cash, short-term investments, receivables, etc.) and procedures to control them. In this chapter you are introduced to merchandising businesses and some topics unique to them. One of the most important is merchandise inventory, including procedures to account for and control this current asset. The learning objectives for this chapter are to

1. Use the cost-of-goods-sold model
2. Apply the various inventory methods: specific unit cost, weighted-average, FIFO, and LIFO
3. Identify the income effects and the tax effects of the inventory methods
4. Measure the effects of inventory errors on cost of goods sold and net income
5. Use the gross profits percentage and the rate of inventory turnover to evaluate a business
6. Account for inventory transactions
7. Estimate inventory by the gross profit method

CHAPTER REVIEW

Objective 1 - Use the cost-of-goods-sold model.

For the past five chapters we have examined financial accounting principles as they apply to service businesses. We now turn our attention to merchandising businesses. This type of business generates revenue by purchasing goods (called inventory) and selling the products to customers. The difference between the selling price of an item and its cost is called the gross margin or gross profit. The term 'gross' is used because the formula does not take into consideration the operating expenses of the period. Operating expenses are deducted from the gross profit to determine the net income, as follows:

Sales - Cost of Goods Sold = Gross Profit

Gross Profit- Operating Expenses = Net Income.

The cost-of-goods-sold model is a term used to describe the relationship between inventories at the beginning and end of each accounting period and the net additions to inventory during the period. The model describes the following relationships:

Goods Available for Sale = Beginning Inventory + Net purchases

Cost of Goods Sold = Goods Available for Sale - Ending Inventory

(See Exhibit 6-3 in your text.)

A merchandiser cannot run out of inventory, so a crucial question is "How much inventory should I keep on hand?" Managers use both a cost of goods sold budget and an ending inventory budget to accurately assess the business's inventory needs.

Two of the topics that need to be addressed for merchandising businesses are related to inventory: specifically, how many units of inventory are on hand, and what is the cost of each of those units?

Quantity on hand is determined by a physical count of all the items of inventory the business owns. Determining unit cost, however, can be more complicated.

Objective 2 - Apply the various inventory methods: specific unit cost, weighted-average, FIFO, and LIFO.

Inventories are initially recorded at historical cost. Inventory cost is what the business pays to acquire the inventory. Inventory cost includes the invoice cost of the goods, less purchase discounts, plus taxes, tariffs, transportation and insurance while in transit.

Determining unit costs is easy when costs remain constant. But prices frequently change. GAAP allows four different methods of assigning costs to each inventory item that is sold: 1) **specific unit cost**, 2) **weighted-average cost**, 3) **first-in, first-out**, and 4) **last-in, first-out**.

Specific unit costing (also called the **specific identification method**) is used by businesses whose inventory items are expensive or have "one-of-a-kind" characteristics—such as automobiles, jewelry, and real estate. Using specific unit cost to determine ending inventory is not practical for many businesses. When this is the case, the accountant has to make an assumption concerning the flow of costs through the inventory. Why is an assumption necessary? Because the actual (i.e., specific) unit cost of each item cannot be determined.

The three cost flow assumptions are **weighted-average, FIFO, and LIFO**.

The **weighted-average cost** method is based on the average cost of all inventory items available for sale during the period. The weighted-average cost method requires the following computation:

$$\text{Average Unit Cost} = \frac{\text{Cost of Goods Available for Sale}}{\text{Number of Units Available for Sale}}$$

Cost of Goods Available for Sale = Beginning Inventory + Net Purchases
Ending Inventory = Number of Units Remaining × Average Unit Cost
Cost of Goods Sold = Cost of Goods Available for Sale - Ending Inventory

Under the **First-In, First-Out (FIFO)** method, the first costs into inventory are the first costs out to Cost of Goods Sold. Therefore, ending inventory reflects unit costs most recently incurred. If beginning inventory is 10 units at $4 each, 60 units were bought at $5 each, 80 more units were bought at $6 each, and there are 50 units left, the 50 remaining units would be assigned the $6 unit cost. Ending inventory would be $300.

Under the **Last-In, First-Out (LIFO)** method, the last costs into inventory are the first costs out to Cost of Goods Sold. Ending inventory is based on the oldest inventory unit costs. If beginning inventory is again 10 units at $4 each, 60 units were bought at $5 each, 80 more units were bought at $6 each, and there were 50 units left, ten of the remaining units would be assigned the $4 unit cost and 40 would be assigned the $5 unit cost. Ending inventory would be $240 (10 × $4 + 40 × $5).

(Helpful hint: Review Exhibit 6-4 in your text.)

Objective 3 - Identify the income effects and the tax effects of the inventory methods.

Review Exhibit 6-6 in your text to be sure that you understand the income effects of the FIFO, LIFO, and weighted-average cost inventory methods.

When inventory costs are increasing:

	FIFO	Weighted-Average Cost	LIFO
Ending Inventory	Highest	Middle	Lowest
Cost of Goods Sold	Lowest	Middle	Highest
Gross Margin	Highest	Middle	Lowest:

When inventory costs are decreasing:

	FIFO	Weighted-Average Cost	LIFO
Ending Inventory	Lowest	Middle	Highest
Cost of Goods Sold	Highest	Middle	Lowest
Gross Margin	Lowest	Middle	Highest

Using LIFO to account for inventories has tax advantages when inventory costs are increasing. This is because using LIFO increases Cost of Goods Sold, and thus decreases Gross Margin and Operating Income. If Operating Income is smaller, total tax payments will be smaller. LIFO matches the most recent inventory costs (last into inventory, first out to Cost of Goods Sold) to revenue, but can result in absurd valuations of ending inventory on the balance sheet. The FIFO method presents an accurate ending inventory on the balance sheet but does not match current cost of inventory to revenue, since the current cost of inventory remains in ending inventory.

Generally, the inventory method used for tax purposes is the one that is used for financial reporting.

Different companies use different inventory methods to achieve a desired result. Notes to the financial statements disclose inventory accounting policies and may also report an alternative inventory amount. For example, if inventories are reported using LIFO in the financial statements, a firm may report inventories using FIFO in the notes to the financial statements. When this is done, substitute the FIFO amounts in place of the LIFO amounts for beginning and ending inventories to convert LIFO Cost of Goods Sold to FIFO Cost of Goods Sold. Note that net purchases will be the same for both methods.

LIFO vs. FIFO—some additional considerations:

a. Because LIFO results in the most recent costs reported on the income statement (as cost of goods sold), it presents the most recent cost/revenue relationship.
b. Because FIFO uses the most recent costs as ending inventory, it presents the most recent value for the asset on the balance sheet.
c. During periods of rising prices, FIFO results in inventory profits because the cost to replace a unit sold has risen.
d. Companies using LIFO can manage the income statement by timing inventory purchases at the end of the accounting period.

e. LIFO liquidation results when inventory quantities fall below the level of the previous period. If inventory costs are rising, the effect of LIFO liquidation is to shift lower cost units to cost of goods sold, resulting in higher net income.

f. FIFO and weighted-average are universally accepted whereas many countries do not permit LIFO valuations.

Four accounting concepts or principles directly impact merchandise inventory. The **consistency principle** states that the cost flow assumption used should be followed over time. The **disclosure principle** requires companies to tell the readers of the financial statements all information that would assist in making knowledgeable decisions about the company. The **materiality concept** requires companies to report significant events while allowing them more leeway in reporting insignificant (immaterial) events. Finally, **conservatism** dictates that no change to historical cost as the basis for inventory values be used when the value of the asset has risen. At the same time, a lower value can be used in certain circumstances.

The **lower-of-cost-or-market** rule (LCM) is a direct application of conservatism. Conservatism means that assets and income figures should not be overstated. Because the cost principle states that assets should be recorded at historical cost, the book value of assets is not reported at amounts higher than historical cost even if the value of the asset has increased.

Conservatism also directs accountants to decrease the reported value of assets that appear overvalued. The LCM rule requires that assets be reported on the financial statements at the lower of (1) historical cost or (2) market value (replacement cost). Thus, if inventory market value decreases below its historical cost, it should be written down to its market value. If ending inventory is written down, then cost of goods sold absorbs the impact of the write-down.

Once the value of inventory is written down to market, it is not written back up even if the market value subsequently increases.

> **Study Tip**: When LCM is applied, the effect will always reduce asset value (on the balance sheet) and net income (on the income statement).

Objective 4 - Measure the effects of inventory errors on cost of goods sold and net income.

If the value of ending inventory is misstated, then cost of goods sold and net income will be misstated. Since the ending inventory for the current period becomes the beginning inventory for the next period, the errors will offset each other and total gross margin and net income for the two periods will be correct. Nevertheless, gross margin and net income for the individual periods will be misstated.

If ending inventory is overstated, then cost of goods sold is understated and net income is overstated. If ending inventory is understated, then cost of goods sold is overstated and net income is understated.

Study Exhibits 6-9 and 6-10 in your text carefully to familiarize yourself with the effect of inventory errors on 1) ending inventory, 2) cost of goods sold, and 3) net income.

Objective 5 - Use the gross profits percentage and the rate of inventory turnover to evaluate a business.

A key measure of profitability for a merchandiser is the **gross profit percentage**.

$$\text{Gross Profit Percentage} = \frac{\text{Gross Profit}}{\text{Net Sales Revenues}}$$

Inventory turnover is a measure of the number of times a company sells its average level of inventory during a year.

$$\text{Inventory Turnover} = \frac{\text{Cost of Goods Sold}}{\text{Average Inventory}}$$

$$\text{Average inventory} = \frac{\text{Beginning Inventory} + \text{Ending Inventory}}{2}$$

Review Exhibits 6-11 and 6-12 and the Decision Guidelines in your text to increase your understanding of these two important statistics.

Objective 6 - Account for inventory transactions.

The two main types of inventory accounting systems are the periodic system and the perpetual system. Both systems require a physical count prior to the preparation of their annual financial statements. However, only the perpetual system maintains a running record of the quantities on hand.

When inventory is acquired, the following transaction is recorded

Inventory	XXX	
Accounts Payable		XXX

If the business incurs a freight charge to acquire the goods, the cost of freight is also included in the debit to the Inventory account. When the business returns inventory to the vendor (called a purchase return and allowance), the entry is

Accounts Payable	XX	
Inventory		XX

Similarly, if the business earns a discount (called a purchase discount) when paying for the inventory, the entry is

Accounts Payable	XX (for the amount of the invoice)	
Inventory		X (the amount of the discount)
Cash		X (the amount of the check)

Combining the above entries means the Inventory account contains a balance representing the total net cost of the goods acquired for resale. If the Inventory account is to maintain a running balance of items on hand it must be updated when a sale is recorded. This requires two entries for each sale. The first entry records the sale, as follows:

Accounts Receivable	XXX	
Sales		XXX

The amounts of the debit and credit reflect the actual selling price of the items. The second entry updates the Inventory account, as follows:

Cost of Goods Sold	XXX	
Inventory		XXX

This entry is based on the cost of the items sold (using one of the costing methods discussed earlier.) Doing so updates the Inventory account so the balance in the account at any time represents the cost of the actual quantities on hand. Of course, the only way to verify the accuracy of the balance is to take a physical inventory. This is an important control feature because it will highlight any differences between what should be on hand and what is actually on hand.

Because inventory is the lifeblood of a merchandising business (and for many companies the largest current asset on the balance sheet), effective internal control procedures dictate:

a. physical counts at least annually
b. efficient purchasing, receiving, and shipping policies
c. protection from theft and loss of value
d. limited access
e. other effective policies to properly manage inventory

Objective 7 - Estimate inventory by the gross profit method.

When a company wants an estimate of ending inventory, the **gross profit method** will calculate the amount quickly.

The gross profit (gross margin) method uses the historical gross margin rate to estimate cost of goods sold. Cost of goods sold is then subtracted from cost of goods available for sale to arrive at estimated ending inventory.

$$\text{Gross Profit Rate} \quad = \quad \frac{\text{Gross Profit}}{\text{Net Sales Revenue}}$$

To use the gross profit method, it is necessary to rearrange ending inventory and cost of goods sold in the cost of goods sold equation as follows:

Beginning Inventory
+ Net Purchases
= Cost of Goods Available for Sale
- Cost of Goods Sold
= Ending Inventory

Cost of goods sold will equal net sales minus the estimated gross profit (sales × gross profit rate) as illustrated in Exhibit 6-15 in your text.

Inventory transactions appear in the operating activities section of the statement of cash flows. Inventory results in an inflow of cash when goods are sold and customers pay their bills. Cash outflows result when the business buys additional inventory and pays for the goods.

APPENDIX TO CHAPTER 6

Accounting for Inventory in the Periodic System

Unlike the perpetual system, a periodic system does not keep a continuous record of inventory on hand. Therefore, the business makes a physical count of the inventory on hand at the end of the period and applies unit costs to the inventory to determine the cost of the ending inventory.

When inventory is acquired under the periodic system, the following entry is recorded:

Purchases	XX	
Accounts Payable		XX

Note that the Inventory account is not affected by this transaction. All additions of inventory are debited into the Purchase account. As a result, the Inventory account, containing the beginning inventory value, remains unchanged throughout the accounting period. At the end of the accounting period, the Inventory account needs to be updated to reflect the ending inventory value. This is accomplished with a dual adjusting entry, as follows:

Cost of Goods Sold	XX	
Inventory		XX
To transfer beginning inventory to Cost of Goods Sold		

Inventory	XX	
Cost of Goods Sold		XX
To establish the ending inventory		

In addition, the Purchase account will also be transferred to the Cost of Goods Sold account, as follows:

Cost of Goods Sold	XX	
Purchases		XX

After these entries have been recorded, the balance in the Cost of Goods Sold account will equal beginning inventory + purchases – ending inventory.

TEST YOURSELF

All the self-testing materials in this chapter focus on information and procedures that your instructor is likely to test in quizzes and examinations.

I. Matching   *Match each numbered term with its lettered definition.*

_____ 1. purchase discount
_____ 2. inventory turnover
_____ 3. consistency principle
_____ 4. inventory cost
_____ 5. gross profit rate
_____ 6. inventory profit
_____ 7. specific-unit-cost method
_____ 8. first-in, first-out (FIFO)
_____ 9. lower-of-cost-or-market rule
_____ 10. gross profit method

_____ 11. weighted-average cost method
_____ 12. last-in, first-out (LIFO)
_____ 13. periodic inventory system
_____ 14. perpetual inventory system
_____ 15. LIFO liquidation
_____ 16. purchase returns and allowances
_____ 17. net purchases
_____ 18. sales returns and allowances
_____ 19. disclosure principle
_____ 20. net sales

A. inventory costing method in which the first costs into Inventory are the first costs out to Cost of Goods Sold
B. requires businesses to use the same accounting principles from period to period
C. a calculation indicating how quickly inventory is sold
D. a way to estimate inventory based on the Cost of Goods Sold model: Beginning Inventory + Net Purchases = Cost of Goods Available for Sale. Cost of Goods Available for Sale - Cost of Goods Sold = Ending Inventory
E. the difference between gross margin figured on the FIFO basis and the gross margin figured on the LIFO basis
F. all costs incurred to make the goods ready for sale
G. requires that an asset be reported in the financial statements at the lower of its historical cost or its market value
H. an inventory system in which the business does not keep a continuous record of the inventory on hand
I. an inventory system in which the business keeps a continuous record for each inventory item to show the inventory on hand at all times
J. inventory costing method based on the average cost of inventory during the period
K. a reduction in the cost of inventory that is offered by the seller as an incentive for the customers to pay promptly
L. inventory costing method in which the last costs into inventory are the first costs out to Cost of Goods Sold
M. inventory cost method based on the cost of particular units of inventory
N. equals to Gross Margin divided by Net Sales Revenue
O. when inventory levels fall below the level of the previous period
P. sales less sales returns/allowance less sales discounts
Q. requires companies to inform others of the methods used to value inventory
R. a decrease in the seller's revenue because the buyer returned merchandise or the seller granted a reduction in the amount the customer owes
S. purchases less purchase discounts less purchase returns and allowances
T. a decrease in the cost of purchases because goods were sent back to the seller and/or the seller granted the buyer a reduction in the amount owed

II. Multiple Choice *Circle the best answer.*

1. To determine the inventory count, a business will count all merchandise that

   A. is physically present
   B. the business owns
   C. is physically present plus merchandise shipped customers
   D. is physically present plus merchandise being shipped to the business

2. An automobile dealer will value inventory using which method?

   A. weighted-average
   B. FIFO
   C. LIFO
   D. specific unit cost

3. When prices are increasing, which inventory method will produce the highest ending inventory cost?

   A. weighted-average cost
   B. FIFO
   C. LIFO
   D. cannot be determined

4. When prices are decreasing, which inventory method will produce the lowest cost of goods sold?

   A. weighted-average cost
   B. FIFO
   C. LIFO
   D. cannot be determined

5. Which inventory method reports ending inventory costs on the balance sheet at a value that reflects current cost?

   A. weighted-average cost
   B. FIFO
   C. LIFO
   D. cannot be determined

6. Which of the following can be used to estimate ending inventory?

   A. weighted-average cost
   B. FIFO
   C. LIFO
   D. gross profit

7. Cost of Goods Sold is debited directly using

   A. only the perpetual inventory system
   B. only the periodic inventory system
   C. only the serial inventory system
   D. both the periodic and perpetual inventory systems

8. Which of the following companies would not be considered a merchandising entity?

   A. a department store
   B. a car dealership
   C. an ice cream shop
   D. an airline

9. To which of the following does the lower-of-cost-or-market rule apply?

   A. disclosure
   B. materiality
   C. conservatism
   D. consistency

10. To calculate the weighted-average unit cost

    A. divide goods available for sale by ending inventory units
    B. divide goods available for sale by total units available for sale
    C. divide cost of goods sold by number of units sold
    D. divide cost of goods sold by number of units available for sale

11. A credit to Purchase Returns and Allowances will:

    A. increase Inventory
    B. increase Net Purchases
    C. increase Sales
    D. decrease Net Purchases

12. A company purchases 80 stereo systems that sell for $250 each. There is a $500 freight charge on the invoice. The journal entry would

    A. debit Inventory $20,000
    B. credit Accounts Payable $20,000
    C. debit Inventory $20,500
    D. credit Cash $10,000

13. A company purchases merchandise on June 1 for $1,200 with terms 2/10, n/30. If it pays for the merchandise on June 8, the entry to record the payment would

A. credit Accounts Payable $1,200
B. credit Inventory $24
C. credit Cash $1,200
D. debit Inventory $1,176

14. A company purchased merchandise for $1,600 on May 1 with terms 1/10 n/30. When it paid the account on May 12, the journal entry

A. debited Accounts Payable $1,584
B. credited Purchase Discounts $32
C. debited Purchases $1,600
D. credited Cash $1,600

15. Gross Profit plus Cost of Goods Sold equals

A. Net Income
B. Cost of Goods Available for Sale
C. Net Sales
D. Operating Income

III. Completion *Complete each of the following.*

1. The largest current asset for most retailers is _____.
2. The largest single expense for most merchandisers is _____.
3. The inventory system that maintains continuous records of items in the inventory is called _____ _____.
4. Which inventory system(s) require(s) physical count of inventory? _____.
5. LIFO liquidation refers to _____.
6. The lower-of-cost-or-market rule for inventory is an example of the_____ principle.
7. During periods of rising prices, _____results in the highest cost of goods sold.
8. The _____method would not be appropriate for a retailer selling a large number of units each with low prices.
9. During periods of falling prices, _____results in the highest value for ending inventory.
10. A seller's request for payment is called a(n)_____.
11. A company debits the Purchases account when goods are acquired. It is using a _____ inventory system.
12. Sales minus Cost of Goods Sold is called _____.
13. A company credits the Inventory account when merchandise is sold. It is using a _____ _____ inventory system.
14. The gross profit percentage is calculated as follows: _____.
15. Inventory turnover is calculated by _____.

IV. True/False *For each of the following statements, circle T for true or F for false.*

1. T F The LIFO Reserve will show an increase when inventory costs have been rising.
2. T F If a company uses FIFO, the notes to the financial statements will contain information about a LIFO Reserve.
3. T F The accounts Inventory and Cost of Goods Sold are used in the periodic inventory system.
4. T F Cash discounts are used to encourage prompt payment.
5. T F The calculation for cost of goods sold is beginning inventory plus net purchases less ending inventory.
6. T F The gross margin rate is determined by dividing gross profit by cost of goods sold.
7. T F The cash discount term "3/10, eom" means the buyer has until the 10th of the following month to earn the discount.
8. T F Inventory-related transactions appear in the investing activities section of the cash-flows statement.
9. T F A high rate of inventory turnover is preferable to a low rate of inventory turnover.
10. T F An error in ending inventory will cause errors in both the current income statement and the next period's income statement.
11. T F When inventory costs are rising, LIFO results in the highest value for ending inventory.
12. T F LIFO liquidations occur when units on hand fall below the number of units in the beginning inventory.
13. T F LIFO reports the most realistic value for inventory on the balance sheet.
14. T F The specific cost method is an appropriate one for a large grocery store.

V. Exercises

1. The following information is given for Scott's Sport Shoes for the month of March:

		Pairs of shoes	Unit Cost
3/1	Inventory	600	$40
3/7	Purchase	800	44
3/13	Purchase	1,400	48
3/22	Purchase	1,400	50
3/29	Purchase	400	46

During the month, 3,800 pairs of shoes were sold.

A. How many shoes should be in the inventory at the end of March?

B. Using the weighted-average cost method, what are the cost of ending inventory and cost of goods sold?

C. Using the FIFO method, what are the cost of ending inventory and cost of goods sold?

D. Using the LIFO method, what are the cost of ending inventory and cost of goods sold?

2. The De Stefano Co.'s inventory was destroyed by a fire. The company's records show net sales of $720,000, beginning inventory of $160,000, net purchase of $600,000, and a gross profit rate of 50%. What is the estimated value of ending inventory?

3. Assume the following:

	X1	X2	X3
Beginning Inventory	$ 8,000	$15,000	$12,000
Net Purchases	45,000	50,000	55,000
Goods Available for Sale	53,000	65,000	67,000
Ending Inventory	15,000	12,000	8,000
Cost of Goods Sold	38,000	53,000	59,000

You discover the following errors:
a. Ending inventory X1 was overstated by $6,000
b. Ending inventory X2 was understated by $4,000

Considering these errors, recalculate cost of goods sold for all three years.

4. The following information is available for Epstein Co. for 2002:

Beginning Inventory	$ 4,000
Ending Inventory	2,400
Operating Expenses	3,150
Cost of Goods Sold	19,225
Sales Discounts	360
Sales	28,610
Sales Returns and Allowances	205

Required:

1. What is net sales for 2002?

2. What is gross profit for 2002?

3. What is net income for 2002?

4. What is the gross profit rate?

5. What is the inventory turnover rate?

5. The following information is given for Bill's Burger 2002:

Beginning Inventory	$ 12,250
Gross Margin	7,500
Operating Expenses	3,100
Purchase Returns & Allowance	600
Purchase Discounts	550
Purchases	39,250
Sales Discounts	500
Sales	51,500
Sales Returns & Allowances	1,700

Required

1. Compute net sales.

2. Compute net purchases.

3. Compute cost of goods sold.

4. Compute ending inventory.

5. Compute net income.

6. What is the inventory turnover rate?

7. What is the gross profit rate?

VI. Critical Thinking

Re-examine the facts presented in Exercise 1. A physical count was taken, and ending inventory was determined to be 700 pairs. In re-checking the sales, you verify that 3,800 pairs were sold. How would you explain the 100 pair difference (800 pairs you expected to be on hand less the actual count of 700 pairs), and how would you "account" for it?

_____

_____

_____

_____

_____

VII. Demonstration Problems

Demonstration Problem #1

Bill Joe's Appliance has the following records relating to its May 2002 inventory:

Date	Item	Quantity (units)	Unit Cost	Sale price
5/1	Beginning inventory	25	10	--
5/3	Purchase	40	11	--
5/9	Sale	45	--	18
5/11	Purchase	50	13	--
5/18	Sale	30	--	21
5/22	Purchase	20	14	--
5/28	Sale	30	--	25

Company accounting records indicate that the related operating expense for the month of May was $960.

Required:
1. Assume that Billy Joe uses a periodic inventory system and a FIFO cost flow assumption, record the May 3 through May 28 transactions (omit explanations).
2. Assume Billy Joe uses a perpetual inventory system and a FIFO cost flow assumption, record the May 3 through May 28 transactions (omit explanations).

Requirement 1 (Periodic Inventory System)

Date	Accounts and Explanation	PR	Debit	Credit

Requirement 2 (Perpetual Inventory System)

Date	Accounts and Explanation	PR	Debit	Credit

Demonstration Problem #2

Requirement 1

Refer to the information in Demonstration Problem #1. Assuming Billy Joe uses a periodic system, complete the income statement columns below. (Round income statement figures to whole dollar amounts.)

Billy Joe Appliance

Income Statement

Month Ended May 31, 2002

	LIFO	FIFO	Weighted-Average
Sales revenue			
Cost of goods sold:			
Beginning inventory			
Net purchases			
Cost of goods available for sale			
Ending inventory			
Cost of goods sold			
Gross margin			
Operating expenses			
Operating income (loss)			

Requirement 2

Refer to Demonstration Problem #1, and assume the same facts in the problem *except* the company uses the perpetual inventory system. Complete the income statement below, through operating income. (Round income statement figures to whole dollar amounts.)

Billy Joe Appliance

Income Statement

Month Ended May 31, 2002

	LIFO	FIFO	Weighted-Average
Sales revenue			
Cost of goods sold			
Gross margin			
Operating expenses			
Operating income (loss)			

(Helpful hint: Before starting, think carefully about which income statement figures will change as a result of using the perpetual inventory system rather than the periodic inventory system. Those amounts that do not change can simply be transferred from your solution to Requirement #1.)

SOLUTIONS

I. Matching

1. K	5. N	9. G	13. H	17. S
2. C	6. E	10. D	14. I	18. R
3. B	7. M	11. J	15. O	19. Q
4. F	8. A	12. L	16. T	20. P

II. Multiple Choice

1. B Answers A, C, and D do not include all the business owns.

2. D Specific unit cost is appropriate for inventory items that may be identified individually such as automobiles, jewels, and real estate.

3. B To obtain the highest ending inventory when prices are increasing it is necessary to have the most recent inventory costs on the balance sheet. The FIFO method accomplishes this.

4. C To obtain the lowest cost of goods sold when prices are decreasing, it is necessary to have the newest inventory costs on the income statement. The LIFO method accomplishes this.

5. B LIFO assigns the most recent inventory costs to the income statement and older inventory cost to the balance sheet. FIFO, on the other hand, assigns the most recent inventory costs to the balance sheet and older inventory costs to the income statement.

6. D Of the items listed, only gross margin is an estimation technique. FIFO, LIFO, and weighted-average cost are techniques for establishing actual ending inventory levels, not estimates.

7. A Under the periodic inventory system, there is no Cost of Goods Sold general ledger account. Rather, cost of goods sold is a calculated amount. Accordingly, no entries can be made to it. Under the perpetual inventory system, Cost of Goods Sold is a general ledger account and inventory purchases are debited directly to it.

8. D An airline is a service business; the other three all sell products.

9. C LCM is an extension of the application of conservatism because it reduces the ending inventory value and therefore net income.

10. B The unit cost for the weighted-average method is calculated by dividing goods available for sale (beginning inventory + net purchases) by the total units available for sale.

11. D Purchase Returns and Allowances is contra to the Purchases account. A credit to Purchase Returns and Allowances increases its balance. Since it is contra to Purchases, this will decrease net purchases.

12. C Freight charges are additions to the purchase price of the goods. Entries to record purchases are based on the total price of the merchandise, which includes all related costs.

13. B   The terms "2/10, n/30" mean that a 2% discount is available if payment is made within ten days of the invoice date; otherwise the net amount of the invoice is due in 30 days. Since payment is made within the ten-day discount period, the journal entry to record the payment is:

Accounts Payable	1,200	
Inventory		24
Cash		1,176

14. D   The terms "1/10, n/30" mean that a 1% discount is available if payment is made within ten days of the invoice date; otherwise, the net amount of the invoice is due in 30 days. Since payment was not made within the ten-day discount period, the net amount is due. The journal entry to record the payment is:

Accounts Payable	1,600	
Cash		1,600

15. C   You are required to work backwards. Since Net Sales - Cost of Goods Sold = Gross Margin; therefore, Net Sales = Gross Margin + Cost of Goods Sold.

III. Completion

1. merchandise inventory
2. Cost of Goods Sold
3. perpetual
4. Both systems require a physical count. In a perpetual inventory system, this verifies that the inventory listed in the accounting records actually exists.
5. The level of inventory falling below the level from the previous period.
6. conservatism (The LCM rule ensures that a business reports its inventory at its replacement cost if that is lower than its original cost. This rule ensures that assets are not overstated and that declines in inventory value are reported on the income statement in the period of the decline.)
7. LIFO (The oldest and therefore lower prices are used to value ending inventory.)
8. specific unit cost
9. LIFO (The oldest and therefore higher prices are used to value ending inventory.)
10. invoice (To the seller, the invoice results in a sale being recorded. To the purchaser, the same invoice results in a purchase being recorded.)
11. periodic (In a periodic system, Purchases is debited and Cash (or Accounts Payable) is credited.)
12. Gross Margin or Gross Profit (The basic income statement formula for a merchandising company is:

> Sales
> - Cost of Goods Sold
> = Gross margin
> - Operating expenses
> = Net income (Net loss)

13. perpetual (Under the perpetual system, all merchandise is debited to the Inventory account when acquired and credited to the Inventory account when sold.)
14. gross margin divided by net sales
15. cost of goods sold divided by average inventory

IV. True/False

1. T
2. F A LIFO Reserve will be present only when the company uses LIFO costing.
3. F Inventory and Cost of Goods Sold accounts are features of a perpetual inventory system.
4. T
5. T
6. F While gross margin and gross profit are synonymous terms, the denominator in the calculation for the gross margin rate is net sales revenue, not cost of goods sold.
7. T
8. F Inventory transactions are operating activities, not investing activities.
9. T
10. T
11. F With rising costs, FIFO results in the highest value for ending inventory because FIFO assigns the most recent costs (and therefore the highest) to ending inventory.
12. T
13. F LIFO reports old cost amounts for ending inventory because it assigns the most recent costs to cost of goods sold.
14. F It would be virtually impossible for a grocery store to trace each item on hand (a large grocery store will have thousands of items on hand) with its actual cost.

V. Exercises

1. A.

	Beginning inventory	600
+	Purchases*	4,000
	Shoes available for sale	4,600
-	Shoes sold	3,800
=	Ending inventory	800

*Sum of purchases on 3/7 (800), 3/13 (1,400), 3/22 (1,400), and 3/29 (400).

B.

3/1	600	pairs at	$40	$ 24,000
3/7	800		44	35,200
3/13	1,400		48	67,200
3/22	1,400		50	70,000
3/29	400		46	18,400
Goods available	4,600			$214,800

Average unit cost = $214,800 ÷ 4,600 = $46.70 (rounded)
Ending inventory = 800 pairs × $46.70 = $37,360
Cost of goods sold = 3,800 pairs × $46.70 = $177,460

C. Ending inventory will be the last 800 pairs purchased.

3/29	400 pairs at $46	$18,400
3/22	400 pairs at $50	20,000
	Ending inventory	$38,400

Cost of goods available for sale	$ 214,800
- Ending inventory	- 38,400
Cost of goods sold	$ 176,400

D. Ending inventory will be the 800 pairs that have been in inventory the longest.

Beginning inventory	600 pairs at $40	$24,000
3/7	200 pairs at $44	8,800
	Ending inventory	$32,800

Cost of goods available for sale	$214,800
- Ending inventory	- 32,800
Cost of goods sold	$182,000

2.

	Beginning inventory	$160,000
+	Purchases	600,000
	Cost of goods available for sale	760,000
-	Cost of goods sold [$720,000 × (1-.50)]	360,000
=	Ending inventory	$400,000

3. For X1, ending inventory decreases to $9,000, so cost of goods sold will increase to $44,000

For X2, beginning inventory decreases to $9,000, and ending inventory increases to $16,000, so:

	Beginning inventory	$ 9,000
+	Net purchases	50,000
	Goods available for sale	59,000
-	Ending inventory	16,000
=	Cost of goods sold	$43,000

For X3, beginning inventory increases to $16,000, so cost of goods sold increases to $63,000

4.

Requirement 1

Sales - Sales Returns & Allowances - Sales Discount = Net Sales
$28,610 - $205 - $360 = $28,045

Requirement 2

Net Sales - Cost of Goods Sold = Gross Profit (or Gross Margin)
$28,045 - $19,225 = $8,820

Requirement 3

Gross Margin - Operating Expenses = Net Income
$8,820 - $3,150 = $5,670

Requirement 4

Gross Margin ÷ Net Sales
$8,820 ÷ $28,045 = 31.4%

Requirement 5

Cost of Goods Sold ÷ Average Inventory
Average Inventory = ($4,000 + $2,400) ÷ 2 = $3,200
$19,225 ÷ $3,200 = 6 times

5.

Requirement 1

Sales - Sales Discounts - Sales Returns & Allowances = Net Sales
$51,500 - $500 - $1,700 = $49,300

Requirement 2

Purchases - Purchase Discounts - Purchase Returns & Allowances = Net Purchases
$39,250 - $550 - $600 = $38,100

Requirement 3

Net Sales - Cost of Goods Sold = Gross Profit
Cost of Goods Sold = $49,300 - $7,500 = $41,800

Requirement 4

Beginning Inventory + Net Purchase - Ending Inventory = Cost of Goods Sold
Therefore, Ending Inventory = Beginning Inventory + Net Purchase - Cost of Goods Sold
Ending Inventory = $12,250 + $38,100 - $41,800 = $8,550

Requirement 5

Gross Profit - Operating Expenses = Net Income
$7,500 - $3,100 = $4,400

Requirement 6

Inventory Turnover Rate = Cost of Goods Sold ÷ Average Inventory
Average Inventory = ($12,250 + $8,550) ÷ 2 = $10,400
Inventory Turnover Rate = $41,800 ÷ $10,400 = 4 times

Requirement 7

Gross Margin Rate = Gross Margin ÷ Net sales
Gross Margin Rate = $7,500 ÷ $49,300 = 15.2%

VI. Critical Thinking

The 100-pair difference is called inventory shrinkage. Since the figure that appears on the balance sheet for ending inventory must represent the actual amount on hand (700 pairs), the shrinkage is accounted for by a larger cost of goods sold figure on the income statement. Possible explanations for the shrinkage are errors in the physical count, theft, and/or errors in recording purchases during the period. Internal control requires that the cause of the difference be investigated and appropriate corrective procedures taken.

VII. Demonstration Problems

Demonstration Problem #1 Solved and Explained

Requirement 1 (Periodic Inventory System)

Date	Accounts and Explanation	PR	Debit	Credit
5/3	Purchases		440	
	Account Payable			440
5/9	Account Receivable		810	
	Sales			810
5/11	Purchases		650	
	Account Payable			650
5/18	Account Receivable		630	
	Sales			630
5/22	Purchases		280	
	Account Payable			280
5/28	Account Receivable		750	
	Sales			750

These six journal entries are pretty straightforward. With a periodic system, the Purchase account is debited as merchandise for resale is acquired, but is not affected when goods are sold.

Study Tip: In a periodic system, the cost flow assumption (in this case FIFO) is irrelevant as far as these transactions are concerned. It becomes important only when you need to determine the value of ending inventory.

Requirement 2 (Perpetual Inventory System)

Date	Accounts and Explanation	PR	Debit	Credit
5/3	Inventory		440	
	Account Payable			440
5/9	Account Receivable		810	
	Sales			810
	Cost of Goods Sold		470	
	Inventory			470
	(25 × $10 + 20 × $11)			
5/11	Inventory		650	
	Account Payable			650
5/18	Account Receivable		630	
	Sales			630
	Cost of Goods Sold		350	
	Inventory			350
	(20 × $11 + 10 × $13)			
5/22	Inventory		280	
	Account Payable			280
5/28	Account Receivable		750	
	Sales			750
	Cost of Goods Sold		390	
	Inventory			390
	(30 × $13)			

In a perpetual system, goods for resale are debited to the Inventory account. When a sale occurs, the entry is identical to those recorded in a periodic system. However, a second entry is required for each sale. This entry transfers the cost of the sale from the Inventory account to a Cost of Goods Sold Account. The amount of the entry is determined by the cost flow assumption used. In this problem, FIFO is assumed. Therefore, the cost of each sale is assigned using the oldest costs in the inventory. For instance, the 5/9 sale was 45 units. How much did these units cost the business? Assuming FIFO, 25 of the units cost $10 each (these are the units from the beginning inventory, i.e., the first units (oldest) in the inventory), and the next 20 units (45-25) cost $11 each (the purchase on 5/3). This same analysis applies to the 5/18 and 5/28 sales. The details for each entry are provided following each entry.

Demonstration Problem #2

Requirement 1

Billy Joe Appliance
Income Statement
Month Ended May 31, 2002

	LIFO	FIFO	Weighted-Average
Sales revenue	$2,190	$2,190	$2,190
Cost of goods sold:			
Beginning inventory	250	250	250
Net purchases	1,370	1,370	1,370
Cost of goods available for sale	1,620	1,620	1,620
Ending inventory	305	410	360
Cost of goods sold	1,315	1,210	1,260
Gross margin	875	980	930
Operating expenses	960	960	960
Operating income (loss)	$ (85)	$ 20	$ (30)

Computations:

Sales Revenue:

Sale Date	Quantity	Price	Total
5/9	45	$18	$ 810
5/18	30	21	630
5/28	30	25	750
	105		$2,190

Sales revenue is unaffected by the firm's method of accounting for inventory costs. Quantity × Price = Total.

Beginning inventory: 5/1 quantity (25 units) × unit cost ($10) = $250

Purchase Date	Quantity	Price	Total
5/3	40	$11	$ 440
5/11	50	13	650
5/22	20	14	280
	110		$1,370

Computation for beginning inventory, purchases, and goods available for sale are identical under the three methods.

	Beginning inventory in units	25
+	Total May purchases in units	110
	Units available for sale	135
-	Units sold	105
=	Ending inventory in units	30

Valued at LIFO:

Purchase Date	Quantity	Price	Total
Beginning inventory	25	$10	$250
5/3	5	11	55
	30		$305

LIFO attains the best matching of current expense with current revenue. The most recently acquired costs (the last items in) are deemed sold first (the first ones out). Logically, ending inventory should consist of the oldest layers of cost.

Valued at FIFO:

Purchase Date	Quantity	Price	Total
5/22	20	$14	$280
5/11	10	13	130
	30		$410

FIFO reports the ending inventory at its most recent cost. The oldest costs are expensed as cost of goods sold. Note that net income under FIFO is larger than that reported under LIFO. In a period of rising prices, LIFO will generally produce a lower net income. The potential tax savings achieved under a LIFO valuation has made it an increasingly popular valuation method in recent years.

Valued at weighted-average cost:

Purchase Date	Quantity	Price	Total
Beginning inventory	25	$10	$ 250
Purchases in May	110	Various	1,370
	135		$1,620

$1,620 inventory cost / 135 units = $12 per unit (rounded)

30 ending inventory units × $12 weighted-average cost per unit = $360

The weighted-average cost method reports ending inventory and produces operating income that falls between the results of FIFO and LIFO. It is not used as a valuation method by as many firms as LIFO and FIFO.

Requirement 2

Billy Joe Appliance
Income Statement
Month Ended May 31, 2002

	LIFO	FIFO	Weighted-Average
Sales revenue	$2,190	$2,190	$2,190
Cost of goods sold	1,290	1,210	1,234
Gross margin	900	980	956
Operating expenses	960	960	960
Operating income (loss)	$ (60)	$ 20	$ (4)

Computations:

Sales—same as Demonstration Problem #1

Cost of Goods Sold:
Remember, in a perpetual system cost of goods sold is an account balance, not a calculation. Therefore, to arrive at the correct amount, you have to trace through each purchase and sale to determine which cost figures have been transferred from Inventory to Cost of Goods Sold, as follows:

LIFO:

Date	Quantity	Price		Total
5/9 Sale	40	$11	$440	
	5	10	50	
				$ 490
5/18 Sale	30	13		390
5/28 Sale	20	14	280	
	10	13	130	
				410
		Cost of goods sold, LIFO		$1,290
	20	10	200	
	10	13	130	
		Ending inventory, LIFO		$ 330*

*Note that this amount is not the same as LIFO periodic.

Merchandise Inventory, Cost of Goods Sold, and Gross Profit   169

FIFO:

Date	Quantity	Price		Total
5/9 Sale	25	$10	$250	
	20	11	220	
				470
5/18 Sale	20	11	220	
	10	13	130	
				350
5/28 Sale	30	13		390
		Cost of goods sold, FIFO		$1,210
	20	14	280	
	10	13	130	
		Ending inventory, FIFO		$410**

**Note that this is the same as FIFO periodic.

Weighted-average cost:
This is even more complicated because it requires you to re-calculate a new average each time there is an addition to inventory (for this reason it is referred to as a moving weighted-average system).

5/9   Sale

25 units at $10 per unit = $250
<u>40</u> units at $11 per unit = <u>440</u>
65                                $690

Average unit cost   = $\frac{\$690}{65}$ = $10.615 per unit, therefore

45 units × $10.615 = $477.69

5/18   Sale

20 units at $10.615 per unit = $212.30   (from above)
<u>50</u> units at $13 per unit =   <u>650.00</u>
70                                 $862.30

Average unit cost   = $\frac{\$862.30}{70}$ = $12.319 per unit, therefore

30 units × $12.319 = $369.56

5/28   Sale

40 units at $12.319 per unit $492.76 (from above)
<u>20</u> units at $14 per unit   =   <u>280.00</u>
60   772.76

Average unit cost   = $\frac{\$772.76}{60}$ = $12.879 per unit, therefore

30 units × $12.879 = $386.37

Cost of goods sold, weighted-average cost $1,233.62

Ending inventory = 30 units × $12.879 = $386.37***

***Note that this amount is not the same as weighted-average periodic.

CHAPTER 7—PLANT ASSETS, INTANGIBLE ASSETS, AND RELATED EXPENSES

CHAPTER OVERVIEW

Beginning with Chapter 4, you have learned more detail about some assets, specifically cash, receivables, and inventory. In this chapter, we examine long-lived assets, both fixed and intangible. The learning objectives for the chapter are to

1. Determine the cost of a plant asset
2. Account for depreciation
3. Select the best depreciation method for income tax purposes
4. Analyze the effect of a plant asset disposal
5. Account for natural resource assets and depletion
6. Account for intangible assets and amortization
7. Report plant asset transactions on the statement of cash flows

CHAPTER REVIEW

Objective 1 - Determine the cost of a plant asset.

Business assets are classified as current or long-lived (long-term) assets. Current assets are considered to be useful for one year or less. Long-lived assets are expected to be useful longer than a year. Plant assets are long-lived assets such as land and equipment. Plant assets are tangible; that is, they have physical form.

The cost of a plant asset is the purchase price plus any other amount paid to acquire it and make it ready for use.

The **cost of land** includes the purchase price, brokerage commission, survey fees, legal fees, transfer taxes, back property taxes, costs to grade or clear the land, and costs to demolish or remove any unwanted buildings or other structures.

The same standard is used to determine the **cost of constructing a building**, namely all costs are included that are necessary to prepare the asset for its intended use. In addition to the actual construction costs you also include professional fees, permits, and other necessary charges.

The **cost of an existing building** includes the purchase price, brokerage commission, taxes, and any expenditure to repair or renovate the building to make it ready for use.

The **cost of machinery and equipment** includes the purchase price less any discounts, plus transportation charges, transportation insurance, commissions, and installation costs.

Improvements to land are not part of the cost of land because the usefulness of the improvement decreases over time. Such improvements include roads, paving, fencing, driveways, parking lots, and lawn sprinkler systems. Improvements to land should be recorded in a separate asset account. The cost of improvements to leased assets are called **leasehold improvements**. **Construction in progress** refers to assets a company has begun building but not yet finished. Capital leases refer to plant assets a company does not own which are being leased over an extended period of time.

Interest costs incurred during the time a plant asset is being constructed are considered a necessary cost to "acquire" the asset and are therefore capitalized (i.e., debited to the asset account).

When a company purchases a group of assets for one single amount (also known as a **lump-sum purchase** or a **basket purchase**), the total cost of the assets is allocated to individual assets by the relative-sales-value method. To use the **relative-sales-value method**, it is necessary to:

1. Determine the market value of each asset by appraisal of the assets.
2. Sum the individual asset market values to obtain the total market value of all assets that have been acquired.
3. Calculate a ratio of the market value of each individual asset to the total market value of all assets (item 1 divided by item 2).
4. Multiply the ratio for each asset (from item 3) by the total purchase price paid for the assets. The resulting amounts will be considered the cost of each of the assets in the basket purchase.

Capital expenditures are expenditures that significantly affect an asset by 1) increasing the asset's productive capacity, 2) increasing the asset's efficiency, or 3) extending the asset's useful life. Capital expenditures are debited to an asset account:

Asset	XX	
Cash		XX

Revenue expenditures are those that maintain the existing condition of an asset or restore an asset to good working order. Revenue expenditures are debited to an expense account:

Expense Account	XX	
Cash		XX

Many expenditures related to plant assets are repairs to the assets. **Extraordinary repairs** are capital expenditures, while ordinary repairs are revenue expenditures.

Depreciation is the process of allocating a plant asset's cost to expense over the useful life of the asset. Note that depreciation is based on an asset's cost, and that depreciation is not in any way related to cash. A contra account called Accumulated Depreciation is used to record the total amount of a plant asset's cost that has been recorded as depreciation expense. The adjusting journal entry to record depreciation is:

Depreciation Expense	XX	
Accumulated Depreciation		XX

To measure depreciation, it is necessary to determine the plant asset's cost, estimated useful life, and estimated residual value (salvage value or scrap value).

Estimated useful life is the length of service a business expects from the plant asset. Useful life may be expressed as a length of time, units of output, or other measures. For example, a computer may be expected to be useful for four years, while a printing press might be expected to print one billion sheets of paper over its useful life. Note that the useful life of an asset is an estimate of the usefulness of an asset and is not necessarily related to the physical life. For example, an asset such as a computer may become obsolete (not economically useful) long before it physically deteriorates.

Estimated residual value is the expected cash value of an asset at the end of its useful life. It is also called scrap or salvage value.

The **depreciable cost** of an asset is its cost minus residual value.

Objective 2 - Account for depreciation.

1. The **straight-line (SL) depreciation method** allocates the depreciable cost of a plant asset to depreciation expense in equal amounts per period over the life of the asset. The formula for straight-line depreciation is:

$$\text{Depreciation expense} = \frac{\text{cost - residual value}}{\text{useful life}}$$

Recall that the adjusting entry to record depreciation expense is:

Depreciation Expense   XX
     Accumulated Depreciation   XX

As accumulated depreciation increases each year, the remaining **book value of the asset** (cost - accumulated depreciation) declines. The final book value of an asset will be its residual value.

(See Exhibit 7-5.)

2. The **units-of-production (UOP) depreciation method** allocates the cost of an asset to depreciation expense based on the output that the asset is expected to produce. The formula for units-of-production depreciation is:

$$\text{UOP depreciation per unit of output} = \frac{\text{cost - residual value}}{\text{useful life in units}}$$

With UOP, the total depreciation expense in a period is:

Depreciation Expense = UOP depreciation per unit of output × units of output in the period

While the straight-line method could be used for any plant asset, the UOP method is not appropriate for all assets. Rather, it is used for assets where the life is a function of use rather than time (for example, an airplane where flying hours is a more accurate measure of life compared with years).

(See Exhibit 7-6.)

3. The **double-declining-balance (DDB) method** is an accelerated depreciation method. **Accelerated depreciation** simply means that a larger portion of an asset's cost is allocated to depreciation expense in the early years of an asset's life, and a smaller portion is allocated to depreciation expense toward the end of the asset's useful life.

To compute double-declining-balance depreciation:

a. Compute the straight-line depreciation rate per year:

$$(1 \,/\, \text{Useful life in years}) = X\%$$

b. Multiply the straight-line depreciation rate per year by 2 (double it) to obtain the double-declining-balance rate:

$$\text{DDB rate} = (1/\text{Useful life in years}) \times 2$$

c. Multiply the asset's beginning book value for a period (remember that book value equals cost minus accumulated depreciation) times the DDB rate. Book value will decrease each period, therefore depreciation expense will decrease each period. Note that the residual value of the asset is ignored until the net book value of the asset approaches the asset's residual value.

$$\text{Depreciation Expense} = \text{DDB rate} \times \text{book value}$$

d. When the net book value of the asset approaches the asset's residual value, adjust the year's depreciation so that the remaining book value of the asset is equal to the residual value. The final year's depreciation amount will be equal to:

Book value at the beginning of the year - Residual value

Depreciation is no longer recorded after the book value of the asset is reduced to the residual value, even if the asset is still in use.

Study Exhibit 7-7 in your text to familiarize yourself with the double-declining-balance method.

Some important points to remember:

1. You never depreciate below the estimated salvage value.
2. Units-of-production ignores time.
3. Double-declining-balance ignores salvage value initially.
4. Double-declining-balance uses book value, while the other methods use depreciable cost.

Study Tip: The method used does not determine the total amount of the asset's cost to recognize as depreciation expense over the asset's life. Rather, the method determines the amount of the total to allocate each accounting period. Regardless of method, accumulated depreciation will be the same when the asset is fully depreciated.

Objective 3 - Select the best depreciation method for income tax purposes.

Although depreciation is a noncash expense, the amount of depreciation recorded affects the amount of income tax a business pays. Higher depreciation expense will reduce taxable income, and therefore income tax payments. Using an accelerated depreciation method will increase depreciation expense in the early years of an asset's life. This will decrease taxable income and income taxes, but only initially. The cash available to the business increases because tax payments are reduced.

Review Exhibit 7-10 in your text to see how accelerated depreciation reduces taxes and increases the cash balance of a business.

For federal income tax purposes, the IRS has in place a **Modified Accelerated Cost Recovery System (MACRS**, pronounced "makers"). MACRS ignores both residual value and estimated useful life, and simply assigns assets to one of eight life classes, most of which (but not all) are based on double-declining-balance.

If a plant asset is held for only part of the year, partial year depreciation is computed by multiplying the full year's depreciation by the fraction of the year that the asset is held.

If a company finds that a change is warranted in its estimate of a plant asset's useful life, it computes revised annual depreciation this way:

$$\frac{\text{Book value - Residual value}}{\text{Remaining life}}$$

If an asset becomes fully depreciated (i.e., book value = residual value) but remains in use, both the asset and contra asset account should remain in the ledger until the business disposes of the asset.

Objective 4 - Analyze the effect of a plant asset disposal.

With the possible exception of land, eventually a plant asset will no longer serve the needs of the business. The business will generally dispose of the asset by junking it, selling it, or exchanging it. The simplest accounting entry occurs when a company junks an asset. If the asset is fully depreciated with no residual value, the entry to record its disposal is:

Accumulated Depreciation—Asset	XX	
Asset		XX

If the asset is not fully depreciated, a loss is recorded for the remaining book value:

Accumulated Depreciation—Asset	XX	
Loss on Disposal of Asset	X	
Asset		XX

These entries have the effect of removing the asset from the books.

When an asset is sold, the first step is to update depreciation for the partial year of service. Depreciation is recorded from the beginning of the accounting period to the date of the sale:

Depreciation Expense	XX	
Accumulated Depreciation—Asset		XX

The second step is to compute the remaining book value:

Book Value = Cost - Accumulated Depreciation

If the cash received is greater than the remaining book value, a gain is recorded:

Cash	XX	
Accumulated Depreciation—Asset	XX	
Asset		XX
Gain on Sale of Asset		XX

If the cash received is less than the remaining book value, a loss is recorded:

Cash	XX	
Loss on Sale of Asset	XX	
Accumulated Depreciation—Asset	XX	
Asset		XX

Note that gains will increase income and losses will decrease income. Therefore, both gains and losses are listed on the income statement.

When plant assets are exchanged or traded in, the balance for the old asset must be removed from the books and the replacement asset must be recorded.

Objective 5 - Account for natural resource assets and depletion.

Depletion expense is that portion of the cost of **natural resources** used up in a particular period. It is computed in the same way as UOP depreciation (refer to Objective 2 for the UOP formula). The appropriate entry is:

Depletion Expense	XX	
Accumulated Depletion		XX

Objective 6 - Account for intangible assets and amortization.

Intangible assets are assets that have no physical substance. Examples include patents, copyrights, trademarks, franchises, leaseholds, and goodwill. The acquisition cost of an intangible asset is recorded as:

Intangible Asset	XX	
Cash		XX

The cost of intangible assets is expensed through **amortization** over the asset's useful life up to a maximum of 40 years. Amortization is usually computed on a straight-line basis, similar to straight-line depreciation. Amortization is recorded as:

Amortization Expense	XX	
Intangible Asset		XX

Note that the book value of the intangible asset is reduced directly. There is no Accumulated Amortization account. Additionally, the residual value of most intangible assets is zero. Finally, the useful life of many amortizable assets is much shorter than the legal life of such assets—for example, copyrights.

One important type of intangible asset is **goodwill**. Goodwill is recorded only when another company is acquired. The amount of goodwill, if any, is equal to the difference between the price paid for the acquired company and the market value of the acquired company's net assets (assets - liabilities):

Goodwill = Price Paid - Market Value of Net Assets

If the purchase price paid is less than the market value of the acquired company's net assets, there is no goodwill.

Objective 7 - Report plant asset transactions on the statement of cash flows.

The statement of cash flows will reflect the acquisition of plant assets, the sale of plant assets, and depreciation (including depletion and amortization). The purchase or sale of plant assets is an investing activity, whereas depreciation (also depletion and amortization) is listed in the operating activities section of the statement of cash flows. Cash inflows result when plant assets are sold for cash while cash outflows result when plant assets are purchased for cash. Depreciation is included in the operating activities section because the expense was listed on the income statement as a deduction to arrive at net income. However, depreciation expense does not require a cash payment and therefore needs to be added back to net income to convert it from an accrual-based amount to cash flows from operating activities.

TEST YOURSELF

All the self-testing materials in this chapter focus on information and procedures that your instructor is likely to test in quizzes and examinations.

I. Matching   *Match each numbered term with its lettered definition.*

_____ 1. accelerated depreciation
_____ 2. extraordinary repairs
_____ 3. double-declining-balance
_____ 4. franchises and licenses
_____ 5. relative-sales-value method
_____ 6. straight-line depreciation
_____ 7. capitalized interest
_____ 8. units-of-production
_____ 9. amortization
_____ 10. copyright

_____ 11. depletion
_____ 12. goodwill
_____ 13. leasehold improvements
_____ 14. capital lease
_____ 15. intangible asset
_____ 16. revenue expenditure
_____ 17. patent
_____ 18. trademarks
_____ 19. MACRS
_____ 20. capitalize

A. the exclusive right to reproduce and sell a book, musical composition, film, or other work of art
B. a method of depreciation for federal income tax purposes
C. that portion of a natural resource's cost that is used up in a particular period
D. an accelerated method of depreciation that computes annual depreciation by multiplying the asset's decreasing book value by a constant percentage, which is two times the straight-line rate
E. repair work that generates a capital expenditure
F. privileges granted by a private business or a government to sell a product or service in accordance with specified conditions
G. excess of the cost of an acquired company over the sum of the market value of its net assets
H. an asset with no physical form
I. a cost a renter incurs to improve rented facilities
J. costs incurred to maintain an asset
K. a grant from the federal government giving the holder the exclusive right to produce and sell an invention
L. an allocation technique for identifying the cost of each asset purchased in a group for a single amount
M. a depreciation method that writes off a relatively large amount of an asset's cost nearer the start of its useful life than does the straight-line method
N. an allocation of cost that applies to intangible assets
O. a lease which covers an extended period of time
P. depreciation method in which an equal amount of depreciation expense is assigned to each year (or period) of asset use
Q. interest cost incurred while an asset is being constructed
R. distinctive identifications of a product or service
S. a depreciation method in which a fixed amount of depreciation is assigned to each unit of output produced by the plant asset
T. to include a related cost as part of an asset's cost

II. Multiple Choice   *Circle the best answer.*

1. All of the following are intangible assets *except*

   A. building
   B. patent
   C. leasehold
   D. trademark

2. Which of the following long-lived assets is not depreciated?

   A. vehicles
   B. building
   C. machinery
   D. oil field

3. The cost of equipment includes all of the following *except*

   A. sales tax
   B. repairs that occur one year after installation
   C. freight charges
   D. installation costs

4. Depreciation expense for an asset is the same every year. The depreciation method is

   A. double-declining-balance
   B. MACRS
   C. straight-line
   D. units-of-production

5. A depreciation method that is not related to specific periods of time is

   A. double-declining-balance
   B. MACRS
   C. straight-line
   D. units-of-production

6. You are computing depreciation for the first year of an asset's life. Which depreciation method ignores time?

   A. double-declining-balance
   B. MACRS
   C. straight-line
   D. units-of-production

7. Which of the following methods is most closely associated with intangible assets?

   A. double-declining-balance
   B. units-of-production
   C. straight-line
   D. MACRS

8. Which depreciation method will usually result in the lowest income tax expense in the first year of an asset's life?

   A. double-declining-balance
   B. MACRS
   C. straight-line
   D. units-of-production

9. The depreciable cost of an asset equals

   A. cost - salvage value
   B. cost - accumulated depreciation
   C. cost - residual value
   D. cost - the current year's depreciation expense

10. Depletion is computed using which of the following depreciation methods?

   A. double-declining-balance
   B. MACRS
   C. straight-line
   D. units-of-production

11. The cost of repairing a gear on a machine would probably be classified as

   A. capital expenditure
   B. extraordinary repair expense
   C. intangible asset
   D. revenue expenditure

12. Which of the following costs should be capitalized?

   A. gas and oil for a delivery van
   B. repainting the interior of the sales floor
   C. research and development costs for new products
   D. the cost of borrowing money to construct a new shopping center

III. Completion   *Complete each of the following.*

1. Two distinguishing characteristics of plant assets are that they are _____ and
   _____ .
2. Depreciation is defined as _____ .
3. Depreciation is a _____ expense.
4. Most companies use _____ depreciation for tax purposes.
5. The maximum time period over which an intangible asset can be amortized is _____ years.
6. When two or more assets are purchased in a group, the total cost of the assets is allocated to individual assets
   by the _____ method.
7. To calculate depreciation, you must know the following four items: 1)_____ ,
   2)_____ , 3)_____ , and 4)_____ .
8. Depreciation is an example of the _____ principle.
9. _____ relates to natural resources, while _____ relates to
   intangible assets.
10. _____ is used to depreciate assets for federal tax purposes.
11. Proceeds from the sale of plant assets are listed in the _____ activities section of the statement of
    cash flows.
12. The most widely used depreciation method for financial statements is _____ .
13. Depreciation expense is listed in the _____ activities section of the statement of cash flows.
14. Costs related to plant assets can be classified as either _____ expenditures or
    _____ expenditures.

IV. True/False   *For each of the following statements, circle* T *for true or* F *for false.*

1. T F Research and development costs are treated as capital expenditure.
2. T F Accelerated depreciation results in higher book value when plant assets are newer.
3. T F The amount of depreciation expense over the life of an asset will be greater if a company
          uses accelerated depreciation.
4. T F Capital leases are reported as assets.
5. T F Revenue expenditures are debited to asset accounts.
6. T F Depreciable cost equals cost less accumulated depreciation.
7. T F Using accelerated depreciation results in increasing amounts of depreciation expense as the
          asset ages.
8. T F Double-declining-balance initially ignores residual value.
9. T F Straight-line depreciation is calculated by dividing useful life into depreciable cost.
10. T F Leasehold improvements are depleted over the life of the lease.
11. T F Capital costs provide future benefit to the company.
12. T F Intangible assets are depreciated over the lesser of the legal life, the economic life, or 40
          years.
13. T F Cash expenditures for plant assets are reported as operating activities on the statement of
          cash flows.
14. T F When calculating depreciation based on a revised life estimate, the formula is book value
          divided by remaining life estimate.
15. T F Residual value, scrap value, and salvage value are synonymous terms.

V. Exercises

1. A company buys Machines 1, 2, and 3 for $90,000. The market values of the machines are $30,000, $36,000, and $54,000, respectively. What cost will be allocated to each machine?

2. Mangia Macaroni Co. purchased equipment for $54,000 on January 4, 2002. Mangia expects the machine to produce 125,000 units over four years and then expects to sell the machine for $14,000. Mangia produced 30,000 units the first year and 45,000 units the second year. Compute the depreciation expense for 2002 and 2003. Round your answer to the nearest dollar.

	2002	2003
Straight-line	_____	_____
Units-of-production	_____	_____
Double-declining-balance	_____	_____

3. On January 2, 2002, Saul's Sweets purchased used equipment for $19,000. Saul expected the equipment to remain in service for 5 years. He depreciated the equipment on a straight-line basis with $2,000 salvage value. On June 30, 2004, Saul sold the equipment for $2,800. Record depreciation expense for the equipment for the six months ended June 30, 2004, and also record the sale of the equipment.

Date	Account and Explanation	PR	Debit	Credit

4. On August 20, 2002, Morrie Amodu, owner of Morrie's Manufacturing, purchased a new drill press for the business. The new equipment carried an invoice price of $9,700 plus a 6% sales tax. In addition, the purchaser was responsible for $460 of freight charges. The sale was subject to 3/15, n/45 discount/credit terms. Upon receipt of the new equipment, Morrie paid $925 to have the press installed and connected. To finance this purchase, Morrie borrowed $11,000 from the bank for 90 days at 10% interest. Morrie paid the invoice within 15 days, earning the 3% discount.

a. Classify each of the following costs as revenue or capital expenditures.

Cost	Classification
a) $9,700 (equipment)	_____
b) $582 (sales tax)	_____
c) $460 (freight)	_____
d) $291 (discount)	_____
e) $925 (installation)	_____
f) $275 (interest on loan)	_____

b. Based on your answer from 1, calculate the fully capitalized cost of the new equipment.

c. Calculate 2002 depreciation using double-declining-balance assuming a six-year life with estimated residual value of $1,000.

5. On October 1, 2002, Roy Company purchased Rogers Company for $10,400,000 cash. The market value of Rogers's assets was $16,200,000, and Rogers had liabilities of $9,000,000.

a. Compute the cost of the goodwill purchased by Roy Company.

b. Record the purchase by Roy Company.

Date	Account and Explanation	PR	Debit	Credit

c. Record the amortization of the goodwill on 12/31/02, assuming a useful life of 6 years.

Date	Account and Explanation	PR	Debit	Credit

VI. Critical Thinking

Evaluate the following statement: "I do not see any problems in paying for next year's budgeted capital expenditures. We have estimated we will need approximately $110,000 for new equipment, and we have more than three times that amount in our depreciation reserves (accumulated depreciation) at the moment."

_____

_____

_____

_____

VII. Demonstration Problems

Demonstration Problem #1

On January 1, 2002, Rosa Cervantes purchased three pieces of equipment. Details of the cost, economic life, residual value, and method of depreciation are shown below:

Equipment	Cost	Useful Life	Residual Value	Depreciation Method
X	$24,000	6 yrs	$3,000	straight-line
Y	16,000	40,000 units	800	units-of-production
Z	18,000	5 yrs	3,000	double-declining-balance

Required:

1. Prepare a schedule computing the depreciation expense for each piece of equipment over its useful life.
2. Prepare the journal entry to record the disposal of Equipment X. Assume that it has been depreciated over its useful life, and that it cannot be sold or exchanged (it is being scrapped).
3. Prepare the journal entry to record the sale of Equipment Y for $1,000. Assume that it has been depreciated over its useful life.

Requirement 1 (Schedule of depreciation)

	X	Y	Z
Asset cost			
Less: Residual value			
Depreciable cost			

Equipment X
Schedule of Depreciation Expense
(Straight-Line Method)

Year	Depreciable Cost	Depreciable Rate	Depreciation Expense

Equipment Y
Schedule of Depreciation Expense
(Units-of-Production)

Year	Depreciable Cost	Units Produced	Depreciation Expense
		12,400	
		10,750	
		11,230	
		6,100	

Equipment Z
Schedule of Depreciation Expense
(Double-Declining-Balance)

Year	Book Value × Rate	Depreciation Expense	Book Value

Requirement 2 (Journal entry—Equipment X)

Date	Account and Explanation	PR	Debit	Credit

Requirement 3 (Journal entry—Equipment Y)

Date	Account and Explanation	PR	Debit	Credit

Demonstration Problem #2

On June 10, 1997, Cutler Catering purchased new kitchen equipment costing $22,500 plus 6% sales tax. The equipment is expected to last eight years and retain an estimated $1,500 residual value. In addition, Cutler paid transportation and insurance charges of $410. The equipment arrived on June 21 and required modification of the existing electrical system. An electrician was scheduled the following day and spent two days installing the new equipment. The electrician's charge was $65 per hour for two 8-hour days, or $1,040 total. The equipment was placed in service on June 24, 1997.

On January 5, 2001, repairs costing $4,500 were made which increased the life of the equipment two additional years. On August 18, 2002, some routine repairs were made costing $480.

On April 10, 2003, Cutler decided the 80-hour work weeks were taking too heavy a toll on his personal life and closed the business. He sold the equipment for $4,200 cash.

The company closes its books on December 31 and uses the straight-line method.

Required:

Present journal entries to record the following:

1. the purchase of the equipment on June 10, 1997
2. payment of the transportation charges
3. payment of the electrician's charges
4. depreciation for 1997
5. the repair on January 5, 2001
6. depreciation for 2001
7. the repair on August 18, 2002
8. depreciation for 2002
9. depreciation up to date of sale
10. the equipment sale on April 10, 2003

Date	Account and Explanation	PR	Debit	Credit

SOLUTIONS

I. Matching

1. M	5. L	9. N	13. I	17. K
2. E	6. P	10. A	14. O	18. R
3. D	7. Q	11. C	15. H	19. B
4. F	8. S	12. G	16. J	20. T

II. Multiple Choice

1.   C   Building is a tangible asset.

2.   D   An oil field is a natural resource and as such is depleted, not depreciated.

3.   B   The cost of equipment includes all amounts paid to acquire the asset and to ready it for its intended use. Repairs to equipment indicate that it is in use and therefore should not be included as part of the equipment's cost .

4.   C   Straight-line depreciation is the only method of depreciation that results in the same amount of depreciation every year. The other methods listed are accelerated (double-declining-balance) or can result in differing amounts of depreciation each year (UOP and MACRS) .

5.   D   Units-of-production depreciation is based on the number of units produced by the depreciable asset. The other methods listed all depend on time in the depreciation calculation .

6.   D   Of all the methods listed, only unit-of-production ignores time in the depreciation calculation.

7.   C   Straight-line is the method used to amortize an intangible asset.

8.   A   The depreciation method that will result in the lowest income tax in the first year is the method that results in the largest depreciation deduction. Double-declining-balance gives the largest deduction in the asset's first year .

9.   A & C   Item B equals the asset's book value. Item D has no significance. Salvage value and residual value are synonymous terms.

10.   D   Both depletion and units-of-production follow the general formula: (cost - residual value) / useful life in units.

11.   D   Capital expenditures are those that increase capacity or efficiency of the asset or extend its useful life. Revenue expenditures merely maintain an asset in its existing condition or restore the asset to good working order.

12.   D   The interest cost on the loan should be capitalized while the shopping center is being developed. The other costs are revenue expenditures and should be debited to expense accounts.

III. Completion

1. long-lived, tangible (The physical form (tangibility) of plant assets provides their usefulness.)
2. a systematic allocation of an asset's cost to expense (Depreciation is not a method of asset valuation.)
3. noncash (Cash is expended either at the acquisition of a plant asset or over time as the asset is paid for. The debit to Depreciation Expense is balanced by a credit to Accumulated Depreciation, not Cash.)
4. accelerated (MACRS) (Accelerated depreciation methods cause larger depreciation deductions in the first years of an asset's life. The larger deductions result in lower taxable income and lower taxes.)

5. 40
6. relative-sales-value (The need to depreciate each asset separately makes it necessary to allocate the purchase price by some reasonable manner.)
7. cost; estimated useful life; estimated residual value; depreciation method (Order is not important.)
8. matching (Matching means to identify and measure all expenses incurred during the period and to match them against the revenue earned during that period.)
9. depletion; amortization
10. MACRS (Modified Accelerated Cost Recovery System)
11. investing
12. straight-line
13. operating
14. capital; revenue (Order not important.)

IV. True/False

1.	F	R&D costs are generally treated as revenue expenditures and therefore debited to an expense account.
2.	F	Accelerated depreciation records larger amounts of depreciation expense when the asset is newer and lesser amounts as the asset ages. Therefore, book value (cost less accumulated depreciation) will be lower when the asset is newer.
3.	F	The amount of total depreciation is not affected by the method used. Instead, the method determines how the depreciable cost is spread.
4.	T	
5.	F	Revenue expenditures are recorded as expenses.
6.	F	Depreciable cost equals cost less residual value.
7.	F	Accelerated depreciation results in the opposite—decreasing amounts as the assets become older.
8.	T	
9.	T	
10.	F	Leasehold improvements are either depreciated or amortized. Depletion relates to natural resources.
11.	T	
12.	F	Amortization, not depreciation, is the term used to spread the cost of an intangible asset over its useful life.
13.	F	The acquisition of plant assets is an investing activity, not an operating activity.
14.	F	The formula is remaining depreciable basis (not book value) divided by remaining useful life.
15.	T	

V. Exercises

1. Machine 1 = [$30,000 / ($30,000 + $36,000 + $54,000)] × $90,000 = $22,500
    Machine 2 = [$36,000 / ($30,000 + $36,000 + $54,000)] × $90,000 = $27,000
    Machine 3 = [$54,000 / ($30,000 + $36,000 + $54,000)] × $90,000 = $40,500
    (Proof: $22,500 + $27,000 + $40,500 = $90,000)

2.

	2002	2003
Straight-line	10,000	10,000
Units-of-production	9,600	14,400
Double-declining-balance	27,000	13,500

Straight-line = ($54,000 - $14,000) / 4 years = $10,000

Units-of-production = (54,000 - 14,000) / 125,000 units = $0.32 per unit
   2002 = $30,000 × $0.32 = $9,600
   2003 = $45,000 × $0.32 = $14,400

Double-declining-balance:
   DDB rate = (1 / 4) × 2 = .50
   2002 = .50 × $54,000 = $27,000
   Book value = $54,000 - $27,000 = $27,000
   2003 = .50 × $27,000 = $13,500

3.

Annual depreciation = ($19,000 - $2,000) / 5 = $3,400
Accumulated depreciation 1/1/04 = 2 years @ $3,400 per year = $6,800

6/30	Depreciation Expense	1,700	
	Accumulated Depreciation		1,700
	Dep. for 6 months (6 / 12 × 3,400) = 1,700		
6/30	Cash	2,800	
	Loss on Sale of Asset	7,700	
	Accumulated Depreciation	8,500	
	Equipment		19,000
	Loss = Cash + Accumulated. Dep. - Cost		

Because cash received ($2,000) is less than book value ($19,000 - $8,500 = $10,500), there is a loss of $7,700 ($10,500 - $2,800) on the sale.

4.
  1.
     a. capital expenditure
     b. capital expenditure
     c. capital expenditure
     d. (capital expenditure)

Study Tip: The discount is in parentheses because it represents a reduction in the cost of the equipment.

     e. capital expenditure
     f. revenue expenditure

Study Tip: The interest on the loan does not qualify as a capital expenditure. Generally, interest is capitalized only on self-constructed assets, and then only during the period it takes to construct the asset.

2. $11,376

Given the answers in part 1, the calculation is $9,700 + 582 + 460 - 291 + 925. The accounts would appear as follows:

Drill Press		Interest Expense	
9,700	291	275	
582			
460			
925			
Bal. 11,376			

3. Double-declining-balance = Book value × Rate
   Book value = $11,376
   Rate = 33 1/3 %
   $11,376 × 33 1/3% = $3,792
   depreciation from 8/20/02 – 12/31/02 = 4 months
   $3,792 × 4/12 = $1,264

Study Tip: Double-declining-balance is the only method which ignores residual value in the formula.

5.

A.

Purchase price for Rogers		$10,400,000
Market value of Rogers	16,200,000	
Less: Rogers's liabilities	9,000,000	
Market value of Rogers's net assets		7,200,000
Goodwill		$3,200,000

B.

Date	Account and Explanation	PR	Debit	Credit
10/1	Assets		16,200,000	
	Goodwill		3,200,000	
	Liabilities			9,000,000
	Cash			10,400,000

C.

Date	Account and Explanation	PR	Debit	Credit
12/31	Amortization expense		133,333	
	Goodwill			133,333
	1/ 6 × $3,200,000 = $533,333 × 1/4 = $133,333			

VI. Critical Thinking

The person making the statement is confused about depreciation reserves (i.e., accumulated depreciation). There is no cash involved in accounting for depreciation; therefore, the balance in accumulated depreciation does not represent any money available for future use. The balance in accumulated depreciation represents the amount of the related assets' cost that has been recognized as an expense because of the assets' loss of usefulness to the business.

VII. Demonstration Problems

Demonstration Problem #1 Solved and Explained

	X	Y	Z
Asset cost	$24,000	$16,000	$18,000
Less: Residual value	3,000	800	3,000
Depreciable cost	$21,000	$15,200	$15,000

Study Tip: Under the double-declining-balance method, the residual value is not considered until the book value approaches residual value.

Equipment X
Schedule of Depreciation Expense
(Straight-Line Method)

Year	Depreciable Cost	Depreciable Rate	Depreciation Expense
2002	$21,000	1/6	$ 3,500
2003	21,000	1/6	3,500
2004	21,000	1/6	3,500
2005	21,000	1/6	3,500
2006	21,000	1/6	3,500
2007	21,000	1/6	3,500
		Total	$21,000

The book value of the equipment after 2007 is $3,000 (cost - accumulated depreciation = $24,000 - $21,000 = $3,000).

Equipment Y
Schedule of Depreciation Expense
(Units-of-Production)

Year	Depreciable Cost	Units Produced	Depreciation Expense
2002	$15,200	12,400	$ 4,712*
2003	15,200	10,750	4,085
2004	15,200	11,230	4,267 (rounded)
2005	15,200	6,100	2,136 (rounded)**
		Total	$15,200

*The per-unit cost is $0.38 ($15,200 / 40,000 units = $0.38)

The book value after 2005 is $800 ($16,000 - $15,200 = $800).

**The original production estimate for the equipment was 40,000 units. The actual production over the life of the equipment was 40,480. Assuming the original estimates (for total production and residual value) are reasonable, the 2004 depreciation should be based on 5,620 units, the number required to total 40,000 units.

> **Study Tip**: The depreciable cost is not affected by the method used. The method simply determines how the depreciable cost will be spread out over the asset's life.

Equipment Z
Schedule of Depreciation Expense
(Double-Declining-Balance)

Year	Book Value × Rate	Depreciation Expense	Book Value
2002	.40 × 18,000	7,200	$10,800
2003	.40 × 10,800	4,320	6,480
2004	.40 × 6,480	2,592	3,888
2005	3,888 – 3,000	888	3,000
2006		0	3,000

The straight-line depreciation rate for an asset with useful life of 5 years is 1/5 per year, or 20%. Double the straight-line rate is 2/5, or 40%. This rate does not change from 2002 through 2006.

> **Study Tip**: The most frequent error made by students in applying double-declining-balance deals with the residual value. Unlike units-of-production, with DDB, the residual value is not taken into account until the final years (in this example, the fourth year) of the asset's life.

Depreciation expense for Equipment Z in the fourth year is not $1,555 ($3,888 × .40) because in the fourth year depreciation expense is the previous year's book value less the residual value ($3,888 - $3,000 = $888). As the asset is fully depreciated at the end of the fourth year, there is no depreciation recorded for the fifth year.

Requirement 2 (Journal entry—Equipment X)

Date	Account and Explanation	PR	Debit	Credit
	Accumulated Depreciation—X		21,000	
	Loss on Disposal of Equipment		3,000	
	Equipment X			24,000

When fully depreciated assets cannot be sold or exchanged, an entry removing them from the books is necessary upon disposal. The entry credits the asset account and debits its related Accumulated Depreciation account. If the fully depreciated asset has no residual value, no loss on the disposal occurs. In most cases, however, it will be necessary to record a debit to a Loss on Disposal account to write off the book value of a junked asset. There can never be a gain on the junking or scrapping of an asset.

Requirement 3 (Journal entry—Equipment Y)

Date	Account and Explanation	PR	Debit	Credit
	Cash		1,000	
	Accumulated depreciation—Y		15,200	
	Equipment Y			16,000
	Gain on Sale of Equipment			200

A gain is recorded when an asset is sold for a price greater than its value. A loss is recorded when the sale price is less than book value. In this case, Equipment Y and its related Accumulated Depreciation account are removed from the books in a manner similar to Equipment X. The gain of $200 is calculated by subtracting the book value of the asset sold ($800) from the cash received ($1,000). The Gain on the Sale of Equipment account is a revenue account and is closed to the Income Summary account at the end of the year.

Demonstration Problem #2 Solved and Explained

Date	Account and Explanation	PR	Debit	Credit
1.	Equipment		23,850	
	Cash			23,850
2.	Equipment		410	
	Cash			410
	Transportation cost.			
3.	Equipment		1,040	
	Cash			1,040
	Installation cost.			

Both the transportation and installation costs are debited to the Equipment account because they are necessary costs incurred to place the asset in service. Therefore, the total cost basis for the equipment is $25,300, not $22,500.

4.	Depreciation Expense—Equipment		1,488	
	Accumulated Depreciation			1,488

($25,300 - $1,500 (see above)) / 8 = 2,975 × 6/12 = $1,488)

Since the asset was acquired on 6/10, but placed in service on 6/24, the first year's depreciation is 6/12 of the company's financial period. Thereafter, annual depreciation is $2,975.

5.	Equipment		4,500	
	Cash (or Accounts Payable)			4,500

This is clearly a capital expenditure because the equipment will last past its original life estimate. Therefore, the cost should be reflected in an asset account, not in an expense account.

6.	Depreciation Expense—Equipment		2,752	
	Accumulated Depreciation			2,752

Accumulated depreciation through 12/31/00 is $10,413. For 1997, depreciation is $1,488; 1998 to 2000 is equal to $2,975 per year × 3 = $8,925. $1,488 + $8,925 = $10,413.

Therefore, on 1/5/01 book value is $14,887 ($25,300 - $10,413). The $4,500 debit in entry (5) increases book value to $19,387, and now life is 2 years more than the original life estimate. As of 1/05/01, the equipment is 3 years, 6 months old. The revised life estimate is now 10 years. Therefore, as of 1/05/01, the asset has 6 years, 6 months of life left (10 years - 3 years, 6 months). To calculate the new depreciation amount, divide book value less residual value ($19,387 - $1,500) by remaining life (6.5 years) or $2,752 per year (rounded).

| 7. | Repair Expense | | 480 | |
| | Cash | | | 480 |

This is clearly a revenue expenditure—one necessary to maintain the asset.

| 8. | Depreciation Expense | | 2,752 | |
| | Accumulated Depreciation | | | 2,752 |

See explanation for 6 above.

| 9. | Depreciation Expense – Equipment | | 688 | |
| | Accumulated Depreciation | | | 688 |

Study Tip: When an asset is disposed of during the fiscal period, first update the depreciation.

Depreciation from 12/31/02 – 4/10/03 = $2,752 × 3/12 = $746 (rounded)

10.	Cash		4,200	
	Accumulated Depreciation		16,605	
	Loss on Sale		8,995	
	Equipment			29,800

The Equipment account and Accumulated Depreciation account appear as follows:

Equipment		Accumulated Depreciation		
(1) 23,850			1,488	12/31/97
(2) 410			2,975	12/98
(3) 1,040			2,975	12/99
(5) 4,500			2,975	12/00
Bal. 29,800			2,752	12/01
			2,752	12/02
			688	4/10/03
			16,605	Bal.

Therefore, on date of disposal book value is $13,195 ($29,800 - $16,605); comparing book value with sales price results in a loss of $8,995.

CHAPTER 8—CURRENT AND LONG-TERM LIABILITIES

CHAPTER OVERVIEW

In the last four chapters, we have concentrated on a detailed examination of assets—specifically cash (Chapter 4), receivables and short-term investments (Chapter 5), inventory (Chapter 6), and plant assets (Chapter 7). We now turn our attention to liabilities, both current and long-term. Whereas assets relate to investing activities, liabilities relate to financing activities. The learning objectives for this chapter are to

1. Account for current liabilities
2. Identify and report contingent liabilities
3. Account for basic bonds payable transactions
4. Measure interest expense by using the effective-interest method
5. Explain the advantages and disadvantages of borrowing
6. Report liabilities on the balance sheet

CHAPTER REVIEW

Liabilities are obligations to transfer assets (for example, to make cash payments for purchases on account) or to provide services in the future (for example, to earn unearned revenue). Current liabilities are due within one year or within the company's operating cycle if it is longer than one year. Long-term liabilities are those not classified as current.

Objective 1 - Account for current liabilities.

Current liabilities include liabilities of a known amount and liabilities that are estimated. Current liabilities of a known amount are: **accounts payable**—amounts owed to suppliers for goods or services purchased on account, **short-term notes payable**—notes due within one year. Companies issue notes payable to borrow cash, to purchase inventory, or to purchase plant assets. Interest expense and interest payable must be accrued at the end of the accounting period.

Suppose a company acquires a plant asset and issues a note payable. The entry is:

Plant Asset	XX	
Notes Payable, Short-Term		XX

Interest expense and interest payable are recorded at the end of the accounting period with this entry:

Interest Expense	XX	
Interest Payable		XX

When the note is paid off at maturity, the entry is:

Notes Payable, Short-Term	XX	
Interest Payable	XX	
Interest Expense	XX	
Cash		XX

Other current liabilities include the following: **sales taxes payable**, the **current portion of long-term debt**, **accrued expenses**, **unearned revenues**, and **contingent liabilities**.

Most states tax retail sales. **Sales tax** is collected in addition to the price of an item. Retailers are actually collecting the tax for the government, and therefore Sales Tax Payable is a current liability.

Sales taxes may be accounted for in one of two ways:

1. Record the tax separately for daily sales:

Cash	XX	
Sales Revenue		XX
Sales Tax Payable		XX

2. Record sales including the taxes collected:

Cash	XX	
Sales Revenue		XX

At the end of each month, an adjusting entry is made to correct the Sales Revenue and Sales Tax Payable accounts:

Sales Revenue	XX	
Sales Tax Payable		XX

In either case, when the taxes are paid to the government the entry is:

Sales Tax Payable	XX	
Cash		XX

Some long-term liabilities, such as notes, bonds, or mortgages are paid in installments. The **current installment of long-term debt** (also called current maturity) is the amount of that debt that is payable within one year. It is reported in the current liabilities section of the balance sheet. The remainder is reported in the long-term liabilities section of the balance sheet.

Accrued expenses (also called **accrued liabilities**) such as interest payable and payroll items are current liabilities. Payroll liabilities refer to both the amount of money owed to the employees (more commonly referred to as net pay) and amounts owed to others based on the salaries and wages earned by employees. Examples of the latter are income taxes (both federal and state), FICA taxes (Social Security and Medicare), in addition to a variety of other amounts earned by employees but withheld from their earnings by the business. At the time these amounts are withheld, they become liabilities of the business. Exhibit 8-1 in your text illustrates a typical entry recorded for payroll.

Unearned revenues (also called **deferred revenues, revenues collected in advance, customer prepayments**) occur when a company receives cash from customers before earning the revenue. As goods are delivered or services are rendered, revenue is recorded. Unearned revenue is recorded as:

Cash	XX	
Unearned Revenue		XX

As the unearned revenue is earned, it is recorded as:

Unearned Revenue	XX	
Revenue		XX

Estimated Current Liabilities

Current liabilities that are estimated include warranties payable, and vacation pay liability. Recall that the matching principle requires that expenses be matched with revenues. A company can reasonably estimate, often as a percentage of sales, the amount of **warranty expense** that will be incurred as a result of defective products. Estimated Warranty Payable is a current liability, recorded as:

Warranty Expense	XX	
Estimated Warranty Payable		XX

Study Tip: When a repair or replacement occurs within the warranty period, the Estimated Warranty Payable (rather than Warranty Expense) is debited.

Many companies provide paid vacations to their employees. The matching principle dictates that the amount of vacation employees have earned be recorded in the period when it was earned and not in a subsequent period when the employee actually takes the time off with pay. Therefore, the company needs to accrue the **estimated vacation pay liability** each period.

Objective 2 - Identify and report contingent liabilities.

A **contingent liability** is a potential liability that depends on a future event that may occur as a result of a past transaction. Contingent liabilities may be difficult to estimate, as in lawsuits, where the amounts are determined by the courts. The disclosure principle requires companies to keep outsiders informed of relevant information about the company.

Some companies report contingent liabilities on the balance sheet after total liabilities, but with no amount listed. An explanatory note usually accompanies a short presentation. Other companies simply report contingent liabilities in supplementary notes only. Contingent liabilities are not required to be presented on the balance sheet. If it is probable that a loss will occur and the amount can be reasonably estimated, then an actual liability should be recorded. If recorded, it will appear as a liability on the balance sheet and as a loss on the income statement.

Financing Operations with Long-term Debt

Corporations issue **bonds** (typically in $1,000 units) to raise large amounts of money from multiple lenders. Bonds are long-term liabilities. The **bond certificate** states the 1) principal amount, 2) interest rate, 3) maturity date, and 4) dates that interest payments are due (which are generally every six months over the life of the bond). See Exhibit 8-2. Companies usually hire a securities firm to underwrite the bonds. The **underwriter** buys the bonds and resells them to clients.

Term bonds mature at the same time. **Serial bonds** mature in installments over a period of time. Unsecured bonds are called **debentures**. The owners of a secured bond have the right to take specified assets of the issuer in the event of default. Other things being equal, debentures will carry a higher interest rate than secured bonds.

Bonds are often traded on bonds markets. Bond prices are quoted at a percentage of their maturity value. For example, a $10,000 bond selling for 97 would sell for $9,700.

> **Study Tip**: Stock prices are quoted in dollars; bond prices are quoted in percentages.

When a bond is issued at a price above the face (par) value, it is being issued at a premium. When the bond is issued at a price below the face (par) value, it is being issued at a discount.

Four factors set the **price of bonds**: 1) the length of time until the bond matures, 2) the company's ability to meet interest and principal payments, 3) the maturity value, and 4) the rates of other available investment plans.

A basic understanding of the concept of **present value** is necessary to understand bond prices. When companies borrow money, they have to pay interest on the debt. To the lender this represents the time value of money. Therefore, a lender would not be interested in giving up $500 today to receive only $500 five years from now. If the lender wants to receive $500 years from now, the question is, how much would the lender be willing to give up today to do so? The answer to the question represents the present value of that future amount ($500). Present value is discussed in detail in Appendix B.

The price at which bonds are sold is determined by the **contract interest (stated) rate** and the **market (effective) interest rate**. The contract rate is the amount (expressed as a percent) listed on the bond certificate. The market rate is the amount that potential investors are currently demanding for their money. When the contract rate is less than the market rate, the bonds have to be sold at less than their face value (called a **discount**) to attract investors. Conversely, when the contract price is greater than the market rate, the bonds will sell at a **premium**. See Exhibit 8-4.

Objective 3 - Account for basic bond payable transactions.

The simplest transaction occurs when bonds are issued on an interest date and no difference exists between the stated rate and the market rate. Debit Cash and credit Bonds Payable. When interest is paid, debit Interest Expense and credit Cash. When the bonds mature and are paid off, debit Bonds Payable and credit Cash.

When **bonds are issued between interest dates**, (or sold "plus accrued interest") the corporation collects the accrued interest from the purchaser, in addition to the selling price of the bonds, as follows:

Cash	XXX (total cash received)
Bonds Payable	XX (selling price of bond)
Interest Payable	XX (accrued interest)

The first interest payment is recorded as follows:

Interest Expense	XXX (actual interest expense since sale date)
Interest Payable	XX (accrued interest collected on sale date)
Cash	XX (full 6 months of interest)

Interest payments are not prorated based on the issue date. The interest payment to the purchaser is composed of the accrued interest collected from the purchaser plus the interest expense from the sale date to the next interest date; in other words, the full six months of interest.

Issuing Bonds at a Discount

If the market interest rate is higher than the stated rate of a bond issue, then the issuer must **sell the bonds at a discount**, that is, at less than face value in order to attract buyers. The entry debits Cash, debits Discount on Bonds Payable, and credits Bonds Payable.

Discount on Bonds Payable is a contra account to Bonds Payable. On the balance sheet, the discount balance is subtracted from Bonds Payable to equal the book value or carrying amount of the bond issue. The issuer will have to repay the face value of the bonds when they mature. Therefore, a discount is an additional cost to the issuer.

Objective 4 - Measure interest expense by using the effective-interest method.

The **effective-interest method** is used to amortize the bond discount over the life of the bond or note. The objective of the effective-interest method is to match interest expense as a constant percentage of the changing carrying value of the bonds rather than as a constant amount each period. The effective-interest rate is the market rate in effect when the bonds are sold. Three steps are followed when using the effective-interest method:

1. Interest expense is calculated by multiplying the effective-interest rate by the carrying value of the bonds. (This amount changes each period.)
2. The cash paid to bondholders is calculated by multiplying the stated interest rate by the principal amount of the bonds. (This amount is the same each period.)
3. The difference between the interest expense and the cash paid is the amount of discount amortized.

Remember that amortization of bond discount will change the carrying value of the bonds before the next calculations are made. When a discount is amortized, the carrying value will increase.

Study Exhibits 8-6, 8-7, and 8-8 in your text in order to understand the effective-interest method. Pay particular attention to the graphs in 8-6 and 8-7.

Issuing Bonds at a Premium

If the market rate is lower than the stated rate of a bond issue, then the issuer can **sell the bonds at a premium**, that is, for more than face value. The entry debits Cash, credits Bonds Payable and credits Premium on Bonds Payable. **Premium on Bonds Payable** is added to Bonds Payable on the balance sheet to show the book value or carrying amount. The issuer will have to repay only the face value of the bonds when they mature. Therefore, a premium is treated as a reduction of the issuer's interest expense. The premium is allocated to reduce interest expense over the life of the bonds, in accordance with the matching principle. See Exhibit 8-9 and 8-10.

Straight-line amortization of the discount or premium is computed by dividing the discount or premium by the number of accounting periods during the life of the bonds. On each interest date, the entry to record interest expense debits Interest Expense, debits Premium on Bonds Payable, or credits Discount on Bonds Payable, and credits Cash.

Sometimes corporations retire bonds prior to the maturity date. **Callable bonds** may be retired at the option of the issuer. **Noncallable bonds** may be bought back on the open market and retired. If interest rates have dropped, the issuer may compare the book value of the bonds to the market price to decide whether to retire the bonds. When bonds are retired and the bonds were initially sold at either a premium or discount, the entry to retire the bonds must also remove the unamortized premium or discount from the books. A **gain (or loss) on retirement** results when the carrying value of the bonds is greater (or lesser for a loss) than the cash paid for the bonds. Any gain or loss on the retirement of bonds payable is an extraordinary item according to GAAP, and reported separately on the income statement.

Bonds which can be converted into common stock are called **convertible bonds**. Investors will convert the bonds when the stock price of the issuing company increases to the point that the stock has a higher market value than the bonds. The entry transfers the bond carrying amount into stockholders' equity:

Bonds Payable	XX	
Premium on Bonds Payable (if applicable)	XX	
Discount on Bonds Payable (if applicable)		XX
Common stock		XX
Paid-in Capital in Excess of Par - Common		XX

Study Tip: Note both Premium and Discount cannot appear in the same entry.

Also, there will never be a gain or loss recorded on the conversion of bonds. The credit to Paid-in Capital is the difference between the carrying value of the bonds (Bonds Payable + Premium or Bonds Payable - Discount) and the par value of the shares issued.

Objective 5 - Explain the advantages and disadvantages of borrowing.

Advantages of borrowing: Trading on the equity usually increases earnings per share. This means that the corporation earns a return on the borrowed funds that is greater than the cost of the borrowed funds.

Disadvantages of borrowing:

1. High interest rates
2. Interest on debt must be paid; dividends on stock are optional.

Review the Decision Guidelines—Financing with Debt or with Stock to become familiar with the issues involved in this decision.

A **lease** is a rental agreement in which the tenant (lessee) agrees to make rent payments to the property owner (lessor) in exchange for the use of some asset. **Operating leases** are usually short term or cancelable. To account for an operating lease, the lessee debits Rent Expense and credits Cash for the amount of the lease payment.

Capital leases are long term and noncancelable. Accounting for capital leases is similar to accounting for the purchase of an asset. Debit the asset leased, credit Cash for the initial payment, and credit Lease Liability for the present value of future lease payments. Because the leased asset is capitalized, it must be depreciated. Leased assets are usually depreciated over the term of the lease. Debit Depreciation Expense and credit the asset's Accumulated Depreciation account.

FASB Statement #13 sets the **guidelines for capital leases**. Only one of the following criteria is required to be present to classify the lease as capital:

1. The lease transfers title (ownership) to the lessee at the end of the lease term .
2. The lease contains a bargain purchase option.
3. The term of the lease is 75% or more of the estimated useful life of the asset.
4. The present value of the lease payments is 90% or more of the market value of the leased asset.

Operating leases are defined by exception: i.e., operating leases are only those which fail to meet all four of these criteria.

In the past, companies were attracted to operating leases because they were not required to list the lease as a liability on the balance sheet—in other words, the company had the use of an asset (or service) without the related debt showing (called **off-balance-sheet financing**). This practice has been curtailed.

Objective 6 - Report liabilities on the balance sheet.

Review the liabilities listed in Exhibit 8-12 in your text to be certain you are familiar with each. Deferred income taxes are tax liabilities that companies are able to postpone for later payment. Deferred gains are unearned revenues (long-term); deferred credits are similar to deferred gains. Minority interest represents outside stockholders interest.

Pensions and **postretirement benefits** are other types of liabilities found on balance sheets. **Pensions** are compensation paid to employees after retirement, usually based on a variety of factors including length of service. Companies are required to report the present value of promised future pension payments to retirees. If the plan assets exceed this amount, the plan is overfunded. Conversely, the fund could be underfunded if assets are less. In addition to pensions, companies are required to report the present value of future payments to retirees for other benefits. The largest of these is health care. At the end of each period, companies accrue the expense and the liability of **postretirement benefits** based on information about the current work force.

Liabilities also affect the statement of cash flows. The issuance of debt (and receipt of cash) is a financing activity, as is the payment of debt. However, interest payments are operating activities because, as an expense, interest appears on the income statement.

TEST YOURSELF

All the self-testing materials in this chapter focus on information and procedures that your instructor is likely to test in quizzes and examinations.

I. Matching   *Match each numbered term with its lettered definition.*

_____ 1. discount (on a bond)
_____ 2. premium (on a bond)
_____ 3. callable bonds
_____ 4. contract interest rate
_____ 5. debentures
_____ 6. lessee
_____ 7. stated interest rate
_____ 8. market interest rate
_____ 9. accrued expense
_____ 10. trading on the equity
_____ 11. off-balance-sheet financing
_____ 12. bond indenture

_____ 13. bonds payable
_____ 14. capital lease
_____ 15. convertible bonds
_____ 16. contingent liability
_____ 17. lessor
_____ 18. short-term note payable
_____ 19. operating lease
_____ 20. serial bonds
_____ 21. term bonds
_____ 22. underwriter
_____ 23. discounting a note payable

A. a potential liability that depends on a future event arising out of a past transaction
B. another name for the contract interest rate
C. acquisition of assets or services with debt that is not reported on the balance sheet
D. an expense incurred but not yet paid by the company, also called accrued liability
E. bonds that may be exchanged for the common stock of the issuing company at the option of the investor
F. bonds that mature in installments over a period of time
G. bonds that the issuer may pay off at a specified price whenever the issuer desires
H. bonds that all mature at the same time for a particular issue
I. note payable due within one year
J. contract under which bonds are issued
K. earning more income than the interest on the borrowed amount
L. excess of a bond's maturity (par) value over its issue price
M. excess of a bond's issue price over its maturity (par) value
N. groups of notes payable issued to multiple lenders, called bondholders
O. interest rate that investors demand in order to lend their money
P. a lease agreement that meets any one of four special criteria
Q. organizations that purchase bonds from an issuing company and resell them to clients, or sell the bonds for a commission and agree to buy all unsold bonds
R. the property owner in a lease agreement
S. the tenant in a lease agreement
T. the interest rate that determines the amount of cash interest the borrower pays
U. unsecured bonds backed only by the good faith of the borrower
V. usually a short-term or cancelable rental agreement
W. a borrowing arrangement in which the bank subtracts the interest amount from the face value of a note payable

II. Multiple Choice   *Circle the best answer.*

1. A $10,000 bond quoted at 104 3/8 has a market price of

   A. $10,000.00
   B. $10,437.50
   C. $10,043.75
   D. $14,375.00

2. All of the following affect the market price of bonds *except*

   A. bond holder's credit rating
   B. bond issuer's credit rating
   C. market interest rate
   D. length of time to maturity

3. Which of the following is not a current liability?

   A. Warranties Payable
   B. Pension Liability
   C. Unearned Revenue
   D. Vacation Liability

4. The interest rate demanded by investors in order to lend their money is the

   A. contract rate
   B. issue rate
   C. effective rate
   D. stated rate

5. The premium on a bond payable

   A. increases the interest expense only in the year the bonds are sold
   B. increases the interest expense over the life of the bonds
   C. reduces interest expense only in the year the bonds mature
   D. is a liability account that is amortized (to expense) over the life of the bonds

6. The book value of Bonds Payable on the balance sheet equals

   A. Bonds Payable + Discount on Bonds Payable or + Premium on Bonds Payable
   B. Bonds Payable - Discount on Bonds Payable or - Premium on Bonds Payable
   C. Bonds Payable + Discount on Bonds Payable or - Premium on Bonds Payable
   D. Bonds Payable - Discount on Bonds Payable or + Premium on Bonds Payable

7. When bonds are issued at a premium, their carrying amount

   A. decreases from issuance to maturity
   B. increases from issuance to maturity
   C. remains constant over the life of the bonds
   D. decreases when the market interest rate increases

8. Gains and losses from early retirement of debt are reported

   A. as operating gains and losses on the income statement
   B. as increases or decreases to Retained Earnings on the statement of retained earnings
   C. as extraordinary items on the income statement
   D. in the footnotes to the financial statements

9. When a convertible bond is exchanged for common stock

   A. stockholders' equity increases
   B. liabilities increase
   C. revenues increase
   D. expenses increase

10. Which of the following is not reported on the balance sheet?

    A. capital lease
    B. pension liabilities
    C. post-retirement benefit liabilities
    D. operating leases

11. Interest expense on a discounted note payable is recorded

    A. at maturity
    B. at the end of the accounting period
    C. in monthly payments
    D. when the note is discounted

12. Which of the following is probably a contingent liability?

    A. Interest Payable
    B. Notes Payable
    C. Lawsuit Claims
    D. Income Tax Payable

13. A contingent liability becomes a real liability when

    A. a loss is probable but cannot be estimated
    B. a loss is possible
    C. a loss is probable and can reasonably be estimated
    D. a loss can be reasonably estimated

14. Which of the following is not an estimated liability?

    A. warranties
    B. postretirement benefits
    C. vacation pay
    D. notes payable

III. Completion   *Complete each of the following.*

1. When the market interest rate is _____ than the stated rate, bonds will sell at a premium.
2. When the premium on bonds payable is reduced, the book value of bonds payable_____.
3. Gains or losses on early retirement of debt is _____ and reported separately on the income statement.
4. The liability to make _____ lease payments is not reported on the balance sheet.
5. If a lease transfers ownership of assets at the end of the lease term, the lease is a(n) _____ lease.
6. The _____ method of interest amortization results in the same amount of discount/premium amortization for identical periods of time.
7. Accruing pension and postretirement benefit liabilities is an example of the _____ principle.
8. When the market interest rate is greater than the stated rate, the bonds will sell at a _____.
9. Convertible bonds give the _____ the right to convert the bonds to common stock.
10. When the effective-interest method of amortization is used, the total amount of interest expense over the life of the bonds is _____.
11. Indicate whether each of the following liabilities is a known amount (K) or an estimated amount (E).

_____	A. Accounts Payable	_____	G. Sales Tax Payable
_____	B. Short-term Notes Payable	_____	H. Liability for Vacation Pay
_____	C. Property Taxes Payable	_____	I. Postretirement Benefits
_____	D. Warranty Liability	_____	J. Interest Payable
_____	E. Salaries Expense	_____	K. Pension Premium Payable
_____	F. Income Taxes Payable		

IV. True/False   *For each of the following statements, circle T for true or F for false.*

1.   T F   A bond listed as selling at 98 means it is selling for $98.
2.   T F   Discount on Bonds Payable is a contra liability account.
3.   T F   The current portion of long-term debt is listed in the current liability section of the balance sheet and includes both the principal and accrued interest.
4.   T F   Accrued expenses and accrued liabilities are synonymous terms.
5.   T F   Salaries Payable represents the amount employees have earned.
6.   T F   Unearned revenue is reported on the income statement after operating income.
7.   T F   The disclosure principle requires businesses to estimate warranty expense.
8.   T F   A debenture is a secured bond.
9.   T F   The carrying amount of a bond will equal its face value if the bond was sold at face value.
10.   T F   When a bond is sold at a premium, the interest expense over the life of the bond is greater than the total interest paid to the bondholder over the life of the bond.
11.   T F   Amortizing a bond discount using the effective-interest method results in a greater amount of interest expense over the life of the bond compared with the straight-line method.
12.   T F   The carrying value of a bond sold at a discount increases over the life of the bond.
13.   T F   A callable bond allows the bondholder to convert the bond into shares of common stock.

14. T F   An example of a capital lease is the lease a tenant signs to rent an apartment.
15. T F   Postretirement benefits are one example of an estimated liability.

V. Exercises

1. Sintax Inc. issued $6,000,000 in 20-year bonds with a stated interest rate of 7 3/4%. The bonds were issued at par on June 1, 2002. Interest is paid December 1 and June 1.

Give the journal entries for:

A. Issuance of the bonds on June 1, 2002.
B. Payment of interest on December 1, 2002.
C. Maturity payment of bonds on June 1, 2022.

	Date	Account and Explanation	Debit	Credit
A.				
B.				
C.				

2. Record journal entries for the following transactions.

A. A company borrows $8,000 on October 1 giving a 10%, 1-year note payable.

GENERAL JOURNAL

Date	Accounts and Explanation	PR	Debit	Credit

B. Record an adjusting entry on December 31 for the note in (A).

GENERAL JOURNAL

Date	Accounts and Explanation	PR	Debit	Credit

3. Radke Corporation issued $500,000 in 7-year bonds with a stated interest rate of 8%. The bonds were sold on January 1, 2002, for $477,956 to yield 9%. Interest is paid July 1 and January 1. Radke uses the straight-line method to amortize Discount on Bonds Payable. (Assume an October 31 year end.)

Record the journal entries for:

A. Issuance of bonds on January 1, 2002.
B. Payment of interest on July 1, 2002.
C. Accrual of interest and related amortization on October 31, 2002 (year end).
D. Payment of interest on January 1, 2003.
E. Maturity payment of bonds on January 1, 2009.

	Date	Account and Explanation	Debit	Credit
A.				
B.				
C.				
D.				
E.				

4. Weston Corporation issued $500,000 in 7-year callable bonds with a stated interest rate of 8%. The bonds were sold on January 1, 2002, for $558,420 to yield 6%. Interest is paid July 1 and January 1. Weston uses the effective-interest method to amortize Premium on Bonds Payable. (Assume a December 31 year end.)

Record the journal entries for:

A. Issuance of bonds on January 1, 2002.
B. Payment of interest on July 1, 2002.
C. Accrual of interest and related amortization on December 31, 2002 (year end).
D. Payment of interest on January 1, 2003.
E. Maturity payment of bonds on January 1, 2009.

Date	Account and Explanation	Debit	Credit
A.			
B.			
C.			
D.			
E.			

5. Review the information in Exercise 4 and assume Weston Corporation exercised its option to call the bonds on July 1, 2004, at 105. Record the 7/1/04 journal entry for

a. the interest payment on 7/1/04

Date	Accounts and Explanation	Debit	Credit

b. the cash payment to the bondholders

Date	Accounts and Explanation	Debit	Credit

VI. Critical Thinking

Review the information in Exercises 3 and 4 above and assume, in each case, that each $1,000 bond is convertible, at the option of the holder, into 31.25 shares of the corporation's common stock. Determine when an investor should seriously consider exercising the option to convert the bonds to stock.

_____
_____
_____
_____
_____
_____
_____
_____
_____

VII. Demonstration Problems

Demonstration Problem #1

The following events occurred in December:

1. On December 1, borrowed $75,000 from the bank, signing a 9-month note at 8% interest.
2. On December 10, the company accepted advance payments from two customers as follows:
    a) A $60,000 payment from Simex for 20 custom-made polishers. As of December 31, six polishers had been produced.
    b) A 10% down payment on a $100,000 contract for a piece of equipment to be delivered by May 1 of the following year. As of December 31, no work had been started on the equipment.
3. During December, a competitor filed a lawsuit against the company alleging violation of anti-trust regulations. If the company loses the suit, it is estimated damages will exceed $1 million.
4. The December payroll totaled $145,000, which will be paid on January 10. Employees accrue vacation benefits at the rate of 2% of monthly payroll. (Ignore payroll deductions and the employer's payroll tax expense).
5. Sales for the month amounted to 1,200 units at $350 each, subject to a retail sales tax of 6%. Each unit carries a 90-day warranty requiring the company to repair or replace the unit if it becomes defective during the warranty period. The estimated cost to the company to honor the warranty is $55, and past experience has shown that approximately 3% of the units will be returned during the warranty period.

Required:

Record the external transactions and, where appropriate, the required adjusting entry at December 31. Use the following format.

Date	Accounts and Explanation	PR	Debit	Credit

Demonstration Problem #2

Master Corporation has outstanding an issue of 10% callable bonds that mature in 2011. The bonds were dated January 1, 2001, and pay interest each July 1 and January 1. Additional bond data:

a. Fiscal year-end for Master Corporation: September 30.
b. Maturity value of the bonds: $500,000.
c. Contract interest rate: 10%.
d. Interest is paid 5% semiannually, $25,000 ($500,000 × .05).
e. Market interest rate at time of issue: 9% annually, 4.5% semiannually.
f. Issue price: 106.

1. Complete the interest method amortization table through January 1, 2003. Round pennies to the nearest dollar. See the form below.

2. Using the amortization table that you have completed, record the following transactions:
   a. Issuance of the bonds on January 1, 2001.
   b. Payment of interest and amortization of premium on July 1, 2001.
   c. Accrued interest and amortization of premium as of September 30, 2001.
   d. Payment of interest and amortization of premium on January 1, 2002.
   e. Retirement of the bonds on January 2, 2002. Callable price of bonds was 108.

Requirement 1

	A	B	C	D	E
Semi-annual Interest Date	Interest Payment (5% of Maturity Value)	Interest Expense (4.5% of Preceding Bond Carrying Value)	Premium Amortiza-tion (A - B)	Premium Account Balance (D - C)	Bond Carrying Value ($500,000 + D)
1/1/01				$30,000	$530,000
7/1/01					
1/1/02					
7/1/02					
1/1/03					

Requirement 2

	Date	Account and Explanation	Debit	Credit
a.				
b.				
c.				
d.				
e.				

SOLUTIONS

I. Matching

1. L	5. U	9. D	13. N	17. R	21. H
2. M	6. S	10. K	14. P	18. I	22. Q
3. G	7. B	11. C	15. E	19. V	23. W
4. T	8. O	12. J	16. A	20. F	

II. Multiple Choice

1. B   The number 104 3/8 means 104.375% (or 1.04375) of the face value: $10,000 × 104.375% = $10,437.50.

2. A   Since anyone may be a bondholder, it does not make sense that a bondholder's credit rating would affect the market price of the bond. All the other listed items do affect the market price of the bond.

3. B   Of the items listed, all are liabilities that are due within one year except for pensions which are long term.

4. C   Effective rate of interest and market rate of interest are synonymous.

5. D   Amortization of the premium on bonds payable serves to reduce the recorded amount of interest expense over the life of the bonds.

6. D   The book value or carrying amount of a bond is equal to the face amount of the bond minus the unamortized discount or plus the unamortized premium.

7. A   The carrying amount of a bond is the face amount of the bond plus (minus) unamortized premium (discount). Since the balance of the premium (discount) account is amortized over the life of the bond, it moves towards zero. Accordingly, the carrying amount of bonds issued at a premium (discount) decreases (increases) over time.

8. C   GAAP identifies gains and losses on early retirement of debt as an extraordinary item.

9. A   The conversion of a bond to common stock converts a liability to stockholders' equity, which increases stockholders' equity.

10. D   Of the items listed, only "operating lease" is not reported on the balance sheet. Operating leases are generally short-term rental agreements that transfer none of the rights of ownership.

11. D   The note payable is discounted (interest is taken out) when the loan is made. The bank subtracts the interest from the note's face amount and the borrower receives the net amount.

12. C   A contingent liability is not an actual liability. It is a potential liability that depends on a future event arising out of a past transaction. Of the items listed, all except "lawsuit claims" are real liabilities.

13.   C   The FASB says to record an actual liability when 1) it is probable that the business has suffered a loss, and 2) its amount can be reasonably estimated.

14.   D   Notes Payable is a known liability, all the others are estimated.

III. Completion

1. lower (when market rate > stated rate, then discount; when market rate < stated rate, then premium)
2. decreases (The book value or carrying value amount of a bond is equal to the face amount of the bond plus (minus) the unamortized premium (discount).)
3. extraordinary (Though not meeting the normal "infrequent and unusual" requirement for other extraordinary items, GAAP specifies that such gains and losses are extraordinary items.)
4. operating (Operating leases are normally short term and transfer none of the rights of ownership to the lessee. Accordingly, neither an asset nor a liability is recorded for such leases.)
5. capital (Capital leases require that the lessee record the leased property as an asset and the obligation to make future lease payments as a liability.)
6. straight-line (This method divides the amount of the discount/premium by the number of time periods resulting in the same figure each period.)
7. matching
8. discount (because the lender expects a greater return on the loan than the stated rate provides)
9. lender (not the borrower; convertibility make the bonds more attractive to prospective lenders because of the potential for greater returns)
10. a constant percentage (as compared with the straight-line method where the amount of discount/ premium is constant). The effective rate is required, although the straight-line method can be used if the difference between the two is not material.
11.

K	A.	Accounts Payable	K	G.	Sales Tax Payable
K	B.	Short-term Notes Payable	E or K	H.	Liability for Vacation Pay
E or K	C.	Property Taxes Payable	E	I.	Post-retirement Benefits
E	D.	Warranty Liability	K	J.	Interest Payable
K	E.	Salaries Expense	E or K	K.	Pension Premium Payable
E or K	F.	Income Taxes Payable			

IV. True/False

1.   F   98 refers to a percent, so it means that the bond is selling for 98% of its face value.

Study Tip: Bond prices are always percentages, while stock prices are always quoted in dollars.

2.   T
3.   F   While it is true that the current portion is listed in the current liability section, it is not true it includes accrued interest. Accrued interest would be reported separately in the current liability section.
4.   T
5.   T
6.   F   Unearned Revenue is a liability account and reported on the balance sheet.
7.   F   The matching principle, not the disclosure principle, requires that warranties expense be estimated and included on the current period's income statement.
8.   F   Debentures are unsecured bonds.

9. T
10. F   The expense will be less than the interest payments—why? Because a part of each interest payment is simply the return to the bondholder of the premium paid when the bond was originally sold.
11. F   The method used for amortizing a bond discount (or premium) does not determine how much interest is recognized over the life of the bond, it simply determines how the total amount of interest is recognized.
12. T
13. F   The callable feature refers to a right of the issuing corporation, not the bondholder.
14. F   An apartment lease is an example of an operating lease.
15. T

V. Exercises

1. A.   Cash   6,000,000
         Bonds Payable   6,000,000

     B.   Interest Expense ($6,000,000 × .0775 × 6/12)   232,500
         Cash   232,500

     C.   Bonds Payable   6,000,000
         Cash   6,000,000

2. A.   Cash   8,000
         Note Payable   8,000

     B.   Adjusting entry on December 31:
         Interest Expense   200
             Interest Payable   200
         ($8,000 × .10 × 3/12)

3. A.   Cash   477,956
         Discount on Bonds Payable   22,044
         Bonds Payable   500,000

     B.   Interest Expense (20,000 + 1,575)   21,575
         Cash (500,000 × .08 × 6/12)   20,000
         Discount on Bonds Payable   1,575
             (22,044 / 14 interest payments)

     C.   Interest Expense (13,333 + 1,050)   14,383
         Interest Payable (500,000 × .08 × 4/12)   13,333
         Discount on Bonds Payable (22,044/14 × 2/3)   1,050
       Note: In this exercise, the year end is October 31, not December 31.

     D.   Interest Expense [(20,000 - 13,333) + 525]   7,192
         Interest Payable   13,333
         Cash (500,000 × .08 × 6/12)   20,000
         Discount on Bonds Payable (22,044/14 × 1/3)   525

E. Bonds Payable   500,000
      Cash   500,000

4. A. Cash   558,420
      Bonds Payable   500,000
      Premium on Bonds Payable   58,420

   B. Interest Expense (558,420 × .06 × 6/12)   16,753
      Premium on Bonds Payable   3,247
         Cash (500,000 × .08 × 6/12)   20,000

   New carrying value of bonds = Bonds Payable + Premium on Bonds Payable =
   500,000 + (58,420 - 3,247) = 555,173

   C. Interest Expense (555,173 × .06 × 6/12)   16,655
      Premium on Bonds Payable   3,345
         Interest Payable (500,000 × .08 × 6/12)   20,000

   New carrying value of bonds = 500,000 + (55,173 – 3,345) = 551,828

   D. Interest Payable   20,000
      Cash   20,000

   E. Bonds Payable   500,000
      Cash   500,000

   Note that after the last interest payment, the account Premium on Bonds Payable
   has a zero balance.

5. In order to record July 1, 2004, interest payment, you need to update the amortization
   of the premium through 7/1/04, as follows:

   Carrying value of bonds on 1/1/03 is $551,828 (see solution to Exercise 4 above).

   Carrying value of bonds on 7/1/03 is $500,000 + ($51,828 - $3,445) = $548,383.

   Carrying value of bonds on 1/1/04 is $500,000 + ($48,383 - $3,549) = $544,834.

   7/1/04   Interest Expense ($544,834 × .06 × 6/12)   16,345
      Premium on Bonds Payable   3,655
         Cash ($500,000 × .08 × 6/12)   20,000

   The carrying value of the bonds is now $500,000 + (44,834 - 3,655) = $541,179

   7/1/04   Bonds Payable   500,000
      Premium of Bonds Payable   41,179
         Cash   525,000
         Extraordinary Gain on Retirement of Bonds   16,179

VI. Critical Thinking

If each $1,000 bond can be converted into 31.25 shares of common stock, then a quick calculation indicates an investor should seriously think about converting when the market price of the stock reaches $32 per share ($1,000 divided by 31.25 shares). However, this assumes the investor paid face value for the bonds. In Exercise 3, investors purchased the bonds at a discount of 89.55% of face value or $895.50 for each $1,000 bond. Therefore, investors in Barnes's bonds could consider converting at a lower price of approximately $28.66 per share ($895.50 divided by 31.25). In Exercise 4, the investors paid a premium for the bonds because they were purchased at 111.68% of face value ($558,420 divided by $500,000). These investors would not be interested in converting until the price rose to $35.74 ($1,116.80 divided by 31.25 shares).

VII. Demonstration Problems

Demonstration Problem #1 Solved and Explained

1.

12/1	Cash		75,000	
	Notes Payable			75,000
12/31	Interest Expense		500	
	Interest Payable			500

The company needs to accrue interest expense for December, calculated as follows: $75,000 \times .08 \times 1/12 = $500

2.

a.

12/10	Cash		60,000	
	Unearned Revenues			60,000
12/31	Unearned Revenues		18,000	
	Revenues Earned			18,000

b.

12/10	Cash		10,000	
	Unearned Revenues			10,000
12/31	No entry as no work had begun on the contract.			

3. No entry required. However, the footnotes to the balance sheet should contain information about this lawsuit. This is an example of a contingent liability.

4.

12/31	Salary Expense		145,000	
	Salary Payable			145,000
	Vacation Pay Expense		2,900	
	Estimated Vacation Pay Liability			2,900

The matching principle requires that the additional expense of vacation pay be included with December's other expenses. The calculation is $145,000 × .02 = $2,900. As employees claim their vacation pay, the entry is:

Estimated Vacation Pay Liability	XX	
Cash		XX

(Of course, vacation pay is subject to taxes just as salaries are.)

5.

Accounts Receivable	445,200	
Sales		420,000
Sales Tax Payable		25,200

12/31	Warranty Expense	1,980	
	Estimated Warranty Liability		1,980

The warranty expense is based on the cost to the company of repairing or replacing each unit. Therefore, the estimate is calculated as follows:

Unit sales × estimate × cost to repair/replace = 1,200 × .03 × $55 = $1,980

Estimating warranty expense is another example of the matching principle.

Demonstration Problem #2 Solved and Explained

Requirement 1

	A	B	C	D	E
Semi-annual Interest Date	Interest Payment (5% of Maturity Value)	Interest Expense (4.5% of Preceding Bond Carrying Value)	Premium Amortization (A - B)	Premium Account Balance (D - C)	Bond Carrying Value ($500,000 + D)
1/1/01				30,000	530,000
7/1/01	25,000	23,850	1,150	28,850	528,850
1/1/02	25,000	23,798	1,202	27,648	527,648
7/1/02	25,000	23,744	1,256	26,392	526,392
1/1/03	25,000	23,688	1,312	25,080	525,080

Study Tip: As the premium is amortized, the carrying amount moves toward the maturity value.

Requirement 2

a.　1/1/01　　Cash ($500,000 × 106/100)　　　　　　　　　　530,000
　　　　　　　　　　Premium on Bonds Payable　　　　　　　　　　　　　30,000
　　　　　　　　　　Bonds Payable　　　　　　　　　　　　　　　　　　500,000
　　　　　　　　To issue 10%, 10-year bonds at a premium.

The bonds were sold at 106, indicating that investors were willing to pay a premium of $30,000 to earn 10% of interest on $500,000 of principal over a 10-year period. This is to be expected because the bond is paying 10% annual interest at a time when the market rate of interest is only 9%.

b.　7/1/01　　Interest Expense ($25,000 - $1,150 amortization)　　23,850
　　　　　　　Premium on Bonds Payable　　　　　　　　　　　1,150
　　　　　　　　　Cash　　　　　　　　　　　　　　　　　　　　　25,000
　　　　　　　　To pay interest and amortize bond premium for six months.

Note that the amortization of the premium has the effect of reducing interest expense from the stated rate ($25,000) to the market rate ($23,850). If the bond is sold at a discount, the interest expense is increased from the stated rate to the market rate.

c.　9/30/01　　Interest Expense ($12,500 - $601 amortization)　　11,899
　　　　　　　Premium on Bonds Payable ($1,202 × 3/6)　　　　601
　　　　　　　　　Interest Payable　　　　　　　　　　　　　　　　12,500
　　　　　　　　To accrue three months' interest and amortize three months' premium.

d.　1/1/02　　Interest Expense ($12,500 - $601 amortization)　　11,899
　　　　　　　Interest Payable　　　　　　　　　　　　　　　12,500
　　　　　　　Premium on Bonds Payable ($1,202 × 3/6)　　　　601
　　　　　　　　　Cash　　　　　　　　　　　　　　　　　　　　　25,000
　　　　　　　　To pay semiannual interest, part of which was accrued, and amortize three months' premium on bonds payable.

In this entry, six months of interest is actually paid to the bondholders on January 1. Note, however, only half (three months' worth) of the interest is current accounting period expense; the remaining amount represents the payment of the September 30 accrual of three months' interest.

e.　1/2/02　　Bonds Payable　　　　　　　　　　　　　　500,000
　　　　　　　Premium on Bonds Payable　　　　　　　　　27,648
　　　　　　　Extraordinary Loss on Retirement on Bonds　　12,352
　　　　　　　　　Cash ($500,000 × 108/100)　　　　　　　　　　540,000
　　　　　　　　To record the retirement of bonds payable at 108, retired before maturity.

This entry removes the Bonds Payable and related Premium account from the corporate records, and records the extraordinary loss on retirement. The carrying value of the bonds ($527,648) is less than the cost to call the bonds ($540,000) resulting in the $12,352 loss. Had the price paid to call the bonds been less than the carrying value, the entry would have recorded an extraordinary gain. Extraordinary gains and losses are reported separately on the income statement.

Points to Remember

The interest rate stated on a debt instrument such as a corporate bond will typically differ from the actual market rate of interest when the bond is ultimately issued to the public. This occurs because of the lag in time that frequently occurs between the approval of the bond by the corporation (and regulatory agencies), its actual printings, and, finally, its issuance to the public. Rather than reprint the bond and potentially miss the rapidly changing market interest rate again, bonds are sold at a discount or premium. Occasionally, bonds are sold at face amount.

A bond is sold at a discount when the stated interest rate of the bond is below the current market rate. A premium is paid when the contract rate is higher than interest rates paid by comparable investments.

Premiums and discounts are, in effect, an adjustment to the interest rates. Thus, premiums and discounts should be amortized over the life of the bond.

Study Tip:

1. A good rule to remember is that Bonds Payable are always recorded at the face amount of the bond. Premiums and discounts are recorded in separate accounts.

2. The actual interest paid to the bondholders at the periodic payment dates (generally, semiannually) will always be the face value of the bond multiplied by the stated interest rate. A discount or premium will not affect these periodic cash payments.

The carrying amount (or book value) of a bond is conceptually similar to the book value of a fixed asset. Premiums are added to the face amount of bonds payable, and discounts are subtracted.

	Bonds Payable
+	Bond Premium or
-	Bond Discount
=	Carrying Value

Note that bonds sold at a premium will have a carrying amount greater than the face amount owed and discounted bonds will have a smaller value. In both cases, the carrying value will always move toward the face amount of the bond as the discount or premium is amortized. (Because of this, it is possible to quickly double-check your amortization entries—be sure the bond carrying value is moving in the right direction.)

CHAPTER 9—STOCKHOLDERS' EQUITY

CHAPTER OVERVIEW

Chapters 4 to 8 have provided a detailed examination of assets and liabilities, two of the three sections on the balance sheet. We now turn our attention to the third section, stockholders' equity. The term refers to one of the three legal forms of business organization—a corporation. The corporate form is more complex than sole proprietorships or partnerships. Although sole proprietorships are greater in number, corporations account for more revenues and total assets than the others. The learning objectives for this chapter are to

1. Explain the advantages and disadvantages of incorporation
2. Measure the effect of issuing stock on a company's financial position
3. Describe how treasury stock transactions affect a company
4. Account for dividends and measure their impact on a company
5. Use different stock values in decision making
6. Evaluate a company's return on assets and return on stockholders' equity
7. Report stockholder equity transactions on the statement of cash flows

CHAPTER REVIEW

Objective 1 - Explain the advantages and disadvantages of incorporation.

1. A corporation is a **separate legal entity** chartered and regulated under state law. The owners' equity of a corporation is held by stockholders as shares of stock.
2. A corporation has **continuous life**. A change in ownership of the stock does not affect the life of the corporation.
3. **Mutual agency of owners is not present** in corporations. A stockholder cannot commit a corporation to a binding contract (unless that stockholder is also an officer of the corporation).
4. Stockholders have **limited liability**. That is, they have no personal obligation for the debts of the corporation.
5. **Ownership and management are separated.** Corporations are controlled by boards of directors who appoint officers to manage the business. Boards of directors are elected by stockholders. Thus, stockholders are not obligated to manage the business; ownership is separate from management.
6. **Corporations pay taxes**: state franchise taxes and federal and state income taxes. Corporations pay dividends to stockholders who then pay personal income taxes on their dividends. This is considered double taxation of corporate earnings.
7. Corporations are subject to more **government regulation** than sole proprietorships or partnerships. States monitor corporations more closely and require them to disclose information to investors and creditors.

Corporations come into existence when a **charter** is obtained from a relevant state official. **Bylaws** are then adopted. The stockholders elect a **board of directors**, who appoint the officers of the corporation. (Review Exhibits 9-1 and 9-2 in your text.)

Stockholders have four basic **rights**:

1. to participate in management by voting their shares
2. to receive a proportionate share of any dividend
3. to a proportionate share of the assets remaining after payment of liabilities in the event of liquidation
4. to maintain a proportionate ownership in the corporation (**preemptive right**)

Stockholders' equity is reported differently than owners' equity of a proprietorship or a partnership because corporations must report the sources of their capital. These sources are **paid-in or contributed capital** from sale of stock, and **retained earnings**. Generally, paid-in capital is not subject to withdrawal. Retained Earnings is the account that at any time is the sum of earnings accumulated since incorporation, minus any losses, and minus all dividends distributed to stockholders.

Owners receive **stock certificates** for their investment. The basic unit of investment is a **share**. A corporation's outstanding stock is the shares held by stockholders. (See Exhibit 9-3 in the text.)

Stocks may be **common** or **preferred** and have a **par value** or **no-par value. Par value** is an arbitrary value that a corporation assigns to a share of stock. Different classes of common or preferred stock may also be issued. Each class of common or preferred stock is recorded separately. Preferred stockholders receive their dividends before common stockholders and take priority over common stockholders in the receipt of assets if the corporation liquidates. (Review Exhibits 9-4 and 9-5 in your text.)

The corporate charter specifies the number of shares a corporation is authorized to issue. The corporation is not required to issue all the stock that has been authorized.

Objective 2 - Measure the effect of issuing stock on a company's financial position.

If a corporation sells common stock for cash equal to the par value, the entry to record the transaction is:

Cash	XX	
Common Stock		XX

Par value is usually set low enough so that stock will not be sold below par. A corporation usually sells its common stock for a price above par value, that is, at a premium. The **premium** is also paid-in capital, but is recorded in a separate account called **Paid-In Capital in Excess of Par Value**. A premium is not a gain, income, or profit to the corporation. A corporation cannot earn a profit or incur a loss by buying or selling its own stock. The entry to record stock issued at a price in excess of par value is:

Cash	XX	
Common Stock		XX
Paid-in Capital in Excess of Par—Common Stock		XX

If no-par common stock has no stated value, the entry is the same as for a cash selling price equal to par value (above). Accounting for no-par common stock with a stated value is identical to accounting for par value stock. When a corporation receives noncash assets as an investment, the assets are recorded by the corporation at their current market value.

Accounting for preferred stock follows the same pattern as accounting for common stock. The difference is that instead of the word "Common," the word "Preferred" will appear in the titles of the general ledger accounts.

When noncash assets are contributed to the corporation in exchange for shares of stock, a potential conflict may arise. Investors may think these contributed assets are "worth" more, which means they would receive more shares of stock. The corporation, however, may think the noncash assets are worth a lesser amount. This poses an ethical dilemma. How do you define (and, in this case, quantify) "current market value"? The ethical course of action is to rely on good-faith estimates from independent appraisers to determine fair market value at the time of the exchange.

Objective 3 - Describe how treasury stock transactions affect a company.

Stock which a corporation issues and later reacquires is called **treasury stock**. Treasury stock does not receive dividends and has no voting rights. Corporations may want treasury stock for distribution within the company, to support or raise the market price, to try to increase net assets by buying low and selling high, or to avoid a takeover. The entry to record the purchase of treasury stock is:

Treasury Stock, Common	XX	
Cash		XX
(Shares × market price per share)		

The debit balance in the Treasury Stock account reduces total stockholders' equity.

> **Study Tip:** Treasury stock is *not* an asset, and the corporation *never* incurs a gain or loss by dealing in its own stock.

The purchase of treasury stock does not alter the number of shares authorized or issued. To determine the number of shares outstanding, take the issued number and deduct the number of shares of treasury stock. The result is the number of shares outstanding.

When treasury stock is sold, the entry to record the transaction depends on the relationship between the selling price and the cost of the treasury stock. The entry to record the sale of treasury stock at cost is:

Cash	XX	
Treasury Stock, Common		XX

The entry to record the sale of treasury stock above cost is:

Cash (Shares × Current price)	XX	
Treasury Stock, Common (Shares × Orig. price)		XX
Paid-in Capital from Treasury Stock		XX

The entry to record the sale of treasury stock below cost is:

Cash	XX	
Paid-in Capital from Treasury Stock	XX	
Treasury Stock, Common		XX

Note that when treasury stock is sold, the Treasury Stock account is credited for the original cost of the treasury stock. Any difference between cost and selling price is recorded in the Paid-in Capital from Treasury Stock account. However, this Paid-In Capital Account cannot have a debit balance. If necessary, the Retained Earnings account may be debited if there is no balance in the Paid-In Capital account and the treasury stock's reissue price is less than its original cost. (Review Exhibit 9-7 in your text.)

A corporation that is replacing issues of stock or is liquidating may repurchase its own stock and retire it. Like treasury stock, retired stock produces neither a gain nor a loss.

Retained Earnings is the account that holds all the corporation's net income less net losses and less dividends declared, accumulated over the life of the business. A deficit or debit balance means net losses have exceeded net incomes. Income Summary is closed to Retained Earnings at the end of each period. Retained Earnings is not a fund of cash.

A **dividend** is a distribution of cash (or stock) to the stockholders of a corporation. A corporation must have Retained Earnings and sufficient cash (or stock) in order to declare a dividend. A dividend must be declared by the board of directors before the corporation can pay it. Once a dividend has been declared, it is a legal liability of the corporation.

On the **date of declaration** the board also announces the **date of record** and the **payment date**. Those owning the shares on the date of record will receive the dividend. The payment date is the date the dividends are actually mailed.

Objective 4 - Account for dividends and measure this impact on a company.

When a dividend is declared, this entry is recorded:

Retained Earnings	XX	
Dividends Payable		XX

Dividends Payable is a current liability.

The date of record falls between the declaration date and the payment date and requires no journal entry. The dividend is usually paid several weeks after it is declared. When it is paid, this entry is recorded:

Dividends Payable	XX	
Cash		XX

Preferred stockholders have priority over common stockholders for the receipt of dividends. In other words, common stockholders do not receive dividends unless the total declared dividend is sufficient to pay the preferred stockholders first.

Preferred stock usually carries a stated percentage rate or a dollar amount per share. Thus, if par value is $100 per share, "6% preferred," stockholders receive a $6 ($100 × 6%) annual dividend. Stockholders holding "$3 preferred" stock would receive a $3 annual cash dividend regardless of the par value of the stock. The dividend to common stockholders will equal:

Common dividend = Total dividend - Preferred dividend

A dividend is passed when a corporation fails to pay an annual dividend to preferred stockholders. Passed dividends are said to be in arrears. **Cumulative preferred stock** continues to accumulate annual dividends until the dividends are paid. Therefore, a corporation must pay all dividends in arrears to cumulative preferred stockholders before it can pay dividends to other stockholders.

Dividends in arrears are not liabilities, but are disclosed in notes to the financial statements. Preferred stock is considered cumulative unless it is specifically labeled as noncumulative. Noncumulative preferred stock does not accumulate dividends in arrears.

Corporations declare **stock dividends** instead of cash dividends when they want to conserve cash or reduce the market price per share of stock. Unlike cash dividends, stock dividends are not distributions of corporate assets. A stock dividend is a proportional distribution of the corporation's stock to its stockholders. Thus, a stock dividend affects only a corporation's stockholders' equity accounts; the result of a stock dividend is a reduction in Retained Earnings, an increase in contributed capital, and total stockholders' equity stays the same.

The effect of declaring a stock dividend is to transfer a portion of Retained Earnings to Common Stock. In the event of a small stock dividend, a portion of Retained Earnings is also transferred to Paid-in Capital in Excess of Par—Common in order to reflect the excess of market value over par. However, large stock dividends are usually accounted for at par value.

Small stock dividends (less than 20-25%) are accounted for at market value on the declaration date. The entry is:

Retained Earnings	XX	
Common Stock Dividend Distributable		XX
Paid-in Capital in Excess of Par—Common		XX

The amount of the debit to Retained Earnings is equal to

No. of Shares Outstanding × Dividend % × Market Price Per Share

The credit to Common Stock Dividend Distributable is equal to

No. of Shares Outstanding × Dividend % × Par Value Per Share

The credit to Paid-in Capital in Excess of Par—Common is equal to

No. of Shares Outstanding × Dividend % × (Market Price - Par)

On the date of distribution of a small stock dividend, the par value of the issued stock is transferred from the Dividend Distributable account to the Stock account:

Common Stock Dividend Distributable	XX	
Common Stock		XX

A **stock split** increases the number of outstanding shares and proportionately reduces the par value of the stock. A stock split affects only the par value of the shares and the number of shares outstanding. No account balances are affected.

Both stock splits and stock dividends increase the number of shares outstanding and may decrease the market price per share. The difference between stock splits and stock dividends is that a stock split changes the par value of the stock, while a stock dividend leaves the par value of the stock unchanged; also a stock dividend requires a transfer from Retained Earnings while a stock split requires no journal entry. (See Exhibit 9-9 in your text.)

Objective 5 - Use different stock values in decision making.

Market value (market price) is the price at which a person could buy or sell a share of the stock. Daily newspapers report the market price of many publicly traded stocks.

Sometimes preferred stock can be redeemed by the corporation for a stated amount per share. This amount, which is set when the stock is issued, is called **redemption value**.

Book value is the amount of stockholders' equity per share of stock. If only common stock is outstanding,

$$\text{Book value} = \frac{\text{Total stockholders' equity}}{\text{Number of shares outstanding}}$$

If both preferred and common stocks are outstanding, preferred stockholders' equity must be calculated first. If preferred stock has no redemption value, then total preferred equity in the equation below is equal to the balance in Preferred Stock. If preferred stock has a redemption value, then total preferred equity in the equation below equals the total redemption value (redemption value per share × number of preferred shares).

$$\text{Preferred book value} = \frac{\text{Total preferred equity + Dividends in arrears}}{\text{Number of preferred shares outstanding}}$$

$$\text{Common book value} = \frac{\text{Total equity - (Total preferred equity + Dividends in arrears)}}{\text{Number of common shares outstanding}}$$

> **Study Tip:** Remember, if there is treasury stock, issued shares and outstanding shares will be different numbers.

Objective 6 - Evaluate a company's return on assets and return on stockholders' equity.

1. $$\text{Rate of return on total assets} = \frac{\text{Net income + Interest expense}}{\text{Average total assets}}$$

The return on total assets (or return on assets) measures how successful the company was in using its (average) assets to earn a profit.

2. $$\text{Rate of return on common stockholders' equity} = \frac{\text{Net income - Preferred dividends}}{\text{Average common stockholders' equity}}$$

The denominator, average common stockholders' equity, is equal to total stockholders' equity minus preferred equity.

The rate of return on common stockholders' equity also measures the profitability of the company. The return on equity should always be higher than the return on assets.

Objective 7 - Report stockholders' equity transactions on the statement of cash flows.

Transactions affecting stockholders' equity are reported on the statement of cash flows as financing activities. These activities fall into three groups: issuing stock, paying dividends, and repurchasing stock. When a company receives cash in exchange for shares of stock, the total amount received is reported as an inflow of cash. When cash dividends are paid (note paid, not declared), the total amount disbursed is reported as a cash outflow.

Study Tip: Stock dividends are not reported on the statement of cash flows because no cash in involved.

When a company repurchases its stock (thereafter called treasury stock), the total amount paid is reported as a cash outflow.

TEST YOURSELF

All the self-testing materials in this chapter focus on information and procedures that your instructor is likely to test in quizzes and examinations.

I. Matching   *Match each numbered term with its lettered definition.*

_____ 1. authorized stock
_____ 2. book value
_____ 3. chairperson of the board
_____ 4. convertible preferred stock
_____ 5. cumulative stock
_____ 6. stockholder
_____ 7. stated value
_____ 8. rate of return on total assets
_____ 9. market value
_____ 10. outstanding stock
_____ 11. stock dividend
_____ 12. preferred stock
_____ 13. stockholders' equity
_____ 14. retained earnings
_____ 15. stock split

_____ 16. board of directors
_____ 17. bylaws
_____ 18. charter
_____ 19. common stock
_____ 20. deficit
_____ 21. dividends
_____ 22. limited liability
_____ 23. paid-in capital
_____ 24. treasury stock
_____ 25. par value
_____ 26. preemptive right
_____ 27. date of record
_____ 28. declaration date
_____ 29. incorporators

A. an increase in the number of authorized, issued, and outstanding shares of stock coupled with a proportionate reduction in the stock's par value
B. the amount of stockholders' equity the company has earned through profitable operations and has not given back to the stockholders
C. the amount of stockholders' equity that stockholders have contributed to the corporation
D. a debit balance in the Retained Earnings account
E. a group elected by the stockholders to set policy for a corporation and to appoint its officers
F. the date on which the liability for a dividend is determined
G. an arbitrary amount assigned to no-par stock
H. a shareholder's right to maintain a proportionate ownership in a corporation
I. an arbitrary amount assigned to a share of stock
J. an elected person on a corporation's board of directors who is usually the most powerful person in the corporation
K. a person who owns the stock of a corporation
L. distributions by a corporation to its shareholders
M. means that the most that a stockholder can lose on his investment in a corporation's stock is the cost of the investment
N. the stockholders' ownership interest in the assets of a corporation
O. a proportional distribution by a corporation of its own stock to its stockholders
P. preferred stock that may be exchanged by the stockholders, if they choose, for another class of stock in the corporation
Q. preferred stock whose owners must receive all dividends in arrears before the corporation pays dividends to the common stockholders
R. persons who organize a corporation
S. shares of stock in the hands of stockholders

T. stock that gives its owners certain advantages such as the priority to receive dividends and the priority to receive assets if the corporation liquidates

U. the maximum number of shares of stock a corporation may issue

V. the amount of owners' equity on the company's books for each share of its stock

W. the sum of net income plus interest expense divided by average total assets

X. the constitution for governing a corporation

Y. a corporation's own stock that it has issued and later reacquired

Z. the document that gives the state's permission to form a corporation

AA. the date that determines who will received a declared dividend

BB. the most basic form of capital stock

CC. the price for which a person could buy or sell a share of stock

II. Multiple Choice   *Circle the best answer.*

1. The corporate board of directors is

    A. appointed by the state
    B. elected by management
    C. elected by the stockholders
    D. appointed by corporate officers

2. A stockholder has no personal obligation for corporation liabilities. This is called

    A. mutual agency
    B. limited agency
    C. transferability of ownership
    D. limited liability

3. The correct order for pertinent dividend dates is

    A. declaration date, record date, payment date
    B. record date, declaration date, payment date
    C. declaration date, payment date, record date
    D. record date, payment date, declaration date

4. A stock certificate shows all of the following *except*

    A. additional paid-in capital
    B. stockholder name
    C. par value
    D. company name

5. The ownership of stock entitles common stockholders to all of the following rights *except*

    A. right to receive guaranteed dividends
    B. voting right
    C. preemptive right
    D. right to receive a proportionate share of assets in a liquidation

6. When a corporation declares a cash dividend

   A. liabilities decrease, assets decrease
   B. assets decrease, retained earnings decreases
   C. assets decrease, retained earnings increases
   D. liabilities increase, retained earnings decrease

7. When a corporation pays a cash dividend

   A. liabilities decrease, assets increase
   B. assets decrease, retained earnings decreases
   C. liabilities decrease, assets decrease
   D. retained earnings decrease, liabilities increase

8. When a company issues stock in exchange for assets other than cash, the assets are recorded at

   A. market value
   B. original cost
   C. book value
   D. replacement cost

9. Dividends Payable is a(n)

   A. expense
   B. current liability
   C. paid-in capital account
   D. stockholders' equity account

10. Dividends in arrears on preferred stock are reported

    A. on the balance sheet
    B. as a reduction of retained earnings
    C. on the income statement
    D. as a footnote to the financial statements

11. Small stock dividends are recorded at

    A. par value
    B. market value
    C. book value
    D. carrying value

12. The market price of a share of Nafpak Corporation's common stock is $90. If Nafpak declares and issues a 50% stock dividend, the market price will adjust to approximately

    A. $45
    B. $180
    C. $135
    D. $60

13. The Common Stock Dividend Distributable account is reported in which section of the balance sheet?

    A. current liabilities
    B. long-term liabilities
    C. current assets
    D. stockholders' equity

14. The purchase of treasury stock will

    A. decrease assets
    B. increase liabilities
    C. increase stockholders' equity
    D. have no effect on stockholders' equity

15. The purchase of treasury stock decreases the number of

    A. authorized shares
    B. outstanding shares
    C. issued shares
    D. both B and C

III. Completion   *Complete each of the following.*

1. Every corporation issues _____ stock.
2. _____ stock does not receive cash dividends.
3. Preferred stockholders have preference over common stockholders in _____ and
   _____.
4. Dividends are declared by _____.
5. A corporation may buy treasury stock in order to _____
   _____
   _____.
6. Stockholders' equity minus preferred equity equals _____.
7. The date of _____ determines who receives the dividend.
8. The date of _____ establishes the liability to pay a dividend.
9. A _____ occurs when a stockholder returns shares to the corporation and
   receives fewer shares in the exchange.
10. Corporations come into existence when a _____ is approved by the
    _____ government.

IV. True/False   *For each of the following statements, circle T for true or F for false.*

1. T F   Dividends paid is a cash outflow reported as a financing activity on the statement of cash flows.
2. T F   To calculate the rate of return on total assets, net income is added to income tax expense then divided by average total assets.
3. T F   Both preferred stock and common stock have stated liquidation values.
4. T F   A 50% stock dividend is the same as a 3 for 2 stock split.
5. T F   Small stock dividends are recorded at market value as of the record date.
6. T F   Noncumulative preferred stock is rare, most preferred stock is cumulative.
7. T F   When a cash dividend is paid, assets and stockholders' equity decrease.

8.   T F   When treasury stock is sold at a price greater than the price at which it was acquired, a gain results.

9.   T F   Treasury stock carries a debit balance and is reported in the asset section of the balance sheet.

10.   T F   Retired stock differs from treasury stock in that retired stock cannot be reissued.

11.   T F   Preferred stock is assumed to be cumulative unless it is specifically labeled as noncumulative.

12.   T F   Issued stock and outstanding stock refer to the same number of shares of stock.

13.   T F   The correct order for items listed in the stockholders' equity section of the balance sheet is preferred stock, common stock, retained earnings.

14.   T F   The preemptive right refers to a shareholder receiving a proportionate share of assets upon liquidation.

15.   T F   When a corporation issues only one class of stock, that stock is called common stock.

V. Exercises

1. Shoppers.com declared a cash dividend of $1.10 a share on common stock on November 10. The dividend was paid on December 20 to stockholders of record on December 1. Shoppers.com has 2,250,000 shares of common stock outstanding.

Prepare the journal entry on November 10.

Date	Accounts and Explanation	PR	Debit	Credit

Prepare the journal entry on December 1.

Date	Accounts and Explanation	PR	Debit	Credit

Prepare the journal entry on December 20.

Date	Accounts and Explanation	PR	Debit	Credit

2. The charter of Estrada-Knox, Inc., authorizes the issuance of 100,000 shares of preferred stock and 5,000,000 shares of common stock. During the first month of operation, Estrada-Knox, Inc., completed the following stock-issuance transactions:

February 1   Issued 600,000 shares of $1 par common stock for cash of $18 per share.
February 10   Issued 20,000 shares of 7%, no-par preferred stock with a stated value of $50 per share. The issue price was $50 per share.
February 28   Received inventory valued at $80,000 and equipment with a market value of $120,000 in exchange for 20,000 shares of $1 par common stock.

Record the necessary journal entries for the above three transactions (omit explanations).

Date	Account	Debit	Credit

3. Using your answers from Exercise 2 above, prepare the stockholders' equity section of the Estrada-Knox, Inc., balance sheet at the end of the first month. Assume Retained Earnings has a balance of $25,000.

Stockholders' Equity	

4. CIFER Corporation has 10,000 shares of $100 par, cumulative, 5% preferred stock outstanding. There were no dividends in arrears at the end of 2000, and no dividends were paid in 2001 or 2002. CIFER also has 20,000 shares of $1 par common stock outstanding.

   A. If CIFER pays a total of $220,000 in dividends in 2003, how much will each class of stockholders receive?

   B. If CIFER pays a total of $140,000 in dividends in 2003, how much will each class of stockholders receive?

5. Indicate the effect of each of the following transactions on Assets, Liabilities, Paid-in Capital, and Retained Earnings. Use + for increase, - for decrease, and 0 for no effect.

	Assets	Liabilities	Paid-in Capital	Retained Earnings
A. Declaration of a cash dividend	_____	_____	_____	_____
B. Payment of a cash dividend	_____	_____	_____	_____
C. Declaration of a stock dividend	_____	_____	_____	_____
D. Issuance of a stock dividend	_____	_____	_____	_____
E. A stock split	_____	_____	_____	_____
F. Cash purchase of treasury stock	_____	_____	_____	_____
G. Sale of treasury stock below cost	_____	_____	_____	_____

6. Major-Minor Corporation had 800,000 shares of $10 par common stock outstanding on March 1. Prepare journal entries for the following transactions:

3/15   Declared a 5% stock dividend. The market price was $60 per share.
3/30   Issued the stock dividend.

Date	Account and Explanation	PR	Debit	Credit

7. Prepare journal entries for the following transactions:

2/10   Purchased 800 shares of $5 par treasury stock for $24 per share.
7/1   Sold 500 shares of treasury stock for $28 per share.
12/12 Sold 300 shares of treasury stock for $16 per share.

Date	Account and Explanation	PR	Debit	Credit

VI. Critical Thinking

Review the facts in Exercise 6 with the following changes:

10/10   Declared a 21-for-20 stock split. The market price was $60 per share.
10/30   Issued the shares.

Present the journal entries for the above stock split.

_____

_____

_____

_____

_____

VII. Demonstration Problems

Demonstration Problem #1

On January 1, 2002, the State of California Corporation Department authorized Audio.com to issue 500,000 shares of 6%, $50 par cumulative preferred stock and 1,000,000 shares of common stock with a no par or stated value. During its start-up phase, the company completed the following selected transactions related to its stockholders' equity:

1/10 Sold 300,000 shares of common stock at $22 per share.
1/11 Issued 10,000 shares of preferred stock for cash of $55 per share.
1/17 Issued 40,000 shares of common stock in exchange for equipment valued at $700,000.
1/24 An old building and small parcel of land were acquired by the corporation for a future office site that would employ 60 people. The site value was $1,000,000; the building was worthless. Audio.com issued 80,000 shares of common stock for the site and building.
1/31 Earned a small profit for January and closed the $12,000 credit balance of Income Summary into the Retained Earnings account.

Required:

1. Record the transactions in the general journal.
2. Post the journal entries into the equity accounts provided.
3. Prepare the stockholders' equity section of Audio.com balance sheet at January 31, 2002.
4. Compute the book value per share of the preferred stock and the common stock. The preferred stock has a liquidation value of $52.50 per share. No dividends are in arrears.

Requirement 1 (journal entries)

Date	Accounts and Explanation	PR	Debit	Credit

Requirement 2 (postings)

Requirements 3 (Stockholders' equity section)

Audio.com
Balance Sheet—Stockholders' Equity Section
January 31, 2002

Requirement 4 (book value per share)

Demonstration Problem #2

Dynamic Dot Com reported the following stockholders' equity:

Stockholders' Equity:
Preferred stock, 8%, $25 par value	
Authorized—1,000,000 shares	
Issued 150,000 shares	$ 3,750,000
Common stock $1 par value	
Authorized—5,000,000 shares	
Issued—800,000 shares	800,000
Paid-in capital in excess of par—common	6,000,000
Retained earnings	6,855,180
Less: Treasury stock, at cost (2,000 common shares)	14,000
Total stockholders' equity	$17,419,180

Required: (Work space to complete each of these questions is provided on the following pages.)

1. What was the average issue price per share of the common stock?
2. What was the average issue price per share of the preferred stock?
3. Assume that net income for the year was $825,000. Journalize the entry to close net income to Retained Earnings.
4. Assume the board of directors declares dividends totaling $1,797,000 to the shareholders. The preferred stock is cumulative and no dividends were declared last year. Calculate the amount per share each class of stock will receive.
5. Journalize the issuance of 10,000 additional shares of common stock at $22.50 per share. Use the same account titles as shown in the problem.
6. How many shares of common stock are outstanding after the 10,000 additional shares have been sold?
7. How many shares of common stock would be outstanding after the corporation split its common stock 2 for 1? What is the new par value?
8. Journalize the declaration of a 10% stock dividend on common stock when the market price of the stock is $11.25 per share. Assume the stock dividend is declared after the 2-for-1 split.
9. Journalize the following treasury stock transactions in the order given:
   A. Dynamic Dot Com purchases 2,500 shares of treasury stock at $25 per share.
   B. One month later, the corporation sells 1,000 shares of the same treasury stock for $27 per share (credit Paid-in Capital from Treasury Stock Transactions).
   C. An additional 1,000 shares of treasury stock acquired in (9A) are sold for $22 per share.

Work Space

1.

2.

3.

Date	Account and Explanation	PR	Debit	Credit

4.

5.

Date	Account and Explanation	PR	Debit	Credit

6.

7.

8.

Date	Account and Explanation	PR	Debit	Credit

9.

A.

Date	Account and Explanation	PR	Debit	Credit

B.

Date	Account and Explanation	PR	Debit	Credit

C.

Date	Account and Explanation	PR	Debit	Credit

SOLUTIONS

I. Matching

1. U	5. Q	9. CC	13. N	17. X	21. L	25. I	29. R
2. V	6. K	10. S	14. B	18. Z	22. M	26. H	
3. J	7. G	11. O	15. A	19. BB	23. C	27. AA	
4. P	8. W	12. T	16. E	20. D	24. Y	28. F	

II. Multiple Choice

1. C   Each share of common stock usually gives the stockholder one vote in the election of the board of directors.

2. D   Mutual agency is a characteristic of partnerships not present in corporations. Transferability of ownership is a characteristic that the corporate form of organization simplifies. Limited agency has no meaning.

3. A   The board of directors declares a dividend on the declaration date, to stockholders of record on the record date that is paid on the payment date.

4. A   Additional paid-in capital is the excess of the price paid to the corporation over the par value of the stock.

5. A   Dividends represent the distribution of the earnings of the corporation and are not guaranteed.

6. D   The declaration of a dividend reduces Retained Earnings and increases the liability account, Dividends Payable.

7. C   The payment of a cash dividend results in cash being paid to stockholders to settle the liability created by the declaration of the dividend.

8. A   When capital stock is issued in exchange for noncash assets, the transaction should be recorded at fair market value.

9. B   The declaration of a dividend by the board of directors creates a current liability.

10. D   Dividends in arrears is not a liability since a dividend must be declared to create a liability. However, dividends in arrears do impair the amount of capital available to common stockholders. Dividends in arrears are usually disclosed by a footnote.

11. B   A small stock dividend is accounted for at market value on the date of declaration.

12. D   If the market price for one share of pre-dividend stock is $90, then approximately the same market value will apply to the 1.5 shares of post-dividend stock since the stockholder's percentage ownership in the corporation has not changed. $90 / 1.5 shares = $60 per share.

13. D   Common Stock Dividend Distributable represents the new shares of stock that will be issued as a result of the declaration of the stock dividend.

14. A   Treasury Stock, a contra stockholders' equity account, is acquired by purchasing it; cash is decreased and stockholder's equity is decreased.

15. B   Treasury stock has been, and still is, authorized and issued, but it is no longer outstanding.

III. Completion

1. common (Corporations may also issue preferred stocks, but that is optional.)
2. Treasury
3. receiving dividends and in event of a liquidation
4. the board of directors
5. avoid a takeover; support the market price of the stock; distribute to employees; buy low and sell high
6. common stockholders' equity
7. record
8. declaration
9. reverse stock split
10. charter; state

IV. True/False

1. T
2. F   Net income is added to interest expense, not income tax expense.
3. F   Only preferred stock will have a liquidation value—common shareholders simply receive a proportionate share of assets remaining after all creditors have been paid and the preferred shareholders have received their cash (liquidation value plus dividends in arrears).
4. F   This is a very "tricky" statement. It is true that a 50% stock dividend will result in the same numbers of shares as a 3 for 2 stock split. However, the stock dividend results in additional shares having the same par (or stated) value as the original shares, whereas the stock split results in shares having a lesser par (or stated) value.
5. F   Small stock dividends are recorded at market value as of the declaration date, the date when the liability is established.
6. T
7. F   The payment of a cash dividend results in a decrease in assets and liabilities—stockholders' equity is not affected.
8. F   A gain (or loss) is never recorded on treasury stock transactions.
9. F   Treasury stock is reported in the stockholders' equity section, as a reduction
10. T
11. T
12. F   Outstanding stock refers to the number of shares of stock held by owners. Issued stock refers to the total number of shares the corporation has ever sold. If there is treasury stock, the outstanding shares will equal issued shares less the treasury shares.
13. T
14. F   The preemptive right allows a current shareholder to purchase additional shares in proportion to the owner's current amount.
15. T

V. Exercises

1.

Date	Accounts and Explanation	Debit	Credit
11/10	Retained Earnings	2,475,000	
	Dividends Payable		2,475,000
	(2,250,000 shares × $1.10)		
12/1	No entry		
12/20	Dividends Payable	2,475,000	
	Cash		2,475,000

2.

Date	Account	Debit	Credit
2/1	Cash	10,800,000	
	Common Stock (600,000 × $1.00)		600,000
	Paid-in Capital in Excess of Par Value [600,000 × ($18 - $1)]		10,200,000
2/10	Cash	1,000,000	
	Preferred Stock (20,000 × $50)		1,000,000
2/28	Merchandise Inventory	80,000	
	Equipment	120,000	
	Common Stock (20,000 × $1)		20,000
	Paid-in Capital in Excess of Par Value ($200,000 - $20,000)		180,000

3.

Stockholders' Equity

Paid-in capital:

Preferred stock, 7%, no-par, $50 stated value, 100,000 shares authorized, 20,000 shares issued	$ 1,000,000
Common stock, $1 par, 5,000,000 shares authorized, 620,000 shares issued	620,000
Paid-in capital in excess of par—common stock	10,380,000
Total paid-in capital	12,000,000
Retained earnings	25,000
Total stockholders' equity	$12,025,000

4.

A. Preferred: 3 years × 10,000 shares × $100 par × 5% = $150,000 (or $15 per share)
   Common: $220,000 - $150,000 = $70,000 (or $3.50 per share)

B. Preferred: 3 years × 10,000 shares × $100 par × 5% = $150,000

Since $140,000 is less than the $150,000 preferred stockholders must receive in dividends before common stockholders receive anything, all $140,000 goes to the preferred stockholders. The common shareholders receive nothing, and the preferred now have $10,000 dividends in arrears.

5.

	Assets	Liabilities	Paid-in Capital	Retained Earnings
A. Declaration of a cash dividend	0	+	0	-
B. Payment of a cash dividend	-	-	0	0
C. Declaration of a stock dividend	0	0	+	-
D. Issuance of a stock dividend	0	0	0	0
E. A stock split	0	0	0	0
F. Cash purchase of treasury stock	-	0	0*	0*
G. Sale of treasury stock below cost	+	0	-**	-**

*While a cash purchase of treasury stock does not affect Paid-in Capital or Retained Earnings, it does reduce stockholders' equity.

**The sale may reduce one or the other, or both. In addition, the sale also increases total stockholders' equity, by the amount of the credit to Treasury Stock.

6.

Date	Account and Explanation	Debit	Credit
3/15	Retained Earnings	2,400,000	
	(800,000 × .05 × $60)		
	Common Stock Dividend Distributable		400,000
	(800,000 × .05 × $10)		
	Paid-in Capital in Excess of Par—Common		2,000,000
	[800,000 × .05 × ($60 - $10)]		
3/30	Common Stock Dividend Distributable	400,000	
	Common Stock		400,000

7.

Date	Account and Explanation	Debit	Credit
2/10	Treasury Stock (800 × $24)	19,200	
	Cash		19,200
7/1	Cash	14,000	
	Treasury Stock (500 × $24)		12,000
	Paid-in Capital from Treasury Stock Transactions		2,000
	[($28 - 24) × 500]		

12/12	Cash (300 × $16)	4,800	
	Paid-in Capital from Treasury Stock Transactions	2,000	
	Retained Earnings	400	
	Treasury Stock (300 × $24)		7,200

The July 1 transaction resulted in a $2,000 balance in the Paid-in Capital account. This credit balance is not large enough to absorb the entire $2,400 difference between the treasury stock cost and its selling price (300 shares × $8). Therefore, the Paid-in Capital account is debited up to its credit balance ($2,000) and the excess is charged against Retained Earnings. The Paid-in Capital account cannot carry a debit balance.

VI. Critical Thinking

No journal entries are required when a company declares a stock split. The outstanding shares are returned to the company and replaced with new shares. Each new share will have a par value of $9.52 ($10 divided by 21/20). The total paid-in capital remains unchanged, however.

VII. Demonstration Problems

Demonstration Problem #1 Solved and Explained

Requirement 1 (journal entries)

1/10	Cash	6,600,000	
	Common Stock (300,000 × $22)		6,600,000
	Sold common stock at $22 per share.		

The receipt of cash is recorded by debiting Cash and crediting Common Stock for the number of shares times the par value of the stock. When the stock has no par or stated value, the Common Stock account is credited for the number of shares times the selling price.

1/11	Cash (10,000 × $55)	550,000	
	Preferred Stock (10,000 × $50)		500,000
	Paid-in Capital in Excess of Par—		
	Preferred Stock (10,000 × $5)		50,000
	Issued preferred stock at a premium.		

Preferred Stock is credited for the shares times par (10,000 × $50). The balance is recorded in the premium account, Paid-in Capital in Excess of Par—Preferred Stock.

1/17	Equipment	700,000	
	Common Stock		700,000
	To issue common stock in exchange for equipment.		

When a corporation issues stock in exchange for an asset other than cash, it debits the asset received (in this case, Equipment) for its fair market value and credits the capital accounts as it would do if cash were the asset received.

1/24	Land	1,000,000	
	Common Stock		1,000,000
	Issued 80,000 shares of common stock for land.		

1/31	Income Summary	12,000	
	Retained Earnings		12,000
	To close Income Summary by transferring net income to Retained Earnings.		

At the end of each month or year, the balance of the Income Summary account is transferred to Retained Earnings. Audio.com earned a small profit in January. The closing entry will debit Income Summary (to reduce it to zero) and credit Retained Earnings (increasing stockholders' equity to reflect profitable operations).

Requirement 2 (posting)

Preferred Stock	
	1/11 500,000
	Bal. 500,000

Common Stock	
	1/10 6,600,000
	1/17 700,000
	1/24 1,000,000
	Bal. 8,300,000

Paid-in Capital in Excess of Par— Preferred Stock	
	1/11 50,000
	Bal. 50,000

Retained Earnings	
	1/31 12,000
	Bal. 12,000

Requirement 3 (stockholders' equity section)

Audio.com
Balance Sheet—Stockholders' Equity Section
January 31, 2002

Stockholders' equity:	
Preferred stock, 6%, $50 par, 500,000 shares authorized	$ 500,000
Paid-in capital in excess of par—Preferred stock	50,000
Common stock, 10,000,000 shares authorized	8,300,000
Total paid-in capital	8,850,000
Retained earnings	12,000
Total stockholders' equity	$8,862,000

Requirement 4 (book value per share)

Preferred:	
Liquidation value (10,000 shares × $52.50)	$ 525,000
Cumulative dividends in arrears	0
Stockholders' equity allocated to preferred	525,000
Book value per share ($525,000 / 10,000 shares)	$ 52.50
Common:	
Total stockholders' equity	$8,862,000
Less: Stockholders' equity allocated to preferred	525,000
Stockholders' equity allocated to common	8,337,000

Book value per share ($8,337,000 / 420,000 shares) $ 19.85

Calculated as follows:

Date	No. of Shares	Transactions
1/10	300,000	Issued
1/17	40,000	Issued
1/24	80,000	Issued
	420,000 shares	

Demonstration Problem #2 Solved and Explained

1. Average issue price of the common stock was $8.50 per share:

Common stock at par ($1 × 800,000 shares)	$800,000
Paid-in capital in excess of par—common	6,000,000
Total paid in for common stock	6,800,000
÷ number of issued shares	÷ 800,000
Average issue price	$8.50

2. Average issue price of the preferred stock was $25 per share:

Preferred stock at par ($25 × 150,000 shares)	$3,750,000
Paid-in capital in excess of par—preferred	0
Total paid in for preferred stock	3,750,000
÷ number of issued shares	÷150,000
Average issue price	$ 25.00

3. Income Summary   825,000
       Retained Earnings   825,000

4. Preferred: $2 per share (8% × $25) × 2 years = $4 per share
                $4 per share × 150,000 shares = $600,000

   Common: $1,197,000 available ($1,797,000 less $600,000 to preferred)
             $1,197,000 ÷ 798,000 shares = $1.50 per share

   Note there are 800,000 shares of common stock issued but only 798,000 outstanding because 2,000 shares are in the treasury. Treasury stock does not receive dividends.

5. Cash (10,000 shares × $22.50 selling price)   225,000
       Common Stock (10,000 × $1)   10,000
       Paid-in Capital in Excess of Par—Common   215,000
   To issue common stock at a premium.

6. Shares outstanding = 808,000
   810,000 shares issued* less 2,000 shares treasury stock = 808,000

* 800,000 shares issued, plus 10,000 shares from answer 5 above.

7. Shares outstanding after 2-for-1 split = 1,616,000:
    808,000 shares outstanding immediately before split × 2/1 = 1,616,000 shares outstanding
    The new par value of the common stock is $0.50 ($1.00 × 1/2)

8.

Retained Earnings (1,616,000 outstanding shares × 10% × $11.25)	1,818,000	
Common Stock Dividend Distributable (161,600 × $.50)		80,800
Paid-in Capital in Excess of Par—Common (161,600 shares × $10.75 premium)		1,737,200
To declare a 10% stock dividend.		

When a *small stock dividend* occurs, Retained Earnings should be capitalized for the *fair market* value of the shares to be distributed (in this case, 1,818,000). Note that 1,616,000 shares were outstanding after answer 7 above, and that the 2-for-1 stock split reduces par value to $0.50 per share. The 10% distribution was for 161,600 shares (1,616,000 × 10% = 161,600).

9. A.

Treasury Stock (2,500 × $25)	62,500	
Cash		62,500
To purchase 2,500 shares of treasury stock at $25 per share.		

B.

Cash (1,000 × $27)	27,000	
Treasury Stock (1,000 × $25)		25,000
Paid-in Capital from Treasury Stock Transactions		2,000
To sell 1,000 shares of treasury stock at $27 per share.		

C.

Cash (1,000 × $22)	22,000	
Paid-in Capital from Treasury Stock Transactions	2,000	
Retained Earnings	1,000	
Treasury Stock (1,000 × $25)		25,000
To sell 1,000 shares of treasury stock at $22 per share.		

A company does not earn income on the purchase and sale of its own stock. The sale of treasury stock results in an increase to paid-in capital, not income. Paid-in Capital from Treasury Stock Transactions (a paid-in capital account is *credited* for sales in excess of cost (as in answer 9b) and *debited* for a sale below cost). If the account balance is not large enough to cover a sale below cost, it may be necessary to debit Retained Earnings (as in answer 9C).

CHAPTER 10—LONG-TERM INVESTMENTS AND INTERNATIONAL OPERATIONS

CHAPTER OVERVIEW

In Chapter 9, you learned about capital stock from the perspective of the issuing corporation. In Chapter 8 we examined long-term liabilities and how corporations account for bonds payable and other obligations. Now we expand these topics but change the perspective. Corporations frequently purchase stocks and bonds as investments. In addition, we learn about parent and subsidiary relationships and foreign currency transactions. The specific learning objectives for this chapter are to

1. Account for available-for-sale investments
2. Use the equity method for investments
3. Understand consolidated financial statements
4. Account for long-term investments in bonds
5. Account for transactions stated in a foreign currency
6. Interpret a foreign-currency translation adjustment
7. Report investing transactions on the statement of cash flows

CHAPTER REVIEW

Objective 1 - Account for available-for-sale investments.

Stocks are traded in markets. Prices are quoted in dollars and one-eighth fractions of a dollar (occasionally you will see quotes in 1/16 and even 1/32 of a dollar). The owner of a stock is the investor. The corporation that issues the stock is the investee.

Stock investments are assets to the investor. **Short-term investments** (sometimes called **marketable securities**) are 1) liquid (readily convertible to cash) and 2) expected to be converted to cash within one year. **Long-term investments** are 1) expected to be held for longer than one year or 2) not readily marketable. Stock investments fall into two categories: 1) trading securities or 2) available-for-sale securities. It is important you understand the distinction between the two types! **Trading securities** are always classified as current assets because the investor's intent is to hold them for only a short time in the hopes of earning profits on price changes. When a stock investment is acquired but the intent is not to capture profits from price changes immediately, the investment is classified as an **available-for-sale security**. Trading securities, by definition, are always current assets whereas available-for-sale securities could be either current or long term.

As with all assets, available-for-sale securities are recorded at cost. Thereafter, however, they are reported at their **current market value**. Any cash dividends received are credited to an appropriate revenue account. Stock dividends do not trigger an entry. Rather, the portfolio is updated to reflect the additional shares. At the end of the accounting period, the market value of the securities is determined and compared with the balance in the investments accounts. If the market value is greater, the following adjusting entry is recorded for the difference:

Allowance to Adjust Investment to Market	XX	
Unrealized Gain on Investment		XX

When the market value of the available-for-sale security is less than the balance in the account, the adjustment is:

Unrealized Loss on Investment	XX	
Allowance to Adjust Investment to Market		XX

The Allowance to Adjust Investment to Market account is a companion account to the Investment account. Recall that a companion account is added to (or subtracted from) a related account. With available-for-sale securities, the Allowance account increases/decreases the Investment account depending on its balance. If the Allowance account has a debit balance the effect is to increase the Investment account. If the Allowance account has a credit balance the effect is to decrease the Investment account.

> **Study Tip**: The Allowance to Adjust Investment to Market account is used regardless of an increase or decrease in the market value. Compare the current market value with the carrying value of the investment and adjust accordingly, always using the Allowance account.

Unrealized gains (losses) occur when there are changes in the value of the investment. They are reported in two places in the financial statements, as (1) other comprehensive income (either on the income statement below net income or on a separate comprehensive income statement) and (2) accumulated other comprehensive income in the stockholders' equity section of the balance sheet.

When a long-term investment is sold, a gain or loss on the sale will result when the proceeds are greater than (a gain) or less than (a loss) the carrying value of the long-term investment. These gains and losses are realized and therefore reported on the income statement as "Other Revenue and Expense" after the operating income.

> **Study Tip**: Realized gains (and losses) only occur when an investment is sold. Unrealized gains (and losses) result from changes in value; however, the investor continues to own the stock.

Objective 2 - Use the equity method for investments.

The **equity method** is used when an investor holds between 20% and 50% of an investee's voting stock because the investor may exert significant influence on the investee's business decisions.

The investment is recorded at cost. Debit Long-Term Investment and credit Cash.

The investor records his proportionate ownership of the investee's net income and dividends. If the investor owns 40% of the voting stock, the investor will record 40% of the net income as revenue and will receive 40% of the dividends. The share of income is recorded with a debit to the Long-Term Investment account and a credit to Equity-Method Investment Revenue. The receipt of cash dividends reduces the investment. Therefore, the dividend is recorded with a debit to Cash and a credit to the Long-Term Investment account. Equity-Method Investment Revenue is reported as "Other Revenue" on the income statement.

When the equity method is used and an investment is sold, the gain (or loss) on the sale is the difference between the proceeds and the balance in the investment account.

Objective 3 – Understand consolidated financial statements.

An investor who owns more than 50% of an investee's voting stock has a controlling (majority) interest. The investor is called the **parent company**, and the investee is called the **subsidiary**. See Exhibits 10-3 and 10-4 in your text. Parent-subsidiary relationships are very common.

Consolidation accounting combines the financial statements of two or more companies that are controlled by the same owners. The assets, liabilities, revenues, and expenses of the subsidiary are added to the parent's accounts.

A separate set of books for the consolidated entity does not exist. The consolidation is accomplished by the use of a work sheet such as Exhibit 10-7 in your text. Transactions that affect both the parent and the subsidiary must be eliminated from the consolidation. These transactions are called **intercompany transactions** and include loans between parent and subsidiary, the parent's investment in the subsidiary, and the subsidiary's equity accounts. **Goodwill** is recorded during the consolidation process if the parent buys the subsidiary for a price above book value.

A **minority interest** will appear on the consolidated balance sheet when the parent company owns more than 50% but less than 100% of the subsidiary's stock. Minority interest usually is recorded as a liability on the consolidated balance sheet. Study Exhibit 10-8 in your text to see how minority interest is recorded in the work sheet for the consolidated balance sheet.

Consolidated income is equal to the net income of the parent plus the parent's proportionate interest in the subsidiary's net income.

Objective 4 - Account for Long-Term Investment in Bonds.

Investors purchase bonds issued by corporations. The investor can purchase short-term (current asset) or long-term (long-term investment) bonds.

Short-term investments in bonds are rare. More commonly, companies purchase bonds as long-term investments, known as **held-to-maturity investments**. When acquired, these held-to-maturity bonds are recorded at cost. Thereafter they are reported on the balance sheet at their **amortized cost**. This means the balance in the Long-Term Investment account reflects both the initial cost of the bond plus or minus a portion of the discount (an addition to the account) or premium (a reduction to the account) on the bond. No Discount or Premium account is used. If the bonds were initially purchased at a discount, the balance in the Long-Term Investment account increases as the bonds approach maturity. If the bonds were initially purchased at a premium, the balance in the Long-Term Investment account decreases as the bonds approach maturity. The amortization of the bond discount would appear as follows:

Long-Term Investment in Bonds	XX	
Interest Revenue		XX

Study Tip: From the buyer's perspective, a discount means additional interest revenue while a premium means less interest revenue. This effect is exactly the opposite from the perspective of the issuer.

Carefully review the Discussion Guideline in your text. It presents an excellent summary of the rules governing stock and bond investments.

Objective 5 - Account for transactions stated in a foreign currency.

International accounting deals with business activities that cross national boundaries. Each country uses its own national currency; therefore, a step has been added to the transaction—one currency must be converted into another.

The price of one nation's currency stated in terms of another country's currency is called the **foreign currency exchange rate**. The conversion of one currency into another currency is called **translation**. Exchange rates are determined by supply and demand. The main factors influencing the supply and demand for a particular country's currency are: 1) the ratio of a country's imports to its exports, and 2) the rate of return available in the country's capital markets.

A strong currency is rising relative to other nations' currencies, and a weak currency is falling relative to other currencies.

When Company A in Country A purchases goods from Company B in Country B, the transaction price may be stated in the currency of either country. Suppose the transaction is stated in Country A's currency. The transaction requires two steps:

1. The transaction price must be translated for recording in the accounting records of Company B.
2. When payment is made, Company B may experience a foreign-currency translation gain or loss. This gain or loss results when there is a change in the exchange rate between the date of the purchase on account and the date of the subsequent payment of cash.

Note that there will be no foreign-currency gain or loss for Company A because the transaction price was stated in the currency of Country A.

The net amount of Foreign-Currency Transaction Gains and Losses are combined for each accounting period and reported on the income statement as Other Revenue and Expense.

Hedging is a means of protecting the company from foreign currency transaction losses by purchasing a **futures contract**, the right to receive a certain amount of foreign currency on a particular date.

Objective 6 - Interpret a foreign currency translation adjustment.

United States companies with foreign subsidiaries must consolidate the subsidiary financial statements into their own for external reporting. This can cause two problems:

1. GAAP may be different in the foreign country. (See Exhibit 10-11)
2. When the foreign subsidiary's financial statements are translated into dollars, there may be a translation adjustment. (See Exhibit 10-10)

A **foreign-currency translation adjustment** arises because of changes in exchange rates over time. Assets and liabilities are translated using exchange rates as of the balance sheet date. Stockholders' equity, including revenues and expenses, are translated using the exchange rates that were in effect when those transactions were executed (this results in stockholders' equity not equaling assets minus liabilities). The adjustment necessary to bring the subsidiary's balance sheet back into balance ("translation adjustment") is reported as part of stockholders' equity on the consolidated balance sheet. The translation adjustment will be positive when the book value of the investment in the foreign subsidiary has increased. A negative amount reflects a reduction.

Objective 7 - Report investing transactions on the statement of cash flows.

The purchase and sale of stock and bond investments are reported on the statement of cash flows in the investing activities section. Revenues from Dividends and Interest Revenue (from bonds) are operating activities because they are reported in the income statement. However, the actual purchase of investments is listed as a cash outflow in the investing activities section of the cash flow statement while the proceeds from the sale of investments will appear as a cash inflow. Carefully review the statement for Campbell Soup Company (Exhibit 10-12) in your text.

TEST YOURSELF

All the self-testing materials in this chapter focus on information and procedures that your instructor is likely to test in quizzes and examinations.

I. Matching   *Match each numbered term with its lettered definition.*

_____ 1.   consolidated statements
_____ 2.   marketable securities
_____ 3.   controlling interest
_____ 4.   held-to-maturity investments
_____ 5.   equity method for investments
_____ 6.   foreign currency exchange rate
_____ 7.   short-term investment
_____ 8.   hedging
_____ 9.   long-term investment
_____ 10. trading securities

_____ 11. minority interest
_____ 12. parent company
_____ 13. available-for-sale securities
_____ 14. strong currency
_____ 15. subsidiary company
_____ 16. foreign-currency translation adjustment
_____ 17. weak currency
_____ 18. market value method

A. short-term investments
B. the balancing figure that brings the dollar amount of the total liabilities and stockholders' equity of a foreign subsidiary into agreement with the dollar amount of total assets
C. stocks and bonds held for the short term with the intent of realizing profits from increases in prices
D. combine the balance sheets, income statements, and other financial statements of the parent with those of the majority-owned subsidiaries into an overall set as if the separate entities were one
E. currency whose exchange rate is rising relative to other nations' currencies
F. investee company in which a parent owns more than 50% of the voting stock
G. investor company that owns more than 50% of the voting stock of a subsidiary company
H. stocks and bonds not held with the intent of realizing profits from increases in prices
I. method used to account for investments in which the investor can significantly influence the decisions of the investee
J. bonds and notes that investors intend to hold to maturity
K. ownership of more than 50% of an investee company's voting stock
L. an investment that is readily convertible to cash and that the investor intends to convert to cash within one year or to use to pay a current liability
M. separate asset category reported on the balance sheet between current assets and plant assets
N. strategy to avoid foreign currency transaction losses
O. subsidiary company's equity that is held by stockholders other than the parent company
P. the price of one country's currency stated in terms of another country's monetary unit
Q. currency whose exchange rate is decreasing relative to other nations' currencies
R. used to account for all available-for-sale securities

II. Multiple Choice   *Circle the best answer.*

1. A stock is listed in *The Wall Street Journal* as having a High of 45 1/4, a Low of 43, a Close of 43 1/2, and a Net Change of +1 1/4. What was the previous day's closing price?

    A. $46.50
    B. $41.75
    C. $44.75
    D. $42.25

2. Assets listed as Short-term Investments on the balance sheet are

    A. only liquid
    B. listed on a national stock exchange
    C. only intended to be converted to cash within one year
    D. liquid and intended to be converted to cash within one year

3. Available-for-sale securities are reported on the balance sheet at

    A. current cost
    B. historical cost
    C. lower of cost or market
    D. market value

4. Intercompany payables and receivables are eliminated in the consolidated entries so that

    A. assets will not be overstated
    B. liabilities will not be understated
    C. stockholders' equity will not be understated
    D. net income will not be overstated

5. All of the following accounts are eliminated in the consolidated work sheet entries *except*

    A. investment in subsidiary
    B. subsidiary's cash
    C. subsidiary's common stock
    D. subsidiary's retained earnings

6. The minority interest account is usually classified as a(n)

    A. revenue
    B. expense
    C. liability
    D. asset

7. The rate at which one unit of a currency can be converted into another currency is called the foreign-currency:

   A. market rate
   B. interest rate
   C. exchange rate
   D. conversion rate

8. A strong currency has an exchange rate that is

   A. inelastic with respect to other nations' currencies
   B. inelastic with respect to its balance of trade
   C. increasing relative to other nations' currencies
   D. decreasing relative to other nations' currencies

9. Available-for-sale securities are

   A. stock investments only
   B. bond investments only
   C. the same as held-to-maturity investments
   D. those other than trading securities

10. An unrealized gain (or loss) results from

    A. available-for-sale securities
    B. trading securities
    C. held-to-maturity securities
    D. all of the above

III. Completion   *Complete each of the following statements.*

1. The price at which stock changes hands is determined by the _____.
2. Two main factors that determine the supply and demand for a particular currency are the country's _____ and _____.
3. Investments in stock are initially recorded at _____.
4. The _____ method is used to account for investments when the investor can significantly influence the actions of the investee.
5. A(n) _____ is ownership of at least 50% of the voting stock of a company.
6. Goodwill is a(n) _____ asset.
7. A change in the currency exchange rates between the date of purchase and the date of payment will result in a(n) _____.
8. Cash used to purchase bonds is reported on the statement of cash flows as a(n) _____ activity.
9. When a parent owns less than 100% of a subsidiary, the other owners are called the _____.
10. Unrealized gains and losses are reported on the _____ in the _____ section.

IV. True/False
For each of the following statements, circle T for true or F for false.

1. T F The interest received on bonds held as a long-term investment is reported as an investing activity on the statement of cash flows.

2. T F Foreign-currency transaction gains/losses are reported on the income statement as other revenues/expenses.

3. T F If the U. S. dollar strengthens relative to a foreign currency between the time a receivable is billed and payment received, a foreign-currency transaction gain will result.

4. T F Foreign-currency translation adjustments are reported on the income statement as other revenues/expenses.

5. T F The presence of a minority interest on a corporation's balance sheet indicates the corporation owns less than 50% of another company.

6. T F When the equity method is used, the parent's investment account is adjusted at the end of the accounting period to reflect the investment's current market value.

7. T F When bonds are purchased at a discount and held as a long-term investment, the carrying value of the investment increases over time.

8. T F When bonds are purchased at a premium and held as a long-term investment, the difference between the face value of the bonds and the premium is reflected in a companion account called Premium on Investment.

9. T F Goodwill results when a business is purchased at a price in excess of the fair market value of the net assets acquired.

10. T F The total amount of stockholders' equity reported on a consolidated balance sheet equals the total parent's stockholders' equity plus the total subsidiary's stockholders' equity.

11. T F A Gain on Sale of Investment is treated as an addition to stockholders' equity on the balance sheet.

12. T F When the equity method is used, it is assumed the investor can influence the investee.

13. T F Unrealized gains result from the sale of available-for-sale investments.

14. T F The Allowance to Adjust to Market account is a companion to the Investment account.

15. T F The receipt of a stock dividend on an available-for-sale investment results in a lower cost per share of the investment.

V. Exercises

1. Martha Company purchased 110,000 shares of Stewart Corporation on January 1, 2002, for $600,000. Stewart Corporation has 1,375,000 shares outstanding. Stewart earned income of $300,000 and paid dividends of $100,000 during 2002. Stewart Corporation stock was trading at 9 3/8 on 12/31/02.

   A. What method should be used to account for the investment in Stewart?

   B. How much revenue will be recorded by Martha in 2002 from the investment in Stewart?

   C. What is the balance in Martha's Investment account at the end of 2002?

2. Wanker Company purchased 40% of Jo Corporation on January 1, 2002, for $12,000,000. Jo Corporation earned income of $1,600,000 and paid dividends of $400,000 during 2002.

   A. What method should be used to account for the investment in Jo Corporation?

   B. How much revenue will be recorded by Wanker Co. in 2002 from the investment in Jo Corporation?

   C. What is the balance in the Investment account at the end of 2002?

3. Peanut Company invested in Brittle Corporation on January 1, 2002, by purchasing 60% of the total stock of Brittle Corporation for $675,000. Brittle Corporation had common stock of $400,000 and retained earnings of $725,000.

   A. What amount of Minority Interest will appear on a consolidated balance sheet prepared on January 1, 2002?

   B. If Peanut Company owes Brittle Corporation $72,000 on a note payable, prepare the two elimination entries in general journal form.

Date	Account and Explanation	Debit	Credit

4. Hunter Company purchased 100% of the common stock of Prey Corporation for $1,315,000. Prey Corporation showed common stock of $280,000 and retained earnings of $510,000. Compute the amount of goodwill resulting from the purchase.

5. Prepare journal entries for the following available-for-sale stock investment:

6/10   Purchased 6,000 shares of Amazing.com common stock at 35 1/4, plus a broker's commission of $200.

10/2   Received a $.90 per share cash dividend.

11/15   Sold 1,000 shares at 40 1/4 per share, less a commission of $80.

12/31   Amazing.com stock closed at $42 1/8.

Date	Account and Explanation	Debit	Credit

6. Prepare journal entries for the following foreign currency transactions.

1/5   Purchased 5,000 cases of dry cider from a British wholesaler for 4.55 pounds sterling per case. Today's exchange rate is $1.67 = 1 pound sterling.

1/20   Purchased 2,000 cases of red wine from a cooperative in Coustouge, France. The price was 64 francs per case. Today's exchange rate is $1.00 = 5.50 French francs.

2/10   Paid the British wholesaler. Today's exchange rate is $1.61 = 1 pound sterling.

3/20   Paid for the French wine. Today's exchange rate is $1.00 = 5.10 French francs.

Date	Account and Explanation	Debit	Credit

VI. Critical Thinking

Review the information in Exercise 5 and change the 10/2 entry to the following:

10/2 Received a 15% stock dividend. The stock was trading at $38 per share.

Prepare journal entries for 6/10, 10/2, 11/15, and 12/31.

Date	Account and Explanation	Debit	Credit

VII. Demonstration Problems

Demonstration Problem #1

On 12/31/02, Global Corporation paid $375,000 for 90% of the common stock of Local Corporation. Local owes Global $60,000 on a note payable. Complete the following work sheet:

	Global Company	Local Company	Eliminations Debit	Credit	12/31/02 Consolidated Amounts
Assets:					
Cash	58,000	26,000			
Note receivable from Local	60,000	-			
Investment in Local	375,000	-			
Goodwill	-	-			
Plant & equipment, net	218,000	328,000			
Other assets	37,000	92,000			
Total	748,000	446,000			
Liabilities and Stockholders' Equity:					
Accounts payable	38,000	41,000			
Notes payable	170,000	125,000			
Minority interest					
Common stock	500,000	110,000			
Retained earnings	40,000	170,000			
Total	748,000	446,000			

Requirement 2

Using the following form, present a consolidated balance sheet for Global Corporation.

Global Corporation
Consolidated Balance Sheet
12/31/02

Demonstration Problem #2

At 12/31/01, Meyer Corporation had the following long-term investments in its portfolio:

	Cost	Market Value
Available-for-sale securities		
4,000 shares Ajax, Inc.	$25 1/8	$28
10,000 shares Dot.com	10 3/8	18 ½
3,800 shares Handy Co.	48	37 3/4
2,500 shares TJCO	63 ½	66 1/4
Held-to-maturity bonds		
$100,000, 9% BioLabs, Inc., due 10/1/2008	$100,000	$100,000

Requirement 1

In the space below, present the long-term investments as they would appear on Meyer Corporation's 12/31/01 balance sheet. None of the stock investments are influential. The bonds pay interest semi-annually on 4/1 and 10/1.

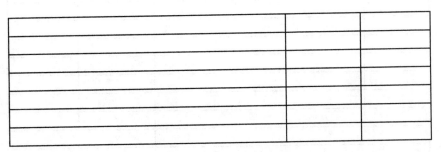

Requirement 2

Record the following 2002 events related to Meyer Corporations' long-term investments:

Ajax, Inc.—these shares paid quarterly dividends of $.15/share on 2/10 and 5/10. The shares were sold on 7/2 for $32/share, less a broker's commission of $185.

Dot.com—these shares pay no cash dividends; however, a 10% stock dividend was received on 8/10. The investment remained in the portfolio at the end of the year, at which time its market value was $24 1/4 per share.

Handy Co.—these shares continued to decline in value throughout January, and management decided to sell them on 2/8 for $31/share, less a commission of $205.

TJCO—these shares remained in the portfolio throughout the year. On 9/15 the stock split 3 for 2. At year end, the shares were trading for $55/share.

BioLabs, Inc.—checks for interest were received 4/1 and 10/1. The bonds remained in the portfolio at year end.

On 6/5/02, Meyer Corporation paid $9.50 a share for 300,000 shares of iTight.com. This ownership represents 30% of the iTight.com outstanding shares and is influential. iTight.com paid 2 cents per share dividends on 8/10 and 11/10 and reported an $850,000 net loss at year end. The stock was trading at $9 on 12/31/02.

On 11/1/99 Meyer Corporation purchased $250,000, 10-year, 6% bonds from Wood, Inc. The bonds pay semiannual interest on 5/1 and 11/1 and were purchased at 97.

Date	Account and Explanation	Debit	Credit

Requirement 3

Record the necessary adjusting entries.

Date	Account and Explanation	Debit	Credit

Requirement 4

Present the long-term investments as they would appear on Meyer Corporation's 12/31/02 balance sheet, taking into consideration the events described in Requirement 2 above.

SOLUTIONS

I. Matching

1. D	5. I	9. M	13. H	17. Q
2. A	6. P	10. C	14. E	18. R
3. K	7. L	11. O	15. F	
4. J	8. N	12. G	16. B	

II. Multiple Choice

1.   D   The High is the previous day's highest price, the Low is the lowest price of the previous day. The Close is the last price at which the stock traded yesterday. Net Change is the increase (+) or decrease (-) in the Close compared to the previous day. The previous day's close is 43 1/2 - 1 1/4 or $43.50 - $1.25 = $42.25.

2.   D   Note that besides the determinable liquidity of the investment, the intent of management determines an investment's classification as a short-term investment.

3.   D   GAAP requires trading securities to be reported on the balance sheet at market value.

4.   A   Failure to eliminate intercompany payables and receivables would result in the overstatement of both assets and liabilities of the consolidated entity. Accordingly, of the items listed, only A is correct.

5.   B   Elimination is not intended to remove the assets and liabilities of the subsidiary. The intent of elimination is to remove only those things that would double up or be counted twice if not eliminated, such as intercompany payables and receivables and the investment in subsidiary and subsidiary stockholders' equity.

6.   C   The Minority Interest account represents the ownership interest of parties outside of the parent-subsidiary relationship. In actual practice it is most often reported as part of the liability section on the balance sheet.

7.   C   The exchange rate is used to convert one currency into another.

8.   C   Strong currencies are those that increase relative to other currencies.

9.   D   Available-for-sale securities are stock investments other than trading securities and bond investments other than trading securities and held-to-maturity securities.

10.   A   Unrealized gains (or losses) are a result of the market value method applied to available-for-sale securities.

III. Completion

1. market (the market allows buyers and sellers with opposing interests to arrive at a price acceptable to both)
2. import/export ratio, rate of return available in its capital markets

3. cost
4. equity
5. controlling interest
6. intangible
7. foreign-currency transaction gain or loss
8. investing
9. minority interest
10. balance sheet; stockholders' equity

IV. True/False

1. F   The interest is an operating activity. However, the purchase/sale of the bonds is an investing activity.
2. T
3. F   A foreign-currency transaction loss will result if the foreign currency has weakened relative to the U. S. dollar.
4. F   Translation adjustments are reported on the balance sheet (in the stockholders' equity section), not the income statement.

Study Tip: Remember—transactions on the income statement, translations on the balance sheet.

---

5. F   When a minority interest is listed on the balance sheet, it means the parent owns less than 100% of the subsidiary's stock.
6. F   The equity method ignores market value. When the equity method is used, the Investment account balance equals the original cost plus the investor's proportionate share of profits less dividends (and less the proportionate share of any losses).
7. T
8. F   When bonds are purchased at either a premium or discount and held as a long-term investment, the bonds are reported at their amortized cost. No premium or discount account is used.
9. T
10. F   The subsidiary's stockholders' equity is eliminated against the parent's Investment account, not added to the parent's stockholders' equity.
11. F   A gain on sale is a realized gain and therefore reported on the income statement. Only unrealized gains/losses are reported on the balance sheet.
12. T
13. F   Unrealized gains are not the result of external transactions; rather, they reflect an increase in the carrying value of an investment.
14. T
15. T

V. Exercises

1. A. market value
    B. 8% of $100,000 = $8,000 dividend revenue
    C. $1,031,250 ($600,000 balance in the Investment account plus $431,250 (9 3/8 × 110,000 shares less $600,000) in the Allowance to Adjust Investment account)

2. A. equity method
    B. .40 × $1,600,000 = $640,000
    C. $12,000,000 + $640,000 - (.40 × $400,000) = $12,480,000

3. A. .40 × ($400,000 + $725,000) = $450,000
    B. (1) Note Payable to Brittle   72,000
                Note Receivable from Peanut   72,000
        (2) Common stock (Brittle)   400,000
                Retained earnings (Brittle)   725,000
                   Investment in Brittle   675,000
                   Minority Interest   450,000
        (Note: Refer to Exhibit 10-7 in your text.)

4. $1,315,000 - ($280,000 + $510,000) = $525,000

5.

    6/10   Investment—Amazing.com   211,700
           Cash   211,700
        (6,000 shares × $35.25 plus $200)
        Actual cost/share is 211,700 / 6,000 = $35.283

    10/2   Cash   5,400
           Dividend Revenue   5,400

    11/15   Cash   40,170
           Investment—Amazing.com   35,284   (rounded)
           Gain on Sale of Investment   4,886
        The gain is the difference between the proceeds and our cost. Our cost is 1/6 (1,000 / 6,000 shares) × $211,700 (see 6/10).

    12/31   Allowance to Adjust Investment to Market   34,209
           Unrealized Gain on Investment   34,209
        Our cost basis was $176,416 ($211,700 - $35,284). The current market value is 5,000 × $42 1/8 = $210,625; therefore, $34,209 is needed to adjust the Investment to Market account. Since the $34,209 represents an increase in value, it represents an unrealized gain on the investment.

6.

    1/5   Inventory   37,992.50
         Accounts Payable   37,992.50
      (5,000 cases × 4.55 pounds sterling × $1.67)

    1/20   Inventory   23,272.73
         Accounts Payable   23,272.73
      (2,000 cases × 64 francs / 5.50)

2/10	Accounts Payable	37,992.50	
	Foreign Currency Transaction Gain		1,365.00
	Cash		36,627.50

(5,000 cases × $4.55 pounds sterling × $1.61)

3/20	Accounts Payable	23,272.73	
	Foreign Currency Transaction Loss	1,825.31	
	Cash		25,098.04

(2,000 cases × 64 francs / $5.10)

Because the dollar strengthened relative to the British pound (on 1/5 it took $1.67 to purchase 1 pound sterling - a month later the same pound would only cost $1.61) a foreign-currency transaction gain was realized when we paid the bill. Conversely, the dollar weakened relative to the French franc, so we realized a foreign-currency transaction loss. Foreign-currency transaction gains and losses are reported on the income statement as "Other Revenues and Expenses."

VI. Critical Thinking

6/10	Investment - Amazing.com	211,700	
	Cash		211,700

(6,000 shares × $35.25 plus $200)

10/2 No entry - however we need to note the receipt of the additional 900 shares. We now own 6,900 shares which cost us $211,700, or $30.68 (rounded) per share.

> **Study Tip:** the current trading value of the shares is irrelevant from our perspective. It is only relevant to Amazing.com. They used it to record the charge against Retained Earnings when the dividend was declared.

11/15	Cash	40,170	
	Investment—Amazing.com		30,680
	Gain on Sale of Investment		9,490

Our cost per share was $30.68 (rounded)—see 10/2 details. We sold 1,000 shares at $40.25/share, less the $80 commission. The gain is the difference between our proceeds (1,000 shares × $40.25 less $80) and the cost basis of those shares, $30.68 × 1,000.

12/31	Allowance to Adjust Investment to Market	67,525.50	
	Unrealized Gain on Investment		67,525.50

You need to give some thought to this adjustment. Remember our adjusted cost per share is $30.68 and we have 5,900 shares (the original 6,000 plus the 900 share dividend less the 1,000 shares sold on 11/15.) Therefore, our cost basis for those remaining shares is $181,012 (5,900 shares × $30.68/share). On 12/31 the shares were trading at $42 1/8 ($42.125), so their market value is $248,537.50; the unrealized gain is the difference between $248,537.50 and $181,012 or $67,525.50. Available-for-sale stock securities are reported on the balance sheet at their market value. The amount in the Allowance to Adjust account will be added to the balance in the Investment account, thereby reporting the investment in stock at the market value.

VII. Demonstration Problems

Demonstration Problem #1 Solved and Explained

	Global Company	Local Company	Eliminations Debit	Eliminations Credit	Consolidated Amounts
Assets:					
Cash	58,000	26,000			84,000
Note receivable from Local	60,000	-		(a) 60,000	
Investment in Local	375,000	-		(b) 375,000	
Goodwill	-	-	(b) 123,000		123,000
Plant & equipment, net	218,000	328,000			546,000
Other assets	37,000	92,000			129,000
Total	748,000	446,000			882,000
Liabilities and Stockholders' Equity:					
Accounts payable	38,000	41,000			79,000
Notes payable	170,000	125,000	(a) 60,000		235,000
Minority interest				28,000	28,000
Common stock	500,000	110,000	(b) 110,000		500,000
Retained earnings	40,000	170,000	(b) 170,000		40,000
Total	748,000	446,000	463,000	463,000	882,000

Entry (a) eliminated Global's $60,000 intercompany note receivable against the note payable owed by Local. Note that the consolidated total represents the amount owed to outside creditors ($170,000 owed by Global + $125,000 owed by Local less $60,000 intercompany debt = $235,000).

Entry (b) eliminates Global's $375,000 investment balance against the $280,000 in Local's equity. Global acquired a 90% interest, so the minority interest is $28,000 (10% × $280,000). Goodwill is the difference between the investment ($375,000) and 90% of Local's common stock and retained earnings, or $123,000 ($375,000 - 90% × $280,000).

Requirement 2

Global Corporation
Consolidated Balance Sheet
12/31/02

Assets:	
Cash	$ 84,000
Plant and equipment (net)	546,000
Goodwill	123,000
Other assets	129,000
Total assets	$882,000

Liabilities and Stockholders' Equity

Liabilities
Accounts payable	$ 79,000	
Notes payable	235,000	
Minority Interest	28,000	
Total liabilities and minority interest		342,000

Stockholders' Equity

Common stock	500,000	
Retained earnings	40,000	
Total stockholders' equity		540,000
Total Liabilities and Stockholders' Equity		$882,000

Demonstration Problem #2 Solved and Explained

Requirement 1

Long-term Investments (at market value) $706,075

The cost of the combined long-term investments (both equity and debt) is $645,400, while the 12/31/01 market value of the portfolio is $706,075. Recall that long-term investments are reported on the balance sheet at market value. Prior to the preparation of the balance sheet, an adjusting entry would have been recorded, as follows:

Allowance to Adjust Investment to Market	60,675	
Unrealized Gain on Long-term Investments		60,675

The effect of this adjustment is to increase the investments to their market value. Most companies would report the investments at market value, then report the cost in a footnote. The unrealized gain would be added into the stockholders' equity section. Meyer would also have adjusted for the accrued interest on the BioLabs bond; however, the amount ($2,250) is NOT included with the long-term investments, but reported separately as interest receivable in the current asset section.

Requirement 2

Ajax, Inc.

2/10	Cash	600	
	Dividend Revenue		600
5/10	Cash	600	
	Dividend Revenue		600
7/2	Cash	127,815	
	Long-term Investment		100,500
	Gain on Sale of Investment		27,315

The gain is the difference between the proceeds (4,000 shares × $32/share less the $185 commission) and the cost (4,000 shares × $25 1/8).

Dot.com

8/10   no entry—memo only reflecting 11,000 shares now in the portfolio

Handy Co.

2/8	Cash	117,595	
	Loss on Sale of Investment	64,805	
	Long-Term Investment		182,400

The loss is the difference between the cost (3,800 × $48) and the proceeds (3,800 × $31 less the $205 commission).

TJCO

9/15   no entry—memo only reflecting 3,750 shares now in the portfolio

BioLabs

4/1	Cash	4,500	
	Interest Receivable		2,250
	Interest Revenue		2,250
10/1	Cash	4, 500	
	Interest Revenue		4,500

iTight.com

6/5	Long-term Investment – iTight.com	2,850,000	
	Cash		2,850,000
8/10	Cash	6,000	
	Long-term Investment – iTight.com		6,000
11/10	Cash	6,000	
	Long-term Investment – iTight.com		6,000
12/31	Unrealized Loss on Long-term Investment	255,000	
	Long-term Investment – iTight.com		255,000

Because the investment in iTight.com is influential, the equity method, not the market value method, is used; therefore, dividends received reduce the Investment account balance. Because iTight.com reported a net loss for the year, Meyer's proportional "equity" in the loss is also charged against the Investment account. If iTight.com had reported net income, the Investment account would have been increased.

Wood, Inc.

11/1	Long-term Investment	242,500	
	Cash		242,500

As the purchaser of the bonds, we do not record the $7,500 discount in a contra account.

Requirement 3 (adjusting entries)

12/31	Allowance to Adjust Investments to Market	149,825	
	Unrealized Gain on Long-term Investments		149,825

As of the end of 2001, the Allowance to Adjust account has a debit balance of $60,675 (see Requirement 1 Solution). At the end of 2002, the cost and market values of the remaining available-for-sale equity securities are as follows:

	Cost	Market
Dot.com (11,000 shares)	$103,750	$266,750
TJCO (3,750 shares)	158,750	206,250
Totals	$262,500	$473,000

The iTight.com investment is not included in this adjustment. Why? Because the equity method is used, not the market value method.

These totals reflect a difference of $210,500. Given the existing debit balance of $60,675, we need to adjust for $149,825 to increase the Allowance account to the desired $210,500 figure.

12/31	Interest Receivable	2,250	
	Interest Revenue		2,250
	To adjust accrued interest ($100,000 × .09 × 3/12) on BioLabs bonds		

12/31	Interest Receivable	2,500	
	Long-term Investment	125	
	Interest Revenue		2,625
	To adjust for accrued interest ($250,000 × .06 × 2/12) and amortize the discount ($7,500/10 years × 2/12).		

Recall that long-term investments in bonds must be reported on the balance sheet at their fully amortized cost. When bonds are purchased at a discount, the amortized cost will increase over the life of the bonds. At maturity, the amortized cost will equal the bond's face value.

Requirement 4

Long-term Investments (at market)	$815,625
Long-term Investments (at equity)	$2,608,000

The balance in the Long-term Investments (at market) account consists of the following:

Stocks ($262,500 cost + $210,500 allowance)	$473,000
Bonds BioLabs	100,000
Wood, Inc. ($242,500 + $125)	242,625
Total	$815,625

The balance in the Long-term Investments (at equity) comes from the iTight.com account, as follows:

iTight.com			
6/5	2,850,000	8/10	6,000
		11/10	6,000
		12/31	255,000
Balance	2,583,000		

Interest Receivable will be listed among the current assets, Interest Revenue under "Other Revenues" on the Income Statement, and the Unrealized Gain with stockholders' equity on the balance sheet.

CHAPTER 11—USING THE INCOME STATEMENT AND THE STATEMENT OF STOCKHOLDERS' EQUITY

CHAPTER OVERVIEW

Throughout the last four chapters we have examined a variety of topics related to the balance sheet. In Chapter 7, we looked at plant and intangible assets, in Chapter 8 current and long-term liabilities, in Chapter 9 stockholders' equity, and in Chapter 10, long-term investments and international operations. While each of these topics impacts the income statement, the primary focus was the balance sheet. We now turn our attention to an in-depth examination of the corporate income statement. The learning objectives for this chapter are to

1. Analyze a complex income statement
2. Account for a corporation's income tax
3. Analyze a statement of stockholders' equity
4. Understand managers' and auditors' responsibilities for the financial statements

CHAPTER REVIEW

Objective 1 - Analyze a complex income statement.

Investors may want to examine the trend of a company's earnings and the makeup of its net income. Therefore, the corporation income statement starts with income from continuing operations, follows with income or loss from discontinued operations and extraordinary gains and losses, and concludes with earnings per share of common stock.

Continuing operations are expected to continue in the future. Income from continuing operations helps investors make predictions about future earnings. Income from continuing operations is shown both before and after income tax has been deducted.

One way potential investors evaluate income from continuing operations is to determine the present value of a company's future income, then compare this result with the company's market value. To determine present value, an assumption must be made about an appropriate interest rate (also called the **investment capitalization rate**). To determine **market value**, multiply the number of outstanding shares of common stock times the stock's current selling price. Comparing these two values helps investors evaluate the company. If the estimated value of the company (based on the present value of future earnings) is greater than the current market value of the company, an investor would be more likely to consider the company favorably. Rather than evaluating based on the total market value of the company, an investor could do a similar kind of analysis for a single share of stock. Using the same investment capitalization rate, divide it into the estimated annual earnings per share. If the result is greater than the current market price for one share of stock, the company is considered more favorably as an investment.

When a corporation sells one of its segments, the sale is reported in a section of the income statement called **discontinued operations**. Such sales are viewed as one-time transactions and are therefore not a future source of income. Discontinued operations is separated into an operating component and a disposal component. Each is shown net of its related tax effect.

Extraordinary gains and losses (also called **extraordinary items**) are both unusual and infrequent and are reported net of tax. Extraordinary items are those which are unusual and not likely to occur in the future. Examples are natural disasters, expropriations of business assets by foreign governments, gains and losses on early retirement of debt (the latter were covered in Chapter 8).

On occasion, companies change an accounting method. When this occurs, it is difficult for financial statement users to compare consecutive years' activity unless they are informed of changes. For this reason, the cumulative (total) effect of any **changes in accounting principles** is reported separately. This cumulative effect is also reported net of its related tax effect.

Earnings per share (EPS) of common stock is computed for each source of income or loss: continuing operations, discontinued operations, extraordinary items, and changes in accounting principle.

To compute EPS divide net income by the weighted average number of shares of common stock outstanding.

$$\textbf{Weighted Average = Shares outstanding} \times \textbf{Fraction of year that shares were held}$$

Review the example in your text (p. 504) to be certain that you understand how to compute the weighted average number of shares.

When preferred dividends exist, they must be subtracted from income subtotals (income from continuing operations, income before extraordinary items, and net income) in the computation of EPS. Preferred dividends are not subtracted from income or loss from discontinued operations, and they are not subtracted from extraordinary gains and losses.

Dilution must be considered if preferred stock can be converted into common stock (Chapter 9) because there is the potential for more common shares to be divided into net income. Corporations therefore provide **basic EPS** and **diluted EPS** information.

> **Study Tip**: Review this discussion by comparing each topic with the complex income statement in your text (Exhibit 11-1).

Comprehensive income is the company's change in total stockholders' equity from all sources other than the owners of the business. FASB 130 requires certain companies to report comprehensive income, which includes net income plus some specific gains and losses which are not listed on the income statement. An example of the latter is the foreign-currency translation adjustment discussed in the previous chapter (see Exhibit 11-2 in your text.)

To obtain a better understanding of a company, one needs to analyze more than the income statement. For instance, cash flows (discussed in detail in Chapter 12) should be considered, along with the other financial statements.

Objective 2 - Account for a corporation's income tax.

Because corporations have a distinct legal identity (they have the right to contract, to sue, and be sued--just as individuals have these rights), their income is taxed just like individuals'. However, unlike individuals, the amount of tax actually paid will differ from the expense incurred for the period (for individuals, these amounts are generally the same). The difference results from the following:

Income tax expense is calculated by multiplying the applicable tax rate times the amount of pretax accounting income as reported on the income statement, while income tax payable is calculated by multiplying the applicable tax rate times the amount of taxable income as reported on the corporate tax return. Because these results will differ, a third account, **Deferred Income Tax**, is used to reconcile the difference.

Prior-period adjustments usually occur as the result of correcting an error in a previous accounting period. Prior-period adjustments that decrease income from a prior period are debited to Retained Earnings:

Retained Earnings	XX	
Asset or Liability account		XX

Prior-period adjustments that increase prior-period income are credited to Retained Earnings:

Asset or Liability account	XX	
Retained Earnings		XX

Note that, because of the matching principle, prior-period adjustments *never* affect revenue or expense accounts in the current period.

Prior-period adjustments net of related tax effect are reported on the statement of retained earnings:

Retained earnings, beginning, as originally reported	$XX
Prior-period adjustment (plus or minus)	XX
Retained earnings, beginning, as adjusted	XX
Net income for current year	XX
	XX
Dividends for current year	(XX)
Retained earnings, ending	$XX

Many corporations obtain financing through long-term loans. Creditors wish to ensure that funds will be available to repay these loans. Thus, loan agreements frequently **restrict** the amount of retained earnings that can be used to pay dividends and purchase treasury stock. These restrictions are usually reported in notes to the financial statements.

Objective 3 - Analyze a statement of stockholders' equity.

You already know that the two major components of stockholder's equity are paid-in capital and retained earnings. However, you have also learned that there are additional items affecting stockholder's equity, such as treasury stock, unrealized gains and losses, cumulative translation adjustments, and dividends. A **statement of stockholder's equity** presents all of these elements with details about the changes in each during the year. Exhibit 11-5 in your text illustrates a typical format for this statement. The particular elements of stockholder's equity are listed across the top of the statement, with ending balances from the previous year. The sources of change within stockholder's equity are listed down the right-hand side of the statement. This matrix format provides the user with both the dollar amount of specific changes and the item within stockholder's equity affected by the change. For instance, net income increases retained earnings, while dividends decrease retained earnings. After all the changes have been listed under the appropriate stockholders' equity element, each column is summarized, thereby providing an end-of-year amount. Adding these ending amounts together results in total year-end stockholders' equity.

Objective 4 - Understand managers' and auditors' responsibilities for the financial statements.

A **statement of responsibility** from the top managers of the company is included with the financial statements. Within the statement, management states its responsibility for the preparation, integrity, and objectivity of the financial statements. In addition, they will confirm the statement's conformance with generally accepted accounting principles (GAAP), the use of estimates, the presence of a system of internal controls, and the application of high ethical standards. Finally, the statement will refer to the Audit Committee of the board of directors, mentioning its responsibilities and composition.

In addition to the statement by management, every annual report will include a report from the **independent external auditors**. The Securities and Exchange Commission (SEC) requires that only audited financial statements appear in the annual report. This means that a public accounting firm has reviewed the financial statements to determine if they comply with GAAP. The report will contain a reference to the standards used by the public accounting firm in reviewing the financial statements, and an opinion. The opinion will usually fall into one of the following four categories:

1. **Unqualified (clean)** - the statements are reliable
2. **Qualified** - the statements are reliable, except for one or more items for which the opinion is said to be qualified
3. **Adverse** - the statements are unreliable
4. **Disclaimer** - the auditor was unable to reach a professional opinion

Audited financial statements result in many advantages to shareholders, potential investors, and the general public.

TEST YOURSELF

All the self-testing materials in this chapter focus on information and procedures that your instructor is likely to test in quizzes and examinations.

I. Matching *Match each numbered term with its lettered definition.*

_____ 1. earnings per share
_____ 2. investor's total return on investment
_____ 3. segment of a business
_____ 4. investment capitalization rate
_____ 5. taxable income
_____ 6. qualified
_____ 7. disclaimer
_____ 8. extraordinary item

_____ 9. interim reporting
_____ 10. prior-period adjustment
_____ 11. statement of stockholders' equity
_____ 12. pretax accounting income
_____ 13. unqualified
_____ 14. adverse
_____ 15. comprehensive income

A. an audit opinion stating that the auditor was unable to reach a professional opinion regarding the quality of the financial statements
B. an audit opinion stating that the financial statements are unreliable
C. an audit opinion stating that the financial statements are reliable, except for one or more items for which the opinion is said to be qualified
D. an audit opinion stating that the financial statements are reliable
E. the basis for computing the amount of tax payable to the government
F. income before income tax on the income statement
G. an earnings rate used to estimate the value of an investment in the capital stock of another company
H. reports the changes in all categories of stockholders' equity during the period
I. one of various separate divisions of a company
J. a correction to Retained Earnings for an error in an earlier period
K. financial reporting for a period of less than one year
L. change in stock price plus dividends received divided by beginning stock price
M. a gain or loss that is both unusual for the company and infrequent
N. amount of a company's net income per share of its outstanding common stock
O. net income plus certain other non-income statement gains and losses

II. Multiple Choice *Circle the best answer.*

1. When the market price of a share of common stock rises, the P/E ratio will

A. rise
B. remain unchanged
C. fall
D. cannot be determined

2. The correct order for the following income statement items is

    A. income from continuing operations, income from discontinued operations, prior-period adjustments, net income
    B. income from continuing operations, income from discontinued operations, extraordinary items, change in accounting principles, net income
    C. income from continuing operations, extraordinary items, income from discontinued operations, net income
    D. income from continuing operations, income from discontinued items, change in accounting principles, extraordinary items, net income

3. If a company shows $80,000 income from discontinued operations and is subject to a 30% tax rate, the amount added to income from continuing operations will be

    A. $80,000
    B. $104,000
    C. $56,000
    D. cannot be determined

4. Which of the following would be considered a segment of a business?

    A. the human resources department
    B. the company's warehouse
    C. all the offices located in a particular state
    D. a catering business owned by an airline

5. Which of the following events is not considered an extraordinary item?

    A. losses resulting from a strike by the company's employees
    B. gains on the early retirement of debt
    C. a loss resulting from an earthquake
    D. assets seized by a foreign government

6. Which of the following would not be reported on the statement of stockholders' equity?

    A. net income
    B. cash dividends
    C. sale of treasury stock
    D. interest earned on investments

7. All of the following result in an increase in total stockholders' equity except

    A. sale of common stock
    B. purchase of treasury stock
    C. net income
    D. unrealized gains

8. Prior-period adjustments are found on the

   A. statement of cash flows
   B. statement of retained earnings
   C. stockholders' equity statement
   D. income statement

9. An appropriation of retained earnings will

   A. decrease total retained earnings
   B. increase total retained earnings
   C. not affect total retained earnings
   D. reduce net income

10. Which of the following is an audit report category?

    A. unconditional
    B. acceptable
    C. accurate
    D. unqualified

III. Completion   *Complete each of the following statements.*

1. Income tax expense is calculated by multiplying the applicable tax rate times _____.
2. Income tax payable is calculated by multiplying the applicable tax rate times _____.
3. The difference between income tax expense and income tax payable is called _____.
4. Extraordinary gains and losses are both _____ and _____.
5. To calculate earnings per share, divide _____ by _____.
6. Number the following income statement categories to show the order in which they should appear. Use * to indicate those categories that should be shown net of tax.

   _____ A. Effect of change in accounting principle
   _____ B. Discontinued operations
   _____ C. Extraordinary items
   _____ D. Continuing operations

7. The P/E is an abbreviation for the _____.
8. The denominator for the P/E ratio is _____.
9. An error affecting net income in a previous accounting period is called a _____.
10. The four categories of audit reports are _____, _____, _____, and _____.

IV. True/False   *For each of the following statements, circle T for true or F for false.*

1. T F Fully diluted earnings per share will always be lower than primary earnings per share.
2. T F Realized gains on the sale of assets are reported as extraordinary items.
3. T F A company's market value is determined by multiplying the earnings per share times the number of outstanding shares of common stock.
4. T F To qualify as extraordinary, an item/event must be either unusual or infrequent.

5.   T F   To calculate EPS, net income is divided by the number of common shares outstanding at year end.

6.   T F   Deferred Income Taxes could be credited or debited when recording a corporation's income tax expense.

7.   T F   Prior-period adjustments are reported on the income statement as extraordinary gains or losses.

8.   T F   The statement of stockholders' equity will include amounts for net income, dividends, and the sale of investments.

9.   T F   MD & A is an acronym for merchandise discounts and allowances.

10.   T F   Financial information on business segments is found in the notes to the financial statements.

11.   T F   The total return on a stock investment can be a positive or negative value.

12.   T F   Generally, interim statements are unaudited.

13.   T F   Independent auditors are employees of the corporation.

14.   T F   A "clean" auditor's opinion is the same as an unqualified opinion.

15.   T F   An underfunded pension plan results when the fair market value of the plan's assets are less than the accumulated benefit obligations.

V. Exercises

1. For the current year, Mercedes Corporation reported after-tax net income of $420,000. During the year, $63,000 was paid to preferred shareholders and $102,000 was paid to common shareholders. At the beginning of the year, Mercedes had 180,000 shares of common stock outstanding. On 4/1 an additional 60,000 shares were issued. On 10/1, the corporation reacquired 30,000 shares. Calculate earnings per share for the current year.

2. Ulrich-Sample, Inc., reported retained earnings of $1,615,000 as of 12/31/03. During 2004, the company declared and paid $20,000 in preferred dividends and $104,000 in common dividends. Net income for 2004 was $395,000. A prior-period adjustment was recorded, resulting in a charge against retained earnings of $117,000. An extraordinary loss of $186,000 (net of taxes) was also incurred. In the space below, present a Retained Earnings Statement for Ulrich-Sample, Inc., for 2004.

Ulrich-Sample, Inc.
Statement of Retained Earnings
2004

3. Quan-Brown Corporation reported pretax income of $235,000 on their income statement and $198,000 taxable income on their tax return. Assuming a corporate tax rate of 40%, present the journal entry to record Quan-Brown taxes for the year.

Date	Account and Explanation	Debit	Credit

4. Blenkein Corporation reported the following income statement items for the year :

Extraordinary loss	($540,000)
Cumulative effect of change in inventory valuation	$110,000
Income from continuing operations	$410,000
Discontinued operations:	
Operating loss	($12,950)
Loss on sale	($263,000)

Blenkein is subject to a 40% combined income tax rate. Using the form on the following page, show the correct presentation for the above items.

5. Refer to your solution for Exercise 4. Assuming Blenkein Corporation has 75,000 weighted average shares of common stock outstanding, present the earnings per share information.

VI. Critical Thinking

Examine the information in Exercise 1. Assume the following additional facts: the company's preferred stock is convertible into 50,000 shares of common stock and company executives hold options on 100,000 shares of common stock. Calculate fully diluted earnings per share.

VII. Demonstration Problems

Demonstration Problem #1

The following amounts were reported for Villalobos Corporation for the current year.

Administrative expenses	$220,750
Cost of goods sold	1,385,000
Cumulative effect of change in depreciation (debit)	(49,200)
Discontinued operations:	
Gain on sale	22,910
Operating loss	(205,610)
Dividend revenues	31,000
Gain on retirement of bonds	42,000
Gain on sale of short-term investments	87,000
Interest expense	29,040
Loss from hurricane	91,000
Loss on sale of plant assets	101,600
Sales revenue	2,230,000
Selling expenses	362,500

Villalobos Corporation is subject to a combined 40% income tax rate.

Requirement 1

Present a properly classified income statement for Villalobos Corporation for the current year.

Villalobos Corporation		
Income Statement		
Current Year		

Requirement 2

Present earnings per share information for Villalobos Corporation for the current year, assuming an average of 100,000 shares were outstanding throughout the year.

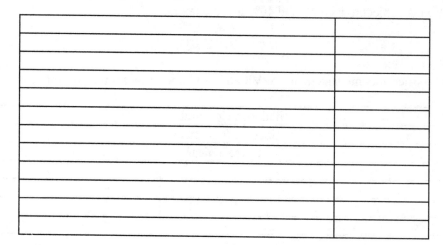

Requirement 3

Assuming Villalobos Corporation's stock was trading for 8 ½ at year end, calculate the P/E ratio based on income from continuing operations and the P/E ratio based on net income.

P/E ratio, based on income from continuing operations.

P/E ratio, based on net income.

Demonstration Problem #2

At the end of 2002, Adachi Applications had the following stockholders' equity:

Preferred stock (6%, $50 par, 1,000,000 shares authorized, 150,000 issued)	$ 7,500,000
Common stock ($1 par, 5,000,000 shares authorized, 2,850,000 issued)	2,850,000
Paid-in capital in excess of par - common	14,250,000
Total paid-in capital	24,600,000
Retained earnings	66,185,000
Less: Treasury stock (45,000 shares)	(990,000)
Cumulative translation adjustment	(1,250,000)
Total stockholders' equity	$88,545,000

Requirement 1

Answer the following questions:

a. What was the average price paid for the preferred shares?

b. What was the average price paid for the common shares?

c. What was the average price paid for the treasury shares?

d. At the end of 2002, the preferred shares were trading at par and the common shares were trading at 31 ¼. What was the market value of Adachi Applications?

Requirement 2

During 2003, the following events occurred:

1. Preferred shareholders received their dividends, as follows:

Declaration Date	Record Date	Payment Date
February 10	March 10	March 30
May 10	June 10	June 30
August 10	September 10	September 30
November 10	November 30	December 30

2. On April 20, a $.90 per share dividend was declared on the common stock to shareholders of record on May 20. The dividend was paid on June 20.

3. On May 29, the corporation paid $36 1/8 per share for 150,000 shares of common stock.
4. On June 5, the depreciation expense for 2002 was re-calculated. The amount reported for 2002 was overstated by $105,000.
5. Certain key employees hold options to purchase 1,000,000 shares of common stock at varying prices. On August 30, options to purchase 240,000 were exercised at $25 per share.
6. On September 5, the board declared a 10% stock dividend on the common stock to shareholders of record on November 5. On September 5, the shares were trading at $45 ¼. The additional shares were distributed on December 5.
7. At the end of 2003, Adachi Applications reported after-tax profits of $2,615,000.

Journalize the required 2003 entries.

Date	Account and Explanation	Debit	Credit

Requirement 3

Using the forms provided, present a Retained Earnings Statement and a Statement of Stockholders' Equity for Adachi Applications for 2003. At the end of 2003, the amount of the cumulative translation adjustment was ($1,004,500).

Adachi Applications	
Statement of Retained Earnings	
For the Year Ended 12/31/03	

Adachi Applications
Statement of Stockholders' Equity
For the Year Ended 12/31/03

	Preferred Stock	Common Stock	Additional Paid-In Capital	Retained Earnings	Treasury Stock	Cumulative Translation Adjustment	Total Stockholders' Equity
Balance, 12/31/02	$7,500,000	$2,850,000	$14,250,000	$66,185,000	($990,000)	($1,250,000)	$88,545,000
Cash dividends							
10% stock dividends							
Prior-period adjustment							
Purchase of treasury stock							
Exercise of stock options							
Net income							
Translation adjustment							
Balance, 12/31/03							

Requirement 4

At the end of 2003, Adachi's preferred stock was trading at par and the common stock was trading at $51 1/8. Calculate Adachi's market value as of the end of 2003.

Requirement 5

Calculate the basic earnings per share for 2003.

Requirement 6

Calculate the diluted earning per share for 2003.

Requirement 7

Calculate the price/earnings ratio as of 12/31/03.

SOLUTIONS

I. Matching

1. N	5. E	9. K	13. D
2. L	6. C	10. J	14. B
3. I	7. A	11. H	15. O
4. G	8. M	12. F	

II. Multiple Choice

1. A   Since the earnings per share figure does not change, an increase in the market price (the numerator) will cause an increase in the P/E ratio.

2. B   The correct order is income from continuing operations, income from discontinued operations, extraordinary items, changes in accounting principles, net income. Prior-period adjustments do not appear on the income statement.

3. C   Income from discontinued operations is reported net of the effects of tax on the income statement; therefore, the $80,000 income amount is reduced by the $24,000 (30% × $80,000) tax expense.

4. D   The other three choices are not considered segments from an accounting perspective.

5. A   The other choices are all unusual and infrequent, whereas strikes by employees are considered normal business events.

6. D   Interest earned on investments is reported on the income statement.

7. B   The purchase of treasury stock reduces total stockholders' equity.

8. B   Prior-period adjustments reflect errors in previous accounting periods. Since these errors affected net income, and net income was closed to retained earnings, a prior-period adjustment only appears on the retained earnings statement.

9. C   When retained earning are appropriated, total retained earnings do not change—the appropriation simply restricts the use of part of the total retained earnings amount.

10. D   The four categories are unqualified, qualified, adverse, and disclaimer.

III. Completion

1. pretax accounting income
2. taxable income
3. deferred income tax
4. unusual and infrequent (order not important)
5. net income less preferred dividends, weighted average number of shares outstanding

6. A. 4*
   B. 2*
   C. 3*
   D. 1 (income from continuing operations is reported both before and after income taxes)
7. price/earnings ratio
8. earnings per share
9. prior-period adjustment
10. unqualified, qualified, adverse, disclaimer (order not important)

IV. True/False

1. T
2. F   Realized gains from the sale of assets are reported separately after income from operations but not as extraordinary items.
3. F   Market value is number of shares outstanding times current market price per share.
4. F   Extraordinary items must be both unusual AND infrequent.
5. F   EPS equals net income (less preferred dividends, if any) divided by the weighted average number of shares outstanding.
6. T
7. F   Prior-period adjustments are reported on the retained earnings statement, not the income statement.
8. F   When investments are sold, gains and losses appear on the income statement not the stockholders' equity statement.
9. F   MD & A stands for Management's Discussion and Analysis.
10. T
11. T
12. T
13. F   Independent auditors are employees of the public accounting firm hired to conduct the audit.
14. T
15. T

V. Exercises

1. earnings per share = net income less preferred dividends / weighted average share of common stock outstanding

   net income - preferred dividends = $420,000 - $63,000
   $$= \$357,000$$
   weighted average common shares outstanding =
   180,000 × 3/12   =   45,000
   240,000 × 6/12   =   120,000
   210,000 × 3/12   =   52,500
   =   217,500
   EPS = $357,000 / 217,500 = $1.64 (rounded)

Study Tip: When calculating EPS, only preferred dividends are deducted.

2.

Ulrich-Sample, Inc.
Statement of Retained Earnings
2004

Retained earnings, 12/31/03 as reported		$1,615,000
Less: Prior-period adjustment		117,000
Retained earnings, 12/31/03 adjusted		1,498,000
Add: Net income		395,000
		1,893,000
Less: Preferred dividends	20,000	
Common dividends	104,000	124,000
Retained earnings, 12/31/04		$1,769,000

Study Tip: The extraordinary loss of $186,000 does not appear on the retained earnings statement. It was listed on the income statement, net of taxes.

3.

Income Tax Expense	94,000	
Deferred Income Taxes		14,800
Income Tax Payable		79,200

Expense = $235,000 × .40 = $94,000
Payable = $198,000 × .40 = $79,200

Study Tip: The expense is based on the financial statement while the liability is based on the tax return. The entry is reconciled (balanced) with a debit or credit to Deferred Income Tax.

4.

Income from continuing operations		$410,000
Less: Income tax expense (.40 × $410,000)		164,000
		246,000
Discontinued operations:		
Operating loss (net of tax benefit)	($7,770)	
Loss on sale (net of tax benefit)	(157,800)	(165,570)
Net income before extraordinary items and cumulative effect of change in inventory valuation		80,430
Extraordinary loss (net of tax benefit)	(324,000)	
Cumulative effect of change in inventory valuation (net of tax)	66,000	(258,000)
Net loss		($177,570)

Study Tip: For all the items "below the line" (i.e., after the income from continuing operations), calculate the tax and **deduct** it. Why? If it's a gain, the tax reduces the amount; if it's a loss, the amount of the loss is reduced because of the tax benefit.

5.

Income from continuing operations (after tax)		$3.28
Discontinued operations:		
Operating income	(.10)	
Loss on sale	(2.10)	(2.20)
		1.08
Extraordinary loss		(4.32)
Cumulative effect of change in inventory valuation		.88
Net income		($2.36)

N. B. Most of these amounts are rounded.

VI. Critical Thinking

Most of the information provided has the effect of diluting primary earnings per share. In other words, if the preferred stock is converted into common stock, the number of outstanding shares will increase, thereby lowering (diluting) the earnings per share. The same is true if the stock options are exercised. To recalculate earnings per share, the denominator changes from 217,000 to 367,500 (217,500 + 50,000 + 100,000). Therefore, EPS (fully diluted) is $357,000 / 367,500 = $.97 (rounded).

> **Study Tip:** Fully diluted EPS will always be lower than primary EPS when the corporation has a complex capital structure.

VII. Demonstration Problems

Demonstration Problem #1 Solved and Explained

Requirement 1 (Income Statement)

Villalobos Corporation
Income Statement
Current Year

Sales revenue		$2,230, 000
Less: Cost of goods sold		1,385,000
Gross margin		845,000
Less: Operating expenses		
Selling expenses	$362,500	
Administrative expenses	220,750	583,250
		261,750
Other revenues (expenses):		
Dividend revenues	31,000	
Gain on sale of short-term investments	87,000	
Interest expense	(29,040)	
Loss on sale of plant assets	(101,600)	(12,640)
Income from continuing operations, before taxes		249,110
Less: Income tax expense ($249,110 × 40%)		99,644
Income from continuing operations		149,466
Discontinued operations:		
Operating income (loss), net of tax benefit	(123,366)	
Gain on sale, net of tax	13,746	(109,620)
Income before extraordinary items and cumulative effect of change in depreciation		39,846
Extraordinary items:		
Gain on retirement of bonds, net of tax	25,200	
Loss from hurricane, net of tax benefit	(54, 600)	(29,400)
Cumulative effect of change in depreciation, net of tax benefit		(29,520)
Net income (loss)		$ (19,074)

Notes: The items above income from continuing operations could be organized in a single-step format, with income tax expense either included with the other deductions or listed separately.

The items following income from continuing operations are ALWAYS listed net of tax. In addition, the order of the items is discontinued operations, extraordinary items, and, lastly, cumulative effects of changes in accounting principles.

Requirement 2 (Earnings Per Share)

Income from continuing operations (after tax)	$1.49
Discontinued operations:	(1.09)
Income before extraordinary items and cumulative effect of change in depreciation	.40
Extraordinary items	(.29)
Cumulative effect of change in depreciation	(.30)
Net income	($.19)

The above amounts are rounded. Note, however, that they reconcile. By far the most important figure above is the EPS from continuing operations. While the corporation did experience a net loss for the year, the items following income from continuing operations should not occur in the future. Therefore, to properly evaluate the company, investors and shareholders will place more emphasis on the continuing operations figure than on the net income amount.

Requirement 3

P/E, based on income from continuing operations:

$8.50 / $1.49 = 5.7

P/E, based on net income:

This value cannot be calculated because the company experienced an overall net loss.

> **Study Tip:** The P/E ratio can only be a positive value. A negative P/E ratio has no meaning.

Demonstration Problem #2 Solved and Explained

Requirement 1

a. $7,500,000 / 150,000 shares = $50 per share
b. ($2,850,000 + $14,250,000) / 2,850,000 shares = $6 per share
c. $990,000 / 45,000 shares = $22 per share
d. Preferred market value = 150,000 shares × $50 ea. = $7,500,000
   Common market value = 2,805,000* shares × $31.25 ea. = $87,656,250
   Total market value = $7,500,000 + $87,656,250 = $95,156,250
   * Common shares outstanding equal issued shares less treasury stock

Requirement 2

2/10	Retained Earnings	112,500	
	Dividends Payable		112,500
	150,000 shares x $.75/share		

> **Study Tip:** No entry is made on date of record.

| 3/30 | Dividends Payable | 112,500 | |
| | Cash | | 112,500 |

| 5/10 | Retained Earnings | 112,500 | |
| | Dividends Payable | | 112,500 |

| 6/30 | Dividends Payable | 112,500 | |
| | Cash | | 112,500 |

| 8/10 | Retained Earnings | 112,500 | |
| | Dividends Payable | | 112,500 |

| 9/30 | Dividends Payable | 112,500 | |
| | Cash | | 112,500 |

| 11/10 | Retained Earnings | 112,500 | |
| | Dividends Payable | | 112,500 |

| 12/30 | Dividends Payable | 112,500 | |
| | Cash | | 112,500 |

4/20	Retained Earnings	2,524,500	
	Dividends Payable		2,524,500
	2,805,000 shares × $.90 per share		

> **Study Tip:** Dividends are only paid on outstanding shares. Treasury stock is NOT outstanding.

5/29	Treasury Stock	5,418,750	
	Cash		5,418,750
	150,000 shares × $36.125		

| 6/5 | Accumulated Depreciation | 105,000 | |
| | Retained Earnings | | 105,000 |

| 6/20 | Dividends Payable | 2,524,500 | |
| | Cash | | 2,524,500 |

8/30	Cash	6,000,000	
	Common Stock		240,000
	Paid-in Capital in Excess of Par-Common		5,760,000

9/5	Retained Earnings	13,099,875	
	Common Stock Dividend Distributable		289,500
	Paid-in Capital in Excess of Par-Common		12,810,375

This requires an explanation! The 10% stock dividend is considered a small stock dividend and, therefore, recorded at the market price per share times the number of shares to be distributed. On the date of declaration, there were 2,895,000 shares outstanding, calculated as follows: at the beginning of the year there were 2,805,000 outstanding (2,850,000 authorized less 45,000 in the treasury). On 5/29, an additional 150,000 shares were added to the treasury, and on 8/30 240,000 shares were sold. As of 9/5 there are 2,895,000 outstanding.

$45.25 \times 2,895,0000 \times 10\% = \$13,099,875$

| 12/5 | Common Stock Dividends Distributable | 289,500 | |
| | Common Stock | | 289,500 |

| 12/31 | Income Summary | 2,615,000 | |
| | Retained Earnings | | 2,615,000 |

Requirement 3

Adachi Applications
Statement of Retained Earnings
For the Year Ended 12/31/03

Retained earnings, 12/31/02		$66,185,000
Add: Prior-period adjustment		105,000
Retained earnings, 12/31/02 adjusted		66,290,000
Net income		2,615,000
		68,905,000
2003 dividends*		
Preferred - cash dividends	$ 450,000	
Common - cash dividends	2,524,500	
Common - stock dividends	13,099,875	16,074,375
Retained earnings, 12/31/03		$52,830,625

* Preferred dividends = 150,000 shares $\times$ $50 par $\times$ 6% = $450,000

Common dividends:
Cash - In April, there were 2,805,000 shares outstanding (2,850,000 issued less 45,000 shares of treasury stock) $\times$ $ .90/share = $2,524,500

Stock - On September 5 there were 2,895,000 shares outstanding (2,805,000 less 150,000 shares purchased on May 29 plus 240,000 shares sold to the key executives on August 30) $\times$ 10% $\times$ $45.25/share = $13,099,875.

There are now 3,184,500 shares outstanding calculated as follows:
2,895,000 + (10% $\times$ 2,895,000) = 2,895,000 + 289,500 = 3,184,500

Small stock dividends are charged against Retained Earnings based on the stock's selling price at the time the dividend is declared.

Adachi Applications
Statement of Stockholders' Equity
For the Year Ended 12/31/03

	Preferred Stock	Common Stock	Additional Paid-In Capital	Retained Earnings	Treasury Stock	Cumulative Translation Adjustment	Total Stockholders' Equity
Balance, 12/31/02	$7,500,000	$2,850,000	$14,250,000	$66,185,000	($990,000)	($1,250,000)	$88,545,000
Cash dividends				(450,000)			(450,000)
				(2,524,500)			(2,524,500)
10% stock dividends		289,500	12,810,375	(13,099,875)			-0-
Prior-period adjustment				105,000			105,000
Purchase of treasury stock					(5,418,750)		(5,418,750)
Exercise of stock options		240,000	5,760,000				6,000,000
Net income				2,615,000			2,615,000
Translation adjustment						245,500	245,500
Balance, 12/31/03	$7,500,000	$3,379,500	$32,820,375	$52,830,625	($6,408,750)	($1,004,500)	$89,117,250

Requirement 4

Preferred market value = 150,000 shares × $50 per share = $7,500,000
Common market value = 3,184,500 shares × $51 1/8 per share = $162,807,563 (rounded)
Total market value = $7,500,000 + $162,807,563 = $170,307,563

Requirement 5

basic earning per share = net income less preferred dividends / weighted average share of common stock
outstanding
= ($2,615,000 - $450,000) / 2,869,875*
= $.75 (rounded)

*	2,805,000 × 5/12	=	1,168,750
	2,655,000 × 3/12	=	663,750 (rounded)
	2,895,000 × 1/12	=	241,250 (rounded)
	3,184,500 × 3/12	=	796,125 (rounded)
			2,869,875

Requirement 6

Basic earnings per share (Requirement 5 above) uses common shares outstanding as the denominator. Diluted earnings per share uses weighted average common shares outstanding PLUS any additional shares that could become outstanding. Remember that 760,000 options could still be exercised (1,000,000 less the 240,000 that were exercised in August.) If those additional options are exercised, the total number of outstanding shares increases to 3,629,875 (2,869,875 + 760,000).

Therefore, diluted earnings per share becomes

$2,615,000/3,629,875 = $.72 (rounded)

Additional items which could "dilute" earnings per share are convertible preferred stock and bonds which have a conversion feature attached to them.

Requirement 7

P/E ratio = market price per share / earnings per share
= $51 1/8 / $.75 (from Requirement 5)
= $68 (rounded)

CHAPTER 12—THE STATEMENT OF CASH FLOWS

CHAPTER OVERVIEW

In each of the preceding chapters, reference has been made to the statement of cash flows and the cash flow effects of selected transactions. Many people think the cash-flow statement is more important than the income statement and the balance sheet, as demonstrated by the opening vignette to this chapter in your text. It is certainly the most complex of the published financial statements. The learning objectives for this chapter are to

1. Identify the purposes of the statement of cash flows
2. Distinguish among operating, investing, and financing activities
3. Prepare a statement of cash flows by the direct method
4. Compute the cash effects of a wide variety of business transactions
5. Prepare a statement of cash flows by the indirect method

CHAPTER REVIEW

Objective 1 - Identify the purposes of the statement of cash flows.

Cash flows are cash receipts and cash payments. The **statement of cash flows** reports all these receipts and disbursements under three categories (operating, investing, and financing) and shows the reasons for changes in the cash balance. The statement is used to:

1. Predict future cash flows
2. Evaluate management decisions
3. Determine the company's ability to pay dividends to stockholders and interest and principal to creditors
4. Show the relationship of net income to the business's cash flows

The term cash is used to include **cash equivalents** which are highly liquid short-term investments (such as T-bills and money market accounts).

Objective 2 - Distinguish among operating, investing, and financing activities.

Operating activities create revenues and expenses in the entity's major line of business. Therefore, operating activities are related to the transactions that make up net income.

Operating activities are always listed first because they are the largest and most important source of cash for a business.

Investing activities increase and decrease the assets with which the business works. Investing activities require analysis of the long-term asset accounts.

Investing activities are critical because they help determine the future course of the business.

Financing activities obtain the funds from investors and creditors needed to launch and sustain the business. Financing activities require analysis of the long-term liability accounts and the stockholders' equity accounts.

Review Exhibit 12-2 in your text and become familiar with both the format and content of a cash-flow statement (direct method).

Objective 3 - Prepare a statement of cash flows by the direct method.

FASB Statement No. 95 permits two different presentations for the cash-flow statement—the direct method and the indirect method. Both formats arrive at the same result; however, the manner in which they do so differs in the operating activities section of the statement. The other two sections (investing activities and financing activities) are the same regardless of the format used. FASB recommends, but does not require, the direct method because it is easier for the user to understand.

The statement of cash flows reports cash flows from operating activities, investing activities, and financing activities, calculates the net increase or decrease in cash over the year, and adds that to the previous year's cash balance in order to arrive at the current year's cash balance. It shows where cash came from and how it was spent.

Preparing the statement of cash flows requires these steps:

1. identify items that affect cash
2. classify the items as operating, investing, or financing activities
3. determine the increase or decrease in cash for each item

Cash flows from operating activities include

1. cash collections from customers
2. cash receipts of interest and dividends
3. payments to suppliers
4. payments to employees
5. payments for interest and income taxes

Although depreciation, depletion, and amortization expense are listed on the income statement and, therefore, affect operating income, they are not listed on the statement of cash flow because no cash is involved.

Cash flows from investing activities include

1. cash payments for plant assets, investments, and loans to other companies
2. cash receipts from the sale of plant assets, investments, and the collection of loans

Cash flows from financing activities include

1. cash receipts from issuing stock and debt
2. cash payments for debt and treasury stock
3. payments for cash dividends

Study Tip: While principal payments on notes and bonds payable are a financing activity, the interest payments are classified as an operating activity.

Objective 4 - Compute the cash effects of a wide variety of business transactions.

Accounts may be analyzed for the cash effects of various transactions using the income statement amounts in conjunction with changes in the balance sheet amounts.

To determine cash flow amounts from operating activities, keep the following in mind:

Revenue/expense from the income statement $\longrightarrow$ Adjust for the change in related balance sheet accounts $\longrightarrow$ Amount for the cash-flow statement

Cash collections from customers can be computed using Sales Revenue from the income statement and the changes in Accounts Receivable from the balance sheet:

$$\begin{array}{ccc} \text{COLLECTIONS} \\ \text{FROM} & = & \text{SALES REVENUE} \\ \text{CUSTOMERS} \end{array} \begin{bmatrix} \text{+ DECREASES IN ACCOUNTS RECEIVABLE} \\ \text{or} \\ \text{- INCREASES IN ACCOUNTS RECEIVABLE} \end{bmatrix}$$

Payments to suppliers computation:

$$\begin{array}{ccc} \text{PAYMENTS} & & \text{COST OF} \\ \text{FOR} & = & \text{GOODS} \\ \text{INVENTORY} & & \text{SOLD} \end{array} \begin{bmatrix} \text{+ INCREASE IN} \\ \text{INVENTORY} \\ \text{or} \\ \text{- DECREASE IN} \\ \text{INVENTORY} \end{bmatrix} \text{and} \begin{bmatrix} \text{+ DECREASE IN} \\ \text{ACCOUNTS PAYABLE} \\ \text{or} \\ \text{- INCREASE IN} \\ \text{ACCOUNTS PAYABLE} \end{bmatrix}$$

Payments for operating expenses computation:

$$\begin{array}{ccc} \text{PAYMENTS} & & \text{OPERATING} \\ \text{FOR} & & \text{EXPENSES OTHER} \\ \text{OPERATING} & = & \text{THAN SALARIES,} \\ \text{EXPENSES} & & \text{WAGES, AND} \\ & & \text{DEPRECIATION} \end{array} \begin{bmatrix} \text{+ INCREASE IN} \\ \text{PREPAID} \\ \text{EXPENSES} \\ \text{or} \\ \text{- DECREASE IN} \\ \text{PREPAID} \\ \text{EXPENSE} \end{bmatrix} \text{and} \begin{bmatrix} \text{+ DECREASE IN} \\ \text{ACCRUED} \\ \text{LIABILITIES} \\ \text{or} \\ \text{- INCREASE IN} \\ \text{ACCRUED} \\ \text{LIABILITIES} \end{bmatrix}$$

Remember that depreciation is not included in operating expenses because depreciation is a noncash expense.

Payments to employees computation:

$$\begin{array}{ccc} \text{PAYMENTS} & & \text{SALARY} \\ \text{TO} & = & \text{AND WAGE} \\ \text{EMPLOYEES} & & \text{EXPENSE} \end{array} \begin{bmatrix} \text{+ DECREASES IN SALARY AND WAGE PAYABLE} \\ \text{or} \\ \text{- INCREASES IN SALARY AND WAGE PAYABLE} \end{bmatrix}$$

Payments of interest and taxes follow the pattern for payments to employees. Exhibit 12-8 summarizes this discussion.

For investing activities we look to the asset accounts (Plant Assets, Investments, Notes Receivable).

Plant asset transactions can be analyzed by first determining book value:

$$
\begin{array}{c}
\text{BEGINNING} \\
\text{PLANT ASSET} \\
\text{BALANCE} \\
\text{(NET)}
\end{array}
+ \text{ACQUISITIONS}
- \text{DEPRECIATION}
-
\begin{array}{c}
\text{BOOK VALUE} \\
\text{OF PLANT} \\
\text{ASSETS SOLD}
\end{array}
=
\begin{array}{c}
\text{ENDING} \\
\text{PLANT} \\
\text{ASSET} \\
\text{BALANCE} \\
\text{(NET)}
\end{array}
$$

In order to compute sale proceeds:

$$
\begin{array}{c}
\text{SALE} \\
\text{PROCEEDS}
\end{array}
=
\begin{array}{c}
\text{BOOK VALUE} \\
\text{SOLD}
\end{array}
+ \text{GAIN}
- \text{LOSS}
$$

Acquisitions will decrease cash, while sale proceeds will increase cash.

Investments and Loans and Notes Receivable are analyzed in a manner similar to Plant Assets; however, there is no depreciation to account for. Review Exhibit 12-9 for a summary of this discussion.

Financing activities affect liability and stockholders' equity accounts.

Long-term debt can be analyzed with this equation:

$$
\begin{array}{c}
\text{BEGINNING} \\
\text{LONG-TERM} \\
\text{DEBT} \\
\text{BALANCE}
\end{array}
+
\begin{array}{c}
\text{ISSUANCE} \\
\text{OF} \\
\text{NEW DEBT}
\end{array}
- \text{PAYMENTS}
=
\begin{array}{c}
\text{ENDING} \\
\text{LONG-TERM} \\
\text{DEBT} \\
\text{BALANCE}
\end{array}
$$

Stock transactions (other than treasury stock) can be analyzed using this equation:

$$
\begin{array}{c}
\text{BEGINNING} \\
\text{STOCK} \\
\text{BALANCE}
\end{array}
+
\begin{array}{c}
\text{ISSUANCE} \\
\text{OF} \\
\text{NEW STOCK}
\end{array}
- \text{RETIREMENTS}
=
\begin{array}{c}
\text{ENDING} \\
\text{STOCK} \\
\text{BALANCE}
\end{array}
$$

Issuances increase cash, while retirements decrease cash.

Treasury stock can be analyzed with this equation:

$$
\begin{array}{c}
\text{BEGINNING} \\
\text{TREASURY STOCK} \\
\text{BALANCE}
\end{array}
+ \text{PURCHASES}
-
\begin{array}{c}
\text{COST OF} \\
\text{TREASURY} \\
\text{STOCK SOLD}
\end{array}
=
\begin{array}{c}
\text{ENDING} \\
\text{TREASURY STOCK} \\
\text{BALANCE}
\end{array}
$$

Purchases will decrease cash. Remember, that cash is increased by the proceeds of treasury stock sold. These proceeds may differ from the cost of treasury stocks sold.

Dividend payments can be computed by analyzing Retained Earnings:

BEGINNING		NET		DIVIDENDS		ENDING
RETAINED	+	INCOME	-	DECLARATIONS	=	RETAINED
EARNINGS						EARNINGS
BALANCE						BALANCE

Remember that stock dividends must be separated from cash dividends. Also, a change in the Dividends Payable account will affect the actual cash dividends paid. Review Exhibit 12-10 in your text.

Noncash investing and financing activities

Some investing and financing activities are noncash. Some typical noncash investing and financing activities include:

1. Acquisition of assets by issuing stock
2. Acquisition of assets by issuing debt
3. Payment of long-term debt by transferring investment assets to the creditor

Noncash activities are included in a schedule or a note to the statement of cash flows.

When the direct method of computing operating cash flows is used, FASB requires companies to include a reconciliation from net income to net cash flows. This reconciliation is identical to the indirect method.

Objective 5 - Prepare a statement of cash flows by the indirect method.

The **indirect** (or **reconciliation method**) reconciles net income to cash flows and affects only the operating activities section of the statement. The investing activities and financing activities sections are identical to the sections prepared using the direct method.

To prepare the operating activities section using the indirect method, we must add and subtract items that affect net income and cash flows differently. Begin with net income from the income statement.

1. Depreciation, amortization, and depletion are noncash expenses which reduce net income. Therefore, we add them back to net income as part of our effort to arrive at cash flow from operations.
2. Gains and losses from the sale of plant assets are reported as part of net income, and the proceeds are reported in the investing activities section. To avoid counting gains and losses twice, we must remove their effect from net income. Therefore, gains are subtracted from net income and losses are added to net income.
3. Changes in current assets and current liabilities:
   a. Increases in current assets, other than cash, are subtracted from net income.
   b. Decreases in current assets, other than cash, are added to net income.
   c. Decreases in current liabilities, other than dividends payable, are subtracted from net income.
   d. Increases in current liabilities are added to net income.

Study Tip: Under the indirect method, only changes in current assets and current liabilities are used.

See Exhibits 12-13 and 12-17. These are examples of the indirect method.

Cash flows are only one source of information creditors and investors use to evaluate a company. The Decision Guidelines in your text provide an excellent summary of questions, factors to consider, and financial statement predictors from both a creditor's and an investor's perspective.

Free cash flows refers to the amount of cash flow that a company could access quickly should a need/opportunity arise. **Free cash flow** is defined as the amount of cash available from operations after paying for planned investments in plant, equipment, and other long-term assets. When net cash flows from operations exceed the amount of cash required for investments in long-term assets, the excess is available for additional investments. Obviously, a positive free cash flow is preferable to a negative amount. Free cash flow is yet another tool to be used in evaluating a company's performance.

TEST YOURSELF

All the self-testing materials in this chapter focus on information and procedures that your instructor is likely to test in quizzes and examinations.

I. Matching   *Match each numbered term with its lettered definition.*

_____ 1.   cash equivalents
_____ 2.   direct method
_____ 3.   indirect method
_____ 4.   operating activity
_____ 5.   cash flows

_____ 6.   financing activity
_____ 7.   investing activity
_____ 8.   statement of cash flows
_____ 9.   free cash flow

A.   a report of cash receipts and cash disbursements classified according to the entity's major activities: operating, investing, and financing
B.   activity that creates revenue or expense in the entity's major line of business
C.   activity that increases or decreases the assets that the business has to work with
D.   activity that obtains from creditors the funds needed to launch and sustain the business or repays such funds
E.   cash receipts and cash disbursements
F.   format of the operating activities section of the statement of cash flows that lists the major categories of operating cash receipts and cash disbursements
G.   format of the operating activities section of the statement of cash flows that starts with net income and shows the reconciliation from net income to operating cash flows
H.   highly liquid short-term investments that can be converted into cash with little delay
I.   the amount of cash available from operations after paying for planned investments in plant, equipment, and other long-term assets

II. Multiple Choice   *Circle the best answer.*

1.   All of the following are uses of the statement of cash flows *except*

   A.   evaluate employee performance
   B.   evaluate management decisions
   C.   predict future cash flows
   D.   relate net income to changes in cash

2.   Activities which increase or decrease business assets such as machinery are called

   A.   financing activities
   B.   investing activities
   C.   operating activities
   D.   reporting activities

3. Transactions involving stockholders' equity or debt activities are called

    A. financing activities
    B. investing activities
    C. operating activities
    D. reporting activities

4. Which of the following is considered a cash equivalent?

    A. accounts receivable
    B. inventory
    C. supplies
    D. treasury bills

5. The receipt of cash dividend revenues would be reported on the

    A. balance sheet
    B. income statement
    C. statement of cash flows only
    D. both the income statement and the statement of cash flows

6. All of the following are examples of operating activities *except*

    A. purchases from suppliers
    B. sales to customers
    C. sales of equipment
    D. recording rent expense

7. All of the following are examples of investing activities *except*

    A. sale of building
    B. payment of dividends
    C. purchase of equipment
    D. receipt of cash from sale of California State bonds

8. All of the following are financing activities *except*

    A. issuing stock
    B. paying dividends
    C. selling equipment
    D. long-term borrowing

9. Cash collections from customers are computed by

    A. Sales Revenue + Increase in Accounts Receivable
    B. Sales Revenue - Increase in Accounts Receivable
    C. Sales Revenues - Decrease in Accounts Receivable
    D. Sales Revenue + Decrease in Accounts Receivable
    E. Either B or D.

10. All of the following are included in the free cash flow calculation except

    A. cash from operating activities
    B. cash payments for bond retirements
    C. cash payments for plant and equipment
    D. all of the above

III. Completion   *Complete each of the following statements.*

1. The _____ is the only financial statement that is dated as of the end of the period.
2. The largest cash inflow from operations is _____.
3. Both the _____ method and the _____ method of preparing the statements of cash flows are permitted by the FASB.
4. Payments of dividends is a(n) _____ activity on the statement of cash flows.
5. Making loans is a(n) _____ activity on the statement of cash flows.
6. Depreciation is included in the _____ activity section on the statement of cash flows when using the indirect method.
7. The purchase of equipment is a(n) _____ activity on the statement of cash flows.
8. While permitting both methods, FASB recommends the _____ method.
9. The _____ method begins with net income.
10. The difference between the direct and indirect method is found in the _____ section of the statement of cash flows.

IV. True/False   *For each of the following statements, circle* T *for true or* F *for false.*

1.   T F   Free cash flow compares cash flows from operations with cash flows from financing activities.
2.   T F   The direct approach reconciles net income to cash flows from operating.
3.   T F   An increase in accounts receivable indicates cash receipts from customers are less than net sales reported on the income statement.
4.   T F   When using the indirect method, increases in current liabilities are deducted from net income.
5.   T F   When using the indirect method, decreases in current assets are added to net income.
6.   T F   Differences between the direct method and indirect method are found in two of the three sections in the statement of cash flows.
7.   T F   Short-term investments are cash equivalents.
8.   T F   Interest received on money market investments is reported as investing activities on the cash-flow statement.
9.   T F   The receipt of dividends and the payment of dividends are reconciled to a net amount and reported as a cash flow from financing activities on the statement of cash flows.
10.   T F   Investing activities focus on the company's long-term assets.
11.   T F   Gains on the sale of plant assets are reported as cash flows from investing activities on the statement of cash flows.
12.   T F   The purchase of treasury stock is reported as a financing activity on the cash-flow statement.
13.   T F   To determine cash paid for interest, begin with Interest Expense and add any decrease in Interest Payable.
14.   T F   An increase in prepaid expenses results in a decrease in cash paid for operating expenses.

15.   T F   The purchase of supplies on account is an example of a noncash investing and financing activity.

V. Exercises

1. Classify each of the following as an operating, investing, or financing activity.

Item	Classification
a) payment to employees	_____
b) lending money	_____
c) receiving dividends on investments	_____
d) selling treasury stock	_____
e) raising funds by selling bonds	_____
f) receiving cash from customers	_____
g) paying taxes	_____
h) purchasing equipment by paying cash	_____
i) purchasing equipment and signing a note payable	_____
j) purchasing inventory on account	_____
k) receiving interest revenue	_____
l) paying dividends to stockholders	_____
m) selling short-term investments	_____
n) selling shares of common stock	_____

2. Hunter Company had interest expense of $54,000 in 2002. The balance in Interest Payable was $2,100 at the beginning of the year and $3,600 at the end of the year. How much cash was paid for interest during 2002?

3. Bollinger Company had cost of goods sold of $600,000, an increase in inventory of $15,000, and an increase in accounts payable of $27,000 in 2002. How much cash was paid to suppliers?

4. MyGuy Company had sales of $2,100,000 in 2002. Ninety percent of sales are on credit. During the year, Accounts Receivable increased from $40,000 to $95,000. How much cash was received from customers during 2002?

5. Saechow Company purchased equipment for $185,000, lent $32,000 to a customer, borrowed $42,000, and sold securities that were not cash equivalents for $12,000. What was the net cash flow from investing activities?

6. From the following list of cash receipts and payments, present the cash flows from the operating activities section of the cash-flow statement, using the direct method.

Cash receipts from interest revenues	$ 1,820
Cash paid for taxes	43,110
Cash payments to suppliers	328,590
Cash receipts from customers	615,200
Cash paid for dividends	12,700
Cash payments to employees	103,200
Cash receipts from dividend revenues	780
Cash payments for interest	4,965

VI. Critical Thinking

Review the information in Exercises 2 and 4. Calculate the same answer using a different approach.

_____

_____

_____

_____

_____

_____

VII. Demonstration Problems

Demonstration Problem #1

The income statement, schedule of current account changes, and additional data for NobleBarn.com follows:

NobleBarn.com
Income Statement
For the Year Ended December 31, 2002

Revenues:		
Net sales revenue	$3,512,500	
Dividend revenue	67,500	$3,580,000
Expenses:		
Cost of goods sold	2,702,500	
Salary expense	322,500	
Other operating expense	77,500	
Depreciation expense	137,500	
Interest expense	162,500	
Amortization expense-patents	12,500	3,415,000
Net income		$165,000

Additional data:

a. Collections exceeded sales by $17,500.
b. Dividend revenue equaled cash amounts received, $67,500.
c. Payments to suppliers were $45,000 less than cost of goods sold. Payments for other operating expense and interest expense were the same as 'Other operating expense' and 'Interest expense'.
d. Payments to employees were less than salary expense by $10,000.
e. Acquisition of plant assets totaled $325,000. Of this amount, $50,000 was paid in cash and the balance was financed by signing a note payable.
f. Proceeds from the sale of land were $212,500.
g. Proceeds from the issuance of common stock were $125,000.
h. Full payment was made on a long-term note payable, $100,000.
i. Dividends were paid in the amount of $40,000.
j. A small parcel of land located in an industrial park was purchased for $185,000.
k. Current asset and liability activity changes were as follows:

	December 31	
	2002	2001
Cash and cash equivalents	580,000	230,000
Accounts receivable	590,000	607,500
Inventory	945,000	960,000
Prepaid expense	30,000	30,000
Accounts payable	535,000	505,000
Salary payable	27,500	17,500
Income tax payable	8,000	8,000

Required

1. Using the direct method, prepare the December 31, 2002, statement of cash flows and accompanying schedule of noncash investing and financing activities for NobleBarn.com.
2. Calculate the corporation's free cash flow.

Requirement 1 (statement of cash flows—direct method)

NobleBarn.com		
Statement of Cash Flows		
For the Year Ended December 31, 2002		

Requirement 2 (free cash flow)

Demonstration Problem #2

Using the information in Problem 1, prepare a statement of cash flows and accompanying schedule of noncash investing and financing activities using the indirect method.

Indirect Method

NobleBarn.com
Statement of Cash Flows
For the Year Ended December 31, 2002

SOLUTIONS

I. Matching

1. H	3. G	5. E	7. C	9. I
2. F	4. B	6. D	8. A	

II. Multiple Choice

1   A   Replace A with "to determine ability to pay dividends and interest" and you have a list of all the purposes for the statement of cash flows.

2.   B   Changes in property, plant, and equipment are investing activities.

3.   A   Changes in capital and debt are financing activities.

4.   D   Cash and cash equivalents are highly liquid, short-term investments that can be converted into cash with little delay and include money market investments and investments in T-bills.

5.   D   Recall that the receipt of a dividend from an investment accounted for under the cost method is treated as income and accordingly will be included in the income statement. For cash-flow statement purposes, the receipt of dividends is considered an operating activity and will be reflected in that portion of the statement.

6.   C   Operating activities create revenues and expenses in the entity's major line of business. Equipment sales are assumed not to be this entity's major line of business.

7.   B   Investing activities increase and decrease the assets the business has to work with. Payment of a dividend is a financing activity. Note that while the receipt of interest on a bond is an operating activity, buying and selling bonds is an investing activity.

8.   C   Financing activities include transactions with investors and creditors needed to obtain funds to launch and sustain the business. Of the items listed, only C, an investing activity, does not fit that definition.

9.   E   Sales revenue is recorded on the accrual basis. To convert this to a cash flow, the net change in accounts receivable must be considered. A decrease in accounts receivable indicates that customers have paid more than they purchased and should be added to sales. An increase in accounts receivable indicates that customers have purchased more than they paid and should be subtracted from sales.

10.   B   Free cash flow refers to net cash flow from operating activities and investing activities.

III. Completion

1. balance sheet (The income statement, statement of retained earnings, and statement of cash flows all cover a period of time. Only the balance sheet is as of a particular date.)
2. collections of cash from customers
3. direct, indirect (order not important)
4. financing
5. investing
6. operating (Recall from our previous discussion that depreciation is a noncash expense.)
7. investing
8. direct
9. indirect
10. operating activities

IV. True/False

1. F Free cash flow begins with cash flows from operating activities then deducts cash flows from investing activities.
2. F The indirect approach begins with net income. The direct approach ignores net income.
3. T
4. F Increases in current liabilities are added, not deducted.
5. T
6. F The differences in presentation between the two approaches is only found in the operating activities section of the cash-flow statement.

> **Study Tip**: Remember, either approach results in the same basic information on cash flows for the period.

7. F Short-term investments includes equity securities held for the short run which are not cash equivalents.
8. F Interest revenue is an operating activity.
9. F Dividend revenue is an operating activity, while dividends paid is a financing activity.
10. T
11. F The cash received from the sale of plant assets is reported, not the gain (or loss).
12. T
13. T
14. T
15. F Changes in both supplies and accounts payable affect the amounts reported in the operating activities section of the cash-flow statement.

V. Exercises

1.
    a) operating activity
    b) investing activity
    c) operating activity
    d) financing activity
    e) financing activity
    f) operating activity
    g) operating activity
    h) investing activity

i) none (this is a noncash investing activity)
j) operating activity
k) operating activity
l) financing activity
m) investing activity
n) financing activity

Study Tip: Remember, operating activities relate to the income statement, investing activities to long-term assets, and financing activities to long-term liabilities and stockholders' equity.

---

2. Note that this exercise and the next ones may be solved using what you learned in earlier chapters.

	Interest Payable (beginning)	$2,100
+	Interest Expense	54,000
=	Subtotal	56,100
-	Cash payments	?
=	Interest Payable (ending)	$3,600

$2,100 + $54,000 - x = $3,600
x = $52,500

3.

	Cost of Goods Sold	$600,000
+	Increase in Inventory	15,000
=	Subtotal	615,000
-	Increase in Accounts Payable	27,000
=	Cash paid to suppliers	$588,000

4. Cash received from credit sales:

	Accounts Receivable (beginning)	$40,000
+	Credit sales (90% × 2,100,000)	1,890,000
=	Subtotal	1,930,000
-	Cash collected from customers	?
=	Accounts Receivable (ending)	$95,000

Cash received from credit sales ($1,930,000 - $95,000)	$1,835,000
Cash collected from cash sales (10% × 2,100,000)	210,000
= Total cash collected from customers	$2,045,000

5.

Purchase of equipment	$(185,000)
Loan made to customer	(32,000)
Sale of securities	12,000
Net cash flow from investing activities	$(205,000)

Borrowing $42,000 is not an investing activity. It is a financing activity.

6.

Cash flows from operating activities:	
Cash receipts from customers	615,200
Cash receipts from dividends	780
Cash receipts from interest	1,820
Cash payments to suppliers	(328,590)
Cash payments to employees	(103,200)
Cash paid for taxes	(43,110)
Cash payments for interest	(4,965)
Net cash inflow from operating	$137.935

The cash paid for dividends is not an operating activity. Dividends paid to shareholders relate to stockholders' equity on the balance sheet and are, therefore, a financing activity.

VI. Critical Thinking

Exercise 2	Interest Expense	$54,000
	* Less increase in Interest Payable	1,500
	Payments for interest	$52,500

*The increase in the related liability is deducted because it represents an expense which has not been paid. Similarly, a decrease in the related liability would be added. Remember we are concerned with <u>cash payments</u>.

Exercise 4	Sales	$2,100,000
	** Less increase in Accounts Receivable	55,000
	Cash received from customers	$2,045,000

**The increase in Accounts Receivable is deducted because it represents credit sales which have not been collected. Similarly a decrease in Accounts Receivable would be added because it represents additional credit sales collected. Remember we are concerned with <u>cash receipts</u>.

VII. Demonstration Problems

Demonstration Problem #1 Solved and Explained

Requirement 1 (direct method)

NobleBarn.com
Statement of Cash Flows
For the Year Ended December 31, 2002

Cash flows from operating activities:		
Receipts:		
Collections from customers	$3,530,000 (A)	
Dividends received on investments in stock	67,500 (B)	
Total cash receipts		$3,597,500
Payments:		
To suppliers	2,735,000 (C)	
To employees	312,500 (D)	
For interest	162,500 (C)	
Total cash payments		3,210,000

Net cash inflow from operating activities		387,500

Cash flows from investing activities:

Acquisition of plant assets	(50,000) (E)	
Proceeds from sale of land	212,500 (F)	
Acquisition of industrial park land	(185,000) (J)	
Net cash outflow from investing activities		(22,500)

Cash flows from financing activities:

Proceeds from common stock issuance	125,000 (G)	
Payment of long-term note payable	(100,000) (H)	
Dividends	(40,000) (I)	
Net cash outflow from financing activities		(15,000)
Net increase in cash		350,000
Cash balance beginning of year		230,000
Cash balance end of year		$580,000

Noncash investing and financing activities:

Acquisition of plant assets by issuing note payable		$275,000 (E)

Computations and Explanations

(A) The largest cash inflow from operations will almost always be the collection of cash from customers. Cash sales obviously will bring in cash immediately. Since sales on account increase Accounts Receivable (not Cash), companies need to know the actual collections from customers. Item (a) of the additional data indicates that collections from customers were more than sales by $17,500. Thus, collections must have been $3,530,000 ($3,512,500 sales plus $17,500).

(B) Dividends do not accrue with the passage of time, but rather are recorded when received. Item (b) of the additional data states that $67,500 was received, the identical amount shown in the income statement. Thus, no adjustment is necessary. Note that dividends received result in a cash inflow reported as an operating activity. Although the origin of the dividend was from an investment activity, in accordance with the FASB, dividends received were accounted for as part of operating activities because they have a direct impact on net income.

(C) Payments to suppliers is a broad category which includes all cash payments for inventory and all operating expenses except disbursements for:

1. employee compensation expense
2. interest expense
3. income tax expense

A review of Item (c) indicates that payments to suppliers were $2,735,000 ($2,657,500 + $77,500) as follows:

Cost of goods sold	$2,702,500
Less: Additional amounts owed to suppliers	45,000
Payments for inventory	$2,657,500
Payments for Other operating expenses	$77,500

Payments to suppliers include all payments (except those listed above as exceptions) to those who supply the business with its inventory and essential services. Note that interest payment equals interest expense, an item that is separately disclosed in the statement of cash flows.

(D) Payments to employees include all forms of employee compensation. The income statement reports the expense (including accrued amounts), whereas the statement of cash flows reports only the payments. Item (d) indicates that actual payments were $312,500, which is $10,000 less than the $322,500 reported in the income statement as salary expense.

(E) The purchase of $325,000 in plant assets used $50,000 in cash. The balance was financed with a $275,000 promissory note. Because the note is not an outflow of cash, it is separately disclosed as a noncash investing activity at the bottom of the statement of cash flows.

The $185,000 industrial park land (Item j) used $185,000 cash and is shown as a cash outflow or "use." A firm's investment in income-producing assets often signals to investors the direction that the firm is taking.

(F) The receipt of $212,500 from the land sale (Item f) is essentially the opposite of the acquisition of a plant asset, and should be reported as a cash inflow from an investment transaction.

(G) Investors and other financial statement users want to know how an entity obtains its financing. The financing activities section of the cash-flow statement for NobleBarn.com discloses the effect of the sale of common stock (inflow of $125,000, Item g), payment of a long-term note (outflow of $100,000, Item h), and payment of cash dividends (outflow of $40,000, Item i).

Requirement 2 (free cash flow)

$365,000

Free cash flow is the difference between cash flows from operating activities and cash flows from investing activities. A review of the cash-flow statement shows cash inflows from operating activities of $387,500 and net cash outflows from investing activities of $22,500. Therefore, free cash flows are $387,500 - $22,500 = $365,000.

Demonstration Problem #2 Solved and Explained

Indirect Method

NobleBarn.com
Statement of Cash Flows
For the Year Ended December 31, 2002

Cash flows from operating activities:		
Net income (from income statement):		$165,000
Add (subtract) items that affect net income and cash flow differently:		
Depreciation	137,500	
Amortization	12,500	
Decrease in accounts receivable	17,500	
Decrease in inventory	15,000	

Increase in accounts payable	30,000	
Increase in salary payable	10,000	222,500
Net cash inflow from operating activities		387,500

Cash flows from investing activities:

Acquisition of plant assets	(50,000)	
Proceeds from sale of land	212,500	
Acquisition of industrial park land	(185,000)	
Net cash outflow from investing activities		(22,500)

Cash flows from financing activities:

Proceeds from common stock issuance	125,000	
Payment of long-term note payable	(100,000)	
Dividends	(40,000)	
Net cash outflow from financing activities		(15,000)
Net increase in cash		$350,000
Cash balance beginning of year		230,000
Cash balance end of year		$580,000

Noncash investing and financing activities:

Acquisition of plant assets by issuing note payable		$275,000

As emphasized many times in this chapter, the difference between the direct method and the indirect method appears only in the presentation of the cash flows from operating activities section of the statement. The indirect method begins with net income, then 'adjusts' the net income figure in order to convert it to a cash based value. Regardless of method, the presentation of cash flows from investing activities and financing activities are the same. FASB No. 95 permits either method, but recommends the direct method because it is thought to be more "user friendly."

CHAPTER 13—FINANCIAL STATEMENT ANALYSIS

CHAPTER OVERVIEW

Financial statements are the primary means an outsider uses to evaluate a particular company. Once completed, the results can be compared with other companies. There are a variety of tools used to evaluate performance. In this chapter you are introduced to some of these techniques. The learning objectives for the chapter are to

1. Perform a horizontal analysis of comparative financial statements
2. Perform a vertical analysis of financial statements
3. Prepare and use common-size financial statements
4. Use the statement of cash flows in decision making
5. Compute the standard financial ratios used for decision making
6. Use ratios in decision making
7. Measure economic value added by a company's operations

CHAPTER REVIEW

Financial statement analysis is based on information taken from the annual report, SEC reports, articles in the business press, and so on. The objective of financial statement analysis is to provide information to creditors and investors to help them 1) predict future returns and 2) assess the risk of those returns. Past performance is often a good indicator of future performance. Three categories of financial statement analysis are: horizontal, vertical, and ratio analysis.

Objective 1 - Perform a horizontal analysis of comparative financial statements.

The study of percentage changes in comparative statements is called **horizontal analysis**. Horizontal analysis highlights changes over time. Computing a percentage change in comparative statements requires two steps: 1) compute the dollar amount of the change from the base period to the later period, and 2) divide the dollar amount of the change by the base period amount.

The **base period** for horizontal analysis is the year prior to the year being considered. Suppose there are three years of data. The change from Year 1 to Year 2 is:

$$\frac{\$\ YEAR\ 2 - \$\ YEAR\ 1}{\$\ YEAR\ 1}$$

and the change from Year 2 to Year 3 is:

$$\frac{\$\ YEAR\ 3 - \$\ YEAR\ 2}{\$\ YEAR\ 2}$$

No percentage changes are computed if the base-year amount is zero or negative. Exhibits 13-2 and 13-3 illustrate horizontal analysis on an income statement and balance sheet.

Trend percentages are a form of horizontal analysis. They indicate the direction of business activities by comparing numbers over a span of several years. Trend percentages are computed by selecting a base year and expressing the amount of each item for each of the following years as a percentage of the base year's amount for that item.

Objective 2 - Perform a vertical analysis of financial statements.

Vertical analysis of a financial statement reveals the percentage of the total that each statement item represents. Percentages on the comparative income statement are computed by dividing all amounts by net sales. Percentages on the comparative balance sheet are shown as either 1) a percentage of total assets or 2) a percentage of total liabilities and stockholders' equity.

Vertical analysis of the income statement highlights changes in such items as the gross profit percentage and net income.

Vertical analysis of the balance sheet shows the composition of balance sheet items. Trend analysis can be used to highlight year-to-year percentage changes.

(Review Exhibits 13-4 and 13-5 in your text.)

Objective 3 - Prepare and use common-size financial statements.

Common-size statements report amounts in percentages only. The common-size statement is a form of vertical analysis. On a common-size income statement, each item is expressed as a percentage of the net sales amount. In the balance sheet, the common size is the total on each side of the accounting equation. Note that common-size percentages are the same percentages shown on financial statements using vertical analysis. (Review Exhibit 13-6 in your text.)

Benchmarking is the practice of comparing to a standard set by other companies. Benchmarking is used to compare a company's results with the average for their industry. In addition, common-size statements can be compared with those of specific competitors within the industry. Exhibits 13-7 and 13-8 in your text illustrate these two uses of benchmarking.

Common-size percentages can be used to compare financial statements of different companies or to compare one company's financial statements to industry averages.

Objective 4 - Use the statement of cash flows in decision making.

The statement of cash flows presents the cash flows from operating, investing, and financing activities.

Questions to consider might include:

1. Does the company generate the majority of its cash from operations, from selling fixed assets, or from borrowing?
2. Does the company retain enough income to finance future operations?

Objective 5 - Compute the standard financial ratios used for decision making.

There are many, many different ratios used in financial analysis. Sometimes a ratio is used alone, but more frequently a group of ratios are calculated and used to analyze a particular issue. The ratios discussed in this section are grouped as follows:

1. Ratios that measure the company's ability to pay current liabilities
2. Ratios that measure the company's ability to sell inventory and collect receivables
3. Ratios that measure the company's ability to pay long-term debt
4. Ratios that measure the company's profitability
5. Ratios used to analyze the company's stock as an investment

1. **Ratios that measure the company's ability to pay current liabilities**

Working capital is used to measure a business's ability to meet its short-term obligations with its current assets.

$$\text{WORKING CAPITAL} = \text{CURRENT ASSETS} - \text{CURRENT LIABILITIES}$$

The **current ratio** is used to measure the availability of sufficient liquid assets to maintain normal business operations.

$$\text{CURRENT RATIO} \quad = \quad \frac{\text{CURRENT ASSETS}}{\text{CURRENT LIABILITIES}}$$

The **acid-test (quick) ratio** measures the ability of a business to pay all of its current liabilities if they came due immediately.

$$\text{ACID-TEST RATIO} \quad = \quad \frac{\text{CASH} + \text{SHORT-TERM INVESTMENTS} + \text{NET CURRENT RECEIVABLES}}{\text{CURRENT LIABILITIES}}$$

> **Study Tip:** Inventory and prepaid expenses are not used to compute the acid-test ratio.

2. **Ratios that measure the company's ability to sell inventory and collect receivables**

Inventory turnover is a measure of the number of times a company sells an average level of inventory during a year.

$$\text{INVENTORY TURNOVER} \quad = \quad \frac{\text{COST OF GOODS SOLD}}{\text{AVERAGE INVENTORY}}$$

$$\text{AVERAGE INVENTORY} \quad = \quad \frac{\text{BEGINNING INVENTORY} + \text{ENDING INVENTORY}}{2}$$

Accounts receivable turnover measures the ability of a company to collect cash from its credit customers.

$$\begin{array}{ccc}
\text{ACCOUNTS} & & \\
\text{RECEIVABLE} & & \dfrac{\text{NET CREDIT SALES}}{\text{AVERAGE NET ACCOUNTS RECEIVABLE}} \\
\text{TURNOVER} & = & \\
\end{array}$$

$$\begin{array}{ccc}
\text{AVERAGE NET} & & \\
\text{ACCOUNTS} & = & \dfrac{\text{BEGINNING ACCOUNTS RECEIVABLE} + \text{ENDING ACCOUNTS RECEIVABLE}}{2} \\
\text{RECEIVABLE} & & \\
\end{array}$$

Days' sales in receivables measures in sales days the value of accounts receivable; it tells how many days' sales remain uncollected (in accounts receivable).

$$\text{ONE DAY'S SALES} = \dfrac{\text{NET SALES}}{365}$$

$$\begin{array}{ccc}
\text{DAYS' SALES IN} & & \\
\text{AVERAGE ACCOUNTS} & = & \dfrac{\text{AVERAGE NET ACCOUNTS RECEIVABLE}}{\text{ONE DAY'S SALES}} \\
\text{RECEIVABLE} & & \\
\end{array}$$

To compute the ratio for the beginning of the year, substitute beginning net Accounts Receivable for average net Accounts Receivable. To compute the ratio for the end of the year, substitute ending net Accounts Receivable for average net Accounts Receivable.

3. **Ratios that measures the company's ability to pay long-term debt**

The **debt ratio** measures the relationship between total liabilities and total assets.

$$\text{DEBT RATIO} = \dfrac{\text{TOTAL LIABILITIES}}{\text{TOTAL ASSETS}}$$

The **times-interest-earned ratio** (also called the **interest-coverage ratio**) measures the ability of a business to pay interest expense.

$$\begin{array}{ccc}
\text{TIMES-} & & \\
\text{INTEREST-EARNED} & = & \dfrac{\text{INCOME FROM OPERATIONS}}{\text{INTEREST EXPENSE}} \\
\text{RATIO} & & \\
\end{array}$$

Remember that income from operations does not include interest revenue, interest expense, or income tax expense.

4. **Ratios that measure the company's profitability**

Rate of return on net sales measures the relationship between net income and sales.

$$\text{RATE OF RETURN ON NET SALES} = \frac{\text{NET INCOME}}{\text{NET SALES}}$$

Rate of return on total assets measures the success a company has in using its assets to earn a profit.

$$\text{RATE OF RETURN ON TOTAL ASSETS} = \frac{\text{NET INCOME + INTEREST EXPENSE}}{\text{AVERAGE TOTAL ASSETS}}$$

$$\text{AVERAGE TOTAL ASSETS} = \frac{\text{BEGINNING TOTAL ASSETS + ENDING TOTAL ASSETS}}{2}$$

The **rate of return on common stockholders' equity** shows the relationship between net income and common stockholders' investment in the company.

$$\text{RATE OF RETURN ON COMMON STOCKHOLDERS' EQUITY} = \frac{\text{NET INCOME - PREFERRED DIVIDENDS}}{\text{AVERAGE COMMON STOCKHOLDERS' EQUITY}}$$

$$\text{AVERAGE COMMON STOCKHOLDERS' EQUITY} = \frac{\text{BEGINNING + ENDING COMMON STOCKHOLDERS' EQUITY}}{2}$$

Earnings per share (EPS) is the amount of net income per share of the company's common stock.

$$\text{EPS} = \frac{\text{NET INCOME - PREFERRED DIVIDENDS}}{\text{NUMBER OF SHARES OF COMMON STOCK OUTSTANDING}}$$

Study Tip: Remember, if the number of shares outstanding has changed during the year, the denominator is changed to reflect the **weighted average** number of shares outstanding.

5. **Ratios used to analyze the company's stock as an investment**

The **price/earnings (P/E) ratio** is the ratio of the market price of a share of common stock to the company's EPS.

$$\text{PRICE/EARNINGS RATIO} = \frac{\text{MARKET PRICE PER SHARE OF COMMON STOCK}}{\text{EARNINGS PER SHARE}}$$

Dividend yield is the ratio of dividends per share of stock to the stock's market price per share.

$$\text{DIVIDENDS YIELD ON COMMON STOCK} = \frac{\text{DIVIDENDS PER SHARE OF COMMON STOCK}}{\text{MARKET PRICE PER SHARE OF COMMON STOCK}}$$

The formula for calculating **book value per share of common stock** is:

$$\text{BOOK VALUE PER SHARE OF COMMON STOCK} = \frac{\text{TOTAL STOCKHOLDERS' EQUITY - PREFERRED EQUITY}}{\text{NUMBER OF SHARES OF COMMON STOCK OUTSTANDING}}$$

Objective 6 - Use ratios in decision making.

Ratios should be 1) evaluated over a period of years, and 2) compared with industry standards.

When a problem is found, the items used to compute the ratio should be analyzed to determine the nature of the problem. At that time, possible solutions to the problem can be suggested.

Objective 7 - Measure economic value added by a company's operations.

Economic value added (EVA) is one measure many companies use to evaluate whether the company has increased stockholder wealth from operations. The formula for EVA is

Net income + interest expense - (capital charge × cost of capital)

Capital charge is notes payable plus loans payable plus long-term debt and stockholders' equity. The **cost of capital** is the weighted average of the returns demanded by the company's stockholders and lenders. Newer companies, because of the added risk, have a higher cost of capital compared with older, more established companies. The underlying assumption behind EVA is that returns to both stockholders and lenders should be greater than the company's capital charge. If the calculation results in a positive value, the result indicates an increase in stockholder wealth. If negative, stockholders may consider selling the stock which, if done in large enough amounts, could lower the price of the stock. Obviously, companies who use this measure strive to achieve a positive result.

In an efficient capital market, stock prices reflect all information that is available to the public. Financial statement analysis helps to identify and evaluate the inherent risks in potential investments.

TEST YOURSELF

All the self-testing materials in this chapter focus on information and procedures that your instructor is likely to test in quizzes and examinations.

I. Matching   *Match each numbered term with its lettered definition.*

_____ 1. accounts receivable turnover
_____ 2. working capital
_____ 3. common-size statements
_____ 4. days' sales in receivables
_____ 5. dividend yield
_____ 6. inventory turnover
_____ 7. return on total assets
_____ 8. times-interest-earned ratio
_____ 9. vertical analysis
_____ 10. acid-test ratio

_____ 11. current ratio
_____ 12. debt ratio
_____ 13. horizontal analysis
_____ 14. price/earnings ratio
_____ 15. return on net sales
_____ 16. book value per share of common stock
_____ 17. return on common stockholders' equity
_____ 18. benchmarking
_____ 19. cost of capital
_____ 20. economic value added

A. analysis of a financial statement that reveals the relationship of each statement item to the total which is the 100% figure
B. common stockholders' equity divided by the number of shares of common stock outstanding
C. current assets divided by current liabilities
D. current assets minus current liabilities
E. financial statements that report only percentages (no dollar amounts)
F. measures the number of times that operating income can cover interest expense
G. measures the number of times a company sells its average level of inventory during a year
H. ratio of the market price of a share of common stock to the company's earnings per share
I. measures the success a company has in using its assets to earn a profit
J. net income minus preferred dividends, divided by average common stockholders' equity; a measure of profitability
K. ratio of average net accounts receivable to one day's sales
L. ratio of dividends per share to the stock's market price per share
M. ratio of net income to net sales; a measure of profitability
N. study of percentage changes in comparative financial statements
O. tells the proportion of a company's assets that it has financed with debt
P. tells whether an entity could pay all its current liabilities if they came due immediately
Q. the ratio of net credit sales to average net accounts receivable; it measures ability to collect cash from credit customers
R. used to measure if a company has increased shareholder wealth from operations
S. the practice of comparing a company with other companies with a view toward improvement
T. a weighted average of the returns demanded by the company's stockholders and lenders

II. Multiple Choice   *Circle the best answer.*

1. In vertical analysis the relationship between net income and net sales is shown by the

    A. income from operations percentage
    B. net income percentage
    C. rate of return on sales
    D. gross profit percentage

2. Which of the following measures profitability?

    A. debt ratio
    B. current ratio
    C. dividend yield
    D. earnings per share common stock

3. Which of the following current assets is not used to compute the acid-test ratio?

    A. accounts receivable
    B. cash
    C. prepaid expenses
    D. short-term investments

4. Which of the following is a common measure of a firm's ability to meet short-term obligations?

    A. working capital
    B. rate of return on sales
    C. net assets
    D. price/earnings ratio

5. The times-interest-earned ratio measures

    A. profitability
    B. ability to pay interest expense on debt
    C. ability to pay current liabilities
    D. ability to collect receivables

6. The proportion of a firm's assets financed by debt is measured by the

    A. current ratio
    B. debt ratio
    C. debt yield ratio
    D. times-interest-earned ratio

7. Assume that a company's current ratio is greater than one. If the company pays current liabilities with cash, the new current ratio will

   A. increase
   B. decrease
   C. remain unchanged
   D. cannot be determined

8. The dividend yield evaluates

   A. the ability to pay current debt
   B. profitability
   C. stock as an investment
   D. ability to pay long-term debt

9. The excess of current assets less current liabilities is

   A. a measure of profitability
   B. economic value added
   C. a measure of short-term liquidity
   D. a measure of long-term debt paying ability

10. Book value measures

   A. profitability
   B. short-term liquidity
   C. long-term debt paying ability
   D. stock as an investment

III. Completion   *Complete each of the following statements.*

1. The study of percentage changes in comparative financial statements is called _____ analysis.

2. Vertical analysis percentages on the income statement are computed by dividing all amounts by _____.

3. Vertical analysis percentages on the balance sheet are computed by dividing all amounts by _____ _____.

4. Working capital is _____.

5. _____ and _____ are the two most common measures of firm size.

6. Leverage _____ the risk to common stockholders.

7. The _____ ratio indicates the market price of one dollar of earnings.

8. The rate of return on total assets equals _____.

9. The most widely quoted of all financial statistics is _____.

10. The _____ is the recorded accounting value of each share of common stock outstanding.

IV. True/False   *For each of the following statements, circle* T *for true or* F *for false.*

1.   T F   Trend percentages are a form of horizontal analysis.
2.   T F   Vertical analysis is one means for analyzing change over time.
3.   T F   Common-size statements contain no dollar amounts, only percentages.
4.   T F   Benchmarking is more closely related to vertical analysis than horizontal analysis.
5.   T F   Rate of return on sales measures a company's ability to pay current debt.
6.   T F   Working capital can be a negative value.
7.   T F   Quick assets consist of cash, short-term investments, net accounts receivable and inventories.
8.   T F   Inventory turnover measures a company's ability to sell on credit and collect cash for those credit sales.
9.   T F   Earnings per share is calculated by dividing net income less preferred dividends by the number of shares outstanding at the end of the year.
10. T F   The price/earnings ratio divides earnings per share into the par value of the common stock
11. T F   The acid-test ratio can never be greater than the current ratio.
12. T F   EVA stands for extra value added.
13. T F   Benchmarking relates one company's results with another company's or the industry's.
14. T F   Generally, the greater the inventory turnover the lower the accounts receivable turnover.
15. T F   Capital charge refers to various liabilities and stockholders' equity.

V. Exercises

1. Net income was $300,000 in Year 1, $500,000 in Year 2, and $400,000 in Year 3. What were the percentage changes in net income?

2. Singh Industries had the following information for 2002:

Cost of goods sold	$600,000
Beginning inventory	40,000
Ending inventory	80,000
Net credit sales	1,125,000
Beginning accounts receivable	85,000
Ending accounts receivable	75,000

A. What is inventory turnover?

B. What is the accounts receivable turnover?

C. What is the days' sales in average receivable?

3. The following information is given for Pradesh Corporation for 2002:

Net sales	$825,000
Net income	60,000
Average common stockholders' equity	3,150,000
Average total assets	4,225,000
Interest expense	75,000
Preferred dividends	20,000
Common dividends	55,000
Common stock outstanding	240,000 shares

A. What is the rate of return on net sales?

B. What is the rate of return on total assets?

C. What is the rate of return on common stockholders' equity?

4. The following information is given for NotNow.com:

Assets:	
Cash	$ 30,000
Marketable securities	59,000
Accounts receivable	107,000
Inventory	70,500
Equipment	120,000
Total assets	$476,500

Liabilities and Stockholders' Equity:	
Accounts payable	$ 52,500
Salary payable	8,500
Long-term bonds payable	82,500
Common stock	100,000
Retained earnings	233,000
Total liabilities and stockholders' equity	$476,500

A. What is the current ratio?

B. What is the acid-test (quick) ratio?

C. What is the debt ratio?

5. Calvin Filger, Inc., has a price/earnings ratio of 12, dividends of $.90 per share, and earnings per share of $1.98.

   A. What is the market price per share?

   B. What is the dividend yield?

VI. Critical Thinking

The operating cycle is the length of time between the purchase of merchandise and its conversion to cash following the sale and receipt of payment (you were introduced to the operating cycle in Chapter 5). Using the information in Exercise 2 above, calculate the operating cycle for Singh Industries.

_____

_____

_____

_____

_____

_____

_____

_____

VII. Demonstration Problems

Demonstration Problem #1

The Granzella Company, headquartered in Richmond, California, manufactures products for the home. Figures from their 2001 annual report (slightly modified for ease of presentation) follow:

The Granzella Company
Statement of Consolidated Earnings
For Year Ended December 31, 2001

	(In thousands)
Net sales	$1,073,022
Cost and expenses	
Cost of products sold	687,103
Selling, delivery, and administration	241,711
Depreciation	15,607
Discount on sales of receivables	3,963
Interest expense	17,546
Other (income) expense, net	1,827
Total costs and expenses	964,103
Earnings before income taxes	108,919
Income Taxes	43,819
Net earnings	$ 65,100
Weighted average shares outstanding	42,600

The Granzella Company
Consolidated Balance Sheet
December 31, 2001

	(In thousands)	
	2001	2000
Assets		
Current assets:		
Cash and short-term investments	8,326	5,225
Accounts receivable, less allowance	125,126	121,763
Inventories	146,002	156,245
Deferred income taxes	20,155	34,038
Prepaid expenses	4,662	3,561
Total current assets	304,271	320,832
Property, plant, and equipment—net	319,677	290,960
Brands, trademarks, patents and other intangibles—net	204,422	202,323
Other assets	32,510	25,831
Total	$860,880	$839,946

Liabilities and Stockholders' Equity
Current liabilities:

Accounts payable	$ 61,168	$ 70,106
Accrued liabilities	110,522	144,863
Income taxes payable	3,474	27,279
Short-term debt	4,013	5,128
Current maturity of long-term debt	116	912
Total current liabilities	179,293	248,288
Long-term debt	199,355	166,279
Other obligations	17,107	18,677
Deferred income taxes	66,300	54,524
Stockholders' equity		
Common stock - authorized, 50,000,000 shares,		
$.01 par value; issued: 43,140,586 shares	431	431
Additional paid-in capital	126,432	121,124
Retained earnings	333,846	278,649
Treasury shares, at cost: 2001, 1,490,000 shares;		
2000, 1,210,700 shares	(52,563)	(40,433)
Cumulative translation adjustments	(9,321)	(7,593)
Total stockholders' equity	398,825	352,178
Total liabilities and stockholders' equity	$860,880	$839,946

Required:

Assume annual dividends of $.80 and a market price of 11 1/8 per share. Compute the following for 2001:

A) working capital

B) current ratio

C) acid-test (quick) ratio

D) inventory turnover

E) accounts receivable turnover

F) days' sales in receivables

G) number of days in operating cycle

H) debt ratio

I) times-interest-earned ratio

J) rate of return on sales

K) rate of return on total assets

L) rate of return on common stockholders' equity

M) earnings per share

N) price/earnings ratio

O) dividend yield

P) book value per share of common stock

Demonstration Problem #2

Vitality Corporation's balance sheets and income statements are presented below:

Vitality Corporation
Balance Sheet
Years 2002 and 2001

	2002	2001
Assets		
Current assets:		
Cash	$ 13,300	$ 20,350
Short-term investments	8,200	8,000
Receivables, net	26,000	24,000
Inventories	45,000	40,000
Prepaid expenses	2,500	4,650
Total current assets	95,000	97,000
Property, plant, and equipment—net	185,680	196,500
Land	40,000	35,000
Intangibles and other assets	2,400	2,400
Total assets	$323,080	$330,900
Liabilities and Stockholders' Equity		
Current liabilities:		
Notes payable	$ 10,000	$ 10,500
Current installments of long-term debt	3,550	3,445
Accounts payable-trade	14,447	18,500
Accrued liabilities	3,670	1,605
Total current liabilities	31,667	34,050
Long-term debt, less current installments	95,500	93,330
Capital lease obligations, less current portion	1,100	2,150
Deferred income and deferred income taxes	4,813	4,370
Total common stockholders' equity	190,000	197,000
Total liabilities and stockholders' equity	$323,080	$330,900

Vitality Corporation
Income Statements
Years 2002 and 2001

	2002	2001
Net sales	$416,500	$406,316
Cost and expenses:		
Cost of goods sold	322,593	315,812
Operating expenses	41,219	43,200
	363,812	359,012
Income from operations	52,688	47,304
Interest expense	3,251	3,150
Earnings before income taxes	49,437	44,154
Income taxes	7,437	6,554
Net income	$ 42,000	$ 37,600

Required:

1. Prepare a horizontal analysis for 2002 of the balance sheet, using the 2001 amounts as the base.

Vitality Corporation				
Balance Sheet				
Years 2002 and 2001				
	2002	2001	Amount Increase (Decrease)	% Change
Assets				
Current assets:				
Cash	$ 13,300	$ 20,350		
Short-term investments	8,200	8,000		
Receivables, net	26,000	24,000		
Inventories	45,000	40,000		
Prepaid expenses	2,500	4,650		
Total current assets	95,000	97,000		
Property, plant, and equipment—net	185,680	196,500		
Land	40,000	35,000		
Intangibles and other assets	2,400	2,400		
Total assets	$323,080	$330,900		

Liabilities and stockholders' equity				
Current liabilities:				
Notes payable	$ 10,000	$ 10,500		
Current installments of long-term debt	3,550	3,445		
Accounts payable-trade	14,447	18,500		
Accrued liabilities	3,670	1,605		
Total current liabilities	31,667	34,050		
Long-term debt, less current installments	95,500	93,330		
Capital lease obligations, less current portion	1,100	2,150		
Deferred income and deferred income taxes	4,813	4,370		
Total common stockholders' equity	190,000	197,000		
Total liabilities and stockholders' equity	$323,080	$330,900		

2. Convert the 2002 and 2001 Income Statements to common-size statements, using net sales as the base figures.

Vitality Corporation				
Income Statements				
Years 2002 and 2001				
	2002		2001	
	Amount	%	Amount	%
Net sales	$416,500		$406,316	
Cost and expenses:				
Cost of goods sold	322,593		315,812	
Operating expenses	41,219		43,200	
Total costs and expenses	363,812		359,012	
Income from operations	52,688		47,304	
Interest expense	3,251		3,150	
Earnings before income taxes	49,437		44,154	
Income taxes	7,437		6,554	
Net income	$ 42,000		$ 37,600	

SOLUTIONS

I. Matching

1. Q	5. L	9. A	13. N	17. J
2. D	6. G	10. P	14. H	18. S
3. E	7. I	11. C	15. M	19. T
4. K	8. F	12. O	16. B	20. R

II. Multiple Choice

1.   C   The rate of return on sale is net income / net sales.

2.   D   Debt ratio measures the ability to pay long-term debts. Current ratio measures ability to pay current liabilities. Dividend yield is used in analyzing stock as an investment.

3.   C   Only the most liquid current assets are used to calculate the acid-test ratio.

4.   A   Working capital is current assets less current liabilities. It measures a firm's ability to meet short-term obligations.

5.   B   Times-interest-earned measures how many times operating income is greater than interest expense.

6.   B   Current ratio measures the ability to pay current liabilities. Debt yield ratio has no meaning. Times-interest-earned ratio measures ability to pay interest on debt. The debt ratio is total liabilities / total assets.

7.   A   Let CA = current assets, CL = current liabilities, and X = the amount of cash paid on current liabilities. Then given that CA > CL (or CL < CA), show that:

$$(CA - X) / (CL - X) > \quad CA / CL$$
$$CL(CA - X) > \quad CA(CL - X)$$
$$CL(CA) - CL(X) > \quad CA(CL) - CA(X)$$
$$-CL(X) > \quad -CA(X)$$

dividing by -X: CL <   CA

> **Study Tip:** In a firm with current assets greater than current liabilities, the current ratio can be improved by using cash to pay current liabilities.

8.   C   Dividend yield compares the amount of dividend per share with the current market price and therefore is one way to evaluate a stock as a potential investment.

9.   C   Working capital (the excess of current assets over current liabilities) measures short-term liquidity.

10.   D   Book value indicates the value of each share of common stock outstanding and is one way to analyze a stock investment.

III. Completion

1. horizontal
2. net sales
3. total assets (or total liabilities plus stockholders' equity)
4. current assets minus current liabilities
5. Net sales, total assets
6. increases (Leverage is the practice of increasing the debt financing of an entity with respect to owner financing. Leverage is a two-edged sword, increasing profits (and returns to stockholders') during good times but compounding losses during bad times.)
7. price/earnings
8. (net income plus interest expense) / average total assets
9. earnings per share
10. book value per share of common stock

IV. True/False

1. T
2. F   Vertical analysis only looks at one year's activity and therefore is not a way to analyze change over time.
3. T
4. T
5. F   Rate of return on sales is a measure of profitability.
6. T

> **Study Tip:** When current liabilities exceed current assets, the result is negative working capital. Negative working capital always exists when the current ratio is less than 1.

7. F   For most industries, inventory is excluded from quick assets.
8. F   Inventory turnover tells you nothing about collecting cash owed from customers.
9. F   The denominator is weighted average number of shares for the year. You would use the year-end figure only when there has been no change in outstanding shares throughout the year.

> **Study Tip:** This is one of the most frequent mistakes students make when calculating ratios. Just remember, net income reflects the entire accounting period - therefore, we should relate it to something with a similar basis.

10. F   The P/E ratio numerator is the current market price per share.
11. T
12. F   EVA stands for economic value added.
13. T
14. F   The two are unrelated.
15. T

V. Exercises

1. Year 2 = $200,000 / $300,000 = 66.7%
   Year 3 = ($100,000) / $500,000 = (20%)

2. A. Cost of goods / Average inventory = [$600,000 / ($40,000 + $80,000) / 2] = 10
   B. Net credit sales / Average accounts receivable = [$1,125,000 / ($85,000 + $75,000) / 2] =

14.06
C. Average accounts receivable / One day's sales = [($85,000 + $75,000) / 2] / ($1,125,000 / 365) = 26 days (rounded)

3. A. Net income / Net sales = $60,000 / $825,000 = .073 = 7.3%
   B. (Net income + Interest expense) / Average total assets = ($60,000 + $75,000) / $4,225,000 = .032 = 3.2%
   C. (Net income - Preferred dividends) / Average common stockholders' equity = ($60,000 - $20,000) / $3,150,000 = .013 = 1.3%

4. A. Current assets / Current liabilities = ($30,000 + $59,000 + $107,000 + $70,500) / ($52,500 + $8,500) = 4.4 (rounded)
   B. (Cash + Short-term investments + Net current receivables) / Current liabilities = ($30,000 + $59,000 + $107,000) / ($52,500 + $8,500) = 3.2

> **Study Tip:** Remember only the assets that will convert to cash "quickly" are called quick assets. Inventory does not do this.

   C. Total liabilities / Total assets = ($52,500 + $8,500 + $82,500) / $476,500 = .301 = 30.1%

5. A. Market price per share of common stock / Earnings per share = P / $1.28 = 12; P = $15.36 or $15 3/8.

   B. Dividends per share of common stock / Market price per share of common stock = $.90 / $15.36 = .058 = 5.8%

VI. Critical Thinking

The operating cycle for Singh Industries is 61.5 days. Instruction (C) in the exercise asked you to calculate the days' sales in average receivables. The correct figure was 26 days. Another way of characterizing this result is to say that it takes approximately 26 days to collect an average account receivable. Instruction (A) asked you to calculate inventory turnover. The correct amount was 10—in other words, inventory "turns" approximately 10 times each year. Divide this result into 365 to convert it to days, or 36.5 days. In other words, on average it takes 36.5 days for an item to sell and 26 days on average to collect a receivable. Therefore, the operating cycle is 61.5 days.

VII. Demonstration Problems

Demonstration Problem #1 Solved and Explained

A) working capital = current assets - current liabilities = $304,271 - $179,293 = $124,978

B) current ratio = current assets / current liabilities = $304,271 / $179,293 = 1.7 (rounded)

C) acid-test (quick)　=　quick assets / current liabilities
　　　　　　　　　　=　($8,326 + $125,126) / $179,293 = 0.74 (rounded)

This means Granzella has 74 cents of quick assets (cash and short-term investment plus net accounts receivable) for every dollar of current liability.

D) inventory turnover = cost of goods sold / average inventory
    = $687,103 / [($156,245 + $146,002) / 2] = 4.55 times

Granzella "turns" its inventory 4.55 times each year. Another way of stating this ratio is to convert it to days by dividing the "turn" into 365. For Granzella, the turnover averages 80 days (365 / 4.55).

E) accounts receivable turnover = net credit sales / average accounts receivable
    = $1,073,022 / [($121,763 + $125,126) / 2] = 8.69 times

F) days' sales in receivables = average net accounts receivable / one day's sales
    = $123,444 / ($1,073,022 / 365) = 42 days

The numerator for this ratio was the denominator for the previous ratio.

G) operating cycle = inventory turn + days' sales in receivables = 80 + 42 = 122 days

H) debt ratio = total liabilities / total assets
    = $462,055 / $860,880
    = 0.537 or 53.7%

This means that 53.7% of the Granzella assets were financed with debt. Notice the numerator (total liabilities) was not presented on the balance sheet but had to be calculated by adding together total current liabilities, long-term debt, other obligations, and deferred income taxes.

I) times-interest-earned = income from operations / interest expense
    = $126,465 / $17,546
    = 7.2 times

Note we used earnings before income taxes plus interest expense as the numerator because interest expense had already been deducted from the earnings before income taxes amount.

J) rate of return on sales = net income / net sales
    = $65,100 / $1,073,022
    = 0.06 or 6%

K) rate of return on total assets = (net income + interest expense) / average total assets
    = ($65,100 + $17,546) / [($839,946 + $860,880) / 2]
    = 0.097 or 9.7%

This ratio measures the return on assets generated by this year's operations.

L) rate of return on common stockholders' equity = (net income - preferred dividends) / average common stockholders' equity
    = ($65,100 - 0) / [($352,178 + $398,825) / 2]
    = 0.173 or 17.3%

Granzella does not have preferred stock outstanding, so the numerator is the same as net earnings.

M) earnings per share = (net income - preferred dividends) / weighted average number of common stock outstanding
   = $65,100 / 42,600
   = $1.53 (rounded)

This should be calculated for each "net earnings" amount. Companies are required to include these per share amounts on the income statement, not in the footnotes.

N) price/earnings ratio = market price per share of common stock / earnings per share
   = $11.125 / $1.53 = 7 (rounded)

O) dividend yield = dividend per share of common stock / market price of common stock
   = $.80 / $11.125
   = 0.0719 or 7.19%

P) book value per share of common stock = (total stockholders' equity - preferred equity) / number of shares of common stock outstanding
   = 398,825 / 41,650,586
   = $9.57 per share

The dollars are presented "in thousands," so you must add three zeroes to the total stockholders' equity amount. To determine the number of shares outstanding, deduct the treasury shares (1,490,000) from the issued shares (43,140,586). As emphasized in your text, these ratios would have more meaning if you did them over consecutive years. In addition, to properly evaluate a company you would also want to compare the ratios with those of competitors and with the industry as a whole.

Demonstration Problem #2 Solved and Explained

1.

Vitality Corporation				
Balance Sheet				
Years 2002 and 2001				
	2002	2001	Amount Increase (Decrease)	% Change
Assets				
Current assets:				
Cash	$ 13,300	$ 20,350	$(7,050)	(34.6)
Short-term investments	8,200	8,000	200	2.5
Receivables, net	26,000	24,000	2,000	8.3
Inventories	45,000	40,000	5,000	12.5
Prepaid expenses	2,500	4,650	(2,150)	(46.2)
Total current assets	95,000	97,000	(2,000)	(2.1)
Property, plant, and equipment—net	185,680	196,500	(10,820)	(5.5)
Land	40,000	35,000	5,000	(14.3)
Intangibles and other assets	2,400	2,400	0	0
	$323,080	$330,900	$(7,820)	(2.4)

Liabilities and stockholders' equity				
Current liabilities:				
Notes payable	$ 10,000	$ 10,500	$ (500)	(5.0)
Current installments of long-term debt	3,550	3,445	105	(3.0)
Accounts payable-trade	14,447	18,500	(4,053)	(21.9)
Accrued liabilities	3,670	1,605	2,065	128.7
Total current liabilities	31,667	34,050	(2,383)	(7.0)
Long-term debt, less current installments	95,500	93,330	2,170	2.3
Capital lease obligations, less current portion	1,100	2,150	(1,050)	(48.9)
Deferred income and deferred income taxes	4,813	4,370	443	10.1
Total common stockholders' equity	190,000	197,000	(7,000)	(3.6)
	$323,080	$330,900	$(7,820)	(2.4)

2.

Vitality Corporation				
Income Statements				
Years 2002 and 2001				
	2002		2001	
	Amount	%	Amount	%
Net sales	$416,500	100.0	$406,316	100.0
Cost and expenses:				
Cost of goods sold	322,593	77.5	315,812	77.7
Operating expenses	41,219	9.9	43,200	10.6
	363,812		359,012	
Income from operations	52,688	12.7	47,304	11.6
Interest expense	3,251	0.8	3,150	.8
Earnings before income taxes	49,437	11.9	44,154	10.8
Income taxes	7,437	1.8	6,554	1.6
Net income	$ 42,000	10.1	$ 37,600	9.2

Points to remember:

1. When presenting horizontal analysis, each year's change is divided by the base-year amount (in this case 2001) and converted to a percentage. While the change in any single item in any single year may not be significant, applying horizontal analysis over a number of years may highlight significant changes.

2. Common-size statements for a single year are only meaningful when the results are compared to other companies or industry data. However, common-size statements covering two or more years permit analysis of the particular company being examined. In this case, we see that 2002 results improved over 2001 due to lower cost of goods sold and lower operating expenses.

3. Financial ratios are mathematical formulas that quantify the relationship between two or more items reported in the financial statements. Ratios are used to assess and compare a firm's liquidity, profitability, rate of return, and ability to meet debt obligations.

Study Tip: One of the most common mistakes students make is forgetting to use the average amount of inventory, accounts receivable, or shares outstanding in some of the formulas. It is important that an average be used to reduce distortions that might occur if only year-end balances were used.

APPENDIX A—ANNUAL REPORT OF GAP, INC.

Appendix A presents the annual report of The Gap, Inc.

APPENDIX B—TIME VALUE OF MONEY: FUTURE VALUE AND PRESENT VALUE

Because you can earn interest on your money over time, the value of invested funds is greater in the future than it is today. This refers to the **time value of money**. To determine what a **future value** will be, you simply apply an interest rate to the amount of your investment and calculate the amount of interest. Add this result to your original amount and the sum becomes the future value at the end of one interest period. Repeat this process for additional interest periods, remembering to add in the interest each time. Therefore, there are three factors involved in determining a future value: 1) the amount of the original investment, 2) the length of time, and 3) the interest rate. Obviously the longer the time, the more calculations are involved. Fortunately, mathematical tables are available to ease your task. Review Exhibit B-2 carefully. This is the table used to determine the future value of a single investment, again assuming time and interest rate.

Instead of investing a single amount for a specific period, you might wish to invest multiple amounts over time. This is an example of an **annuity type investment**. In other words, you invest identical amounts for several years—what will the future value of these multiple investments be? Of course, you could calculate each individually and add the results, or you could consult mathematical tables which do the multiple calculations for you. Review Exhibit B-4 carefully. This is the table used to determine a future value of multiple investments, again assuming time and interest rate. This table is used to answer questions like "If I start setting aside (investing) $500 each year for the next ten years, what will it be worth, assuming I can invest this money at 8%?" Exhibit B-4 shows the value 14.487 at the intersection of 10 and 8%. Multiply this value by your annual investment ($500) and the result is $7,243.50.

Another way to look at present and future values is to begin with the future value and work backwards. In other words, in order to have X amount sometime in the future, how much would one need to set aside today? Again assumptions need to be made about the time and the interest rate (this is always true).

As with the preceding discussions, you could calculate the result manually, but the longer the period the more calculations you would have to complete. Once again, mathematical tables are available to use. Study Exhibit B-6 carefully.

Rather than determining the present value of a single amount, you may be interested in the **present value of an annuity-type investment**. In other words, what is the present value of an investment that will give you the same fixed amount over a number of periods? As with earlier discussions, this value can be calculated manually, but it is time-consuming. Once again, tables are available to simplify the process. Study Exhibit B-7 carefully.

> **Study Tip:** BEFORE PROCEEDING, BE CERTAIN YOU UNDERSTAND IN WHICH CIRCUMSTANCES YOU USE WHICH TABLE. This is vital to understanding the topics which follow.

In Chapter 8 you learned about long-term liabilities, primarily bonds payable. What is a bond? It is a way for a company to borrow funds. When a company issues a bond, what happens? The company promises to pay the face value of the bond at maturity and, during the life of the bond, the company also promises to pay a fixed amount of interest periodically. The face value at maturity is a single value, whereas the interest payments are like an annuity. Therefore, when a company issues bonds, it needs to know what price should be asked (remember bond prices are quoted as percentages of face value) in order to attract investors. To determine this, consult the appropriate tables—in this case B-6 and B-7 in your text. Using the market rate of interest, the first table will give you the present value of a future single amount, the second will give the present value of an annuity. Sum the results and you have an estimate of the market price of the bonds. The market rate of interest is used because this is the rate potential investors will demand for the use of their funds. If the market rate is higher than the contract (or stated) rate of interest, the bonds will have to be sold at a discount to attract investors. Conversely, if the market rate is lower than the contract rate, the bonds will sell at a premium.

In chapter 7, you learned about capital leases. When a company acquires an asset with a capital lease, the company needs to record the asset at "cost." What is the cost when the lease requires payments over the life of the lease? Using present value tables, specifically Exhibit B-7, you can value the asset because the fixed payments over the life of the lease are like annuities and you want to determine the present value (i.e. cost) of all those payments.

Appendix B Exercises

1. When you began college, your aunt, a CPA, set aside $10,000 in a special savings account and promised to give you the total amount in the account when you graduate IF you major in accounting and earn a B average in all your accounting courses. Assuming the savings account earns 5% each year and you meet the terms of her offer, what amount will you receive at graduation?

2. Your uncle, a high school teacher, promised to save $600 annually on your behalf for the four years you are an undergraduate student and give you the total amount at graduation if you choose teaching as a career. The $600 will earn 6% annually. Assuming you choose teaching as a career, what amount will your uncle give you upon graduating?

3. You have just purchased a new car and estimate it will last you for 10 years. Assuming a replacement will cost $20,000 in 10 years, and your present car will have a trade-in value of $2500, what amount should you set aside now to insure you have sufficient cash on hand in 10 years to buy a replacement car? You believe your fund will earn 7% annually.

4. A company needs to borrow $500,000 and decides to offer 10-year debentures carrying 9% interest, payable semi-annually. If the market rate of interest is 8% when the bonds are offered, at what price should the bonds be sold?

5. Assume the same facts as in Exercise 4, but the market rate of interest is 10%. At what price should the bonds be sold?

6. The Levine Laboratories, LLC, has located a warehouse to lease. The company is offered a capital lease for 20 years requiring annual payments of $10,000 in addition to a $25,000 payment upon signing the lease. Present the journal entry to record the cash down payment, assuming a current 6% market rate.

Date	Account and Explanation	Debit	Credit

Appendix B Critical Thinking

Examine the situations presented in Exercises 1 and 2. What decision should you make?

_____
_____
_____
_____
_____

SOLUTIONS

Exercises

1. To answer the question, you have two options: (1) calculate the future value manually or (2) use Table B-2 in the text. Either way, the result should be the same. Calculating it manually requires the following:

    Year 1: $10,000 × 1.05 = $10,500
    Year 2: $10,500 × 1.05 = $11,025
    Year 3: $11,025 × 1.05 = $11,576.25
    Year 4: $11,576.25 × 1.05 = $12,155.06 (rounded)

    Table B-2 lists the value 1.216 at the intersection of 5% and 4 periods. $10,000 times 1.216 equals $12,160.

2. The $600 is like an annuity, so use Table B-4 to calculate the answer. 6% and 4 periods intersect at 4.375 and multiply this value by $600.

    $600 × 4.375 = $2,625

    The answer can also be calculated manually, but would require 10 separate calculations.

3. This exercise requires a present value for a future amount, so use Table B-6. 7% and 10 periods intersect at 0.508. Apply this value to $17,500 to determine the amount of cash that needs to be invested now.

    $17,500 × 0.508 = $8,890

    Note we use $17,500 and not $20,000 because the present car's trade-in value of $2,500 will reduce the amount of cash needed in 10 years time.

4. To determine the asking price of the bonds, we need to know the present value of a future amount and the present value of an annuity. The present value of the $500,000 is determined by consulting Table B-6 while the present value of the annuity (the interest payments) is determined by Table B-7.

    Present value of $500,000 = $500,000 × 0.456 = $228,000

    Use the 4% column and the 20 periods row to find the value 0.456. Because the bonds will pay interest semi-annually and the market rate is 8%, there are 20 periods at 4% each period. Apply this same logic to find the present value of the interest payments by consulting Table B-7. The semi-annual interest payments will be $22,500 ($500,000 and 4.5%) so

    $22,500 × 13.590 = $305,775

    Now add the results as follows:

    $228,000 = $305,775 = $533,775

    Because the bonds carry an interest rate higher than the current market rate, they can be offered for sale at a premium. Therefore, they will be offered for sale at 106.755% ($533,775 divided by $500,000).

5. Following the logic explained in Exercise 4, the calculations are

   $500,000 × 0.377 = $188,500 and $22,500 × 12.462 = $280,395
   These results add to $468,895, so the bonds will be offered at 93.779% ($468,895 divided by $500,000).

6. Use Table B-7 because this is an annuity.

   $10,000 × 11.470 = $114,700; in addition, the lease calls for an initial down payment of $25,000, so the "cost" (present value) of the capital lease is $139,700, recorded as follows:

Warehouse	139,700	
Cash		25,000
Lease Liability		114,700

Critical Thinking

The answer is obvious—become an accounting teacher!

APPENDIX C—SUMMARY OF GENERALLY ACCEPTED ACCOUNTING PRINCIPLES (GAAP)

Generally accepted accounting principles (GAAP) are primarily influenced by the **Financial Accounting Standards Board** (FASB) and its predecessor organization, the **Accounting Principles Board** (APB). However, the **Securities and Exchange Commission** (SEC) has ultimate authority to establish accounting principles for publicly-held companies.

The FASB's pronouncements are called Statements of Financial Standards. These standards determine how to account for certain business transactions. The basic objective of financial reporting is to provide information that is useful for investment and lending decisions. Information should be relevant, reliable, comparable, and consistent. Relevant information is useful. Reliable information is unbiased and free from significant error. Comparable and consistent information can be compared from period to period.

Concepts

The **entity concept** provides that the transactions of the organization be accounted for separately from the transactions of other organizations and persons, including the owner(s) of the entity.

The **going-concern concept** is an assumption that the business will continue to operate in the future. This concept enables accountants to assume that a business will continue long enough to recover the cost of its assets.

The **stable-monetary-unit concept** assumes that the value of the monetary unit never changes. Accountants ignore the effects of inflation and make no accounting adjustments related to changes in the purchasing power of the dollar.

The **time-period concept** provides that financial information be reported at regular intervals so that decision makers can compare business operations over time to assess the success or failure of the business. This concept is the basis for accruals and adjusting entries prepared at the end of an accounting period.

The **conservatism concept** requires that income and assets be reported at their lowest reasonable amounts. This does not mean that assets or income should be deliberately understated. It does mean that when different values can be assigned to a transaction, the less optimistic value should be used. The lower-of-cost-or-market method (LCM) for valuing assets is a clear example of conservatism.

The **materiality concept** requires accountants to accurately account for significant items and transactions. Information is significant (or material) if it is likely to cause a statement user to change a decision because of that information. The accounting treatment for a $3 pencil sharpener is not likely to affect any decisions; the pencil sharpener is immaterial. However, failing to record a $1 million liability would affect the decisions of many users. Thus, the $1 million is material.

Principles

The **reliability (objectivity) principle** states that accounting information should be based on the most reliable data available.

The **cost principle** states that transactions are to be recorded at cost. When assets are purchased, they are recorded at cost, and the accounting records of the asset are maintained at cost. The actual cost of an asset or service is considered to be a verifiable, objective evidence of value.

The **revenue principle** tells the accountant when to record revenue and how much revenue to record. Generally, revenue is recorded when it is earned and not before. Three conditions must be met before revenue is recorded:

1. The seller has done everything necessary to expect to collect from the buyer.
2. The amount of revenues can be objectively measured.
3. Collectibility is reasonably assured.

Generally, these conditions are met when the seller delivers the goods or renders services to the buyer.

The **matching principle**, in conjunction with the revenue principle, governs income recognition. Recall that expenses are matched against revenues.

The **consistency principle** is enhanced by using the same accounting methods from period to period.

The **disclosure principle** requires that a company's financial statements report enough information for users to make knowledgeable decisions about the company. In order to satisfy the disclosure principle, companies add to the financial statements notes that disclose significant accounting policies, probable losses, and accounting changes.

Financial Statements and Notes

The **Balance sheet** presents the accounting equation (assets = liabilities + owners' equity) at a point in time.

The **Income statement** lists revenues and gains less expenses and losses. The difference is either net income or net loss for the period.

The **Statement of cash flows** lists cash receipts and cash disbursements during the period. These are grouped under operating, investing, and financing activities.

The **Statement of retained earnings** lists the changes in retained earnings during the period.

The **Statement of stockholders' equity** explains all changes in each stockholders' equity account during the period.

Financial statement notes provide information that is not included on the face of the financial statement. The notes are an integral part of the statement.